T0211788

Lecture Notes in Computer Science　12849

More information about this subseries at http://www.springer.com/series/7409

Noella Edelmann · Csaba Csáki ·
Sara Hofmann · Thomas J. Lampoltshammer ·
Laura Alcaide Muñoz · Peter Parycek ·
Gerhard Schwabe · Efthimios Tambouris (Eds.)

Electronic Participation

13th IFIP WG 8.5 International Conference, ePart 2021
Granada, Spain, September 7–9, 2021
Proceedings

Springer

Editors
Noella Edelmann (iD)
Danube University Krems
Krems, Austria

Csaba Csáki (iD)
Corvinus University of Budapest
Budapest, Hungary

Sara Hofmann (iD)
University of Agder
Kristiansand, Norway

Thomas J. Lampoltshammer (iD)
Danube University Krems
Krems, Austria

Laura Alcaide Muñoz (iD)
University of Granada
Granada, Spain

Peter Parycek (iD)
Danube University Krems
Krems, Austria

Gerhard Schwabe (iD)
University of Zurich
Zürich, Switzerland

Efthimios Tambouris (iD)
University of Macedonia
Thessaloniki, Greece

ISSN 0302-9743   ISSN 1611-3349   (electronic)
Lecture Notes in Computer Science
ISBN 978-3-030-82823-3   ISBN 978-3-030-82824-0   (eBook)
https://doi.org/10.1007/978-3-030-82824-0

LNCS Sublibrary: SL3 – Information Systems and Applications, incl. Internet/Web, and HCI

This Springer imprint is published by the registered company Springer Nature Switzerland AG
The registered company address is: Gewerbestrasse 11, 6330 Cham, Switzerland

Preface

The EGOV-CeDEM-ePart conference is now in the fourth year of its existence after the successful merger of three formerly independent conferences, that is, the IFIP WG 8.5 Electronic Government (EGOV) conference, the Conference for E-Democracy and Open Government (CeDEM), and the IFIP WG 8.5 IFIP Electronic Participation (ePart) conference. This larger, united conference is dedicated to a broad area of digital or electronic government, open government, smart governance, e-democracy, policy informatics, and electronic participation. Scholars from around the world have found this conference to be a premier academic forum with a long tradition along its various branches, which has given the EGOV-CeDEM-ePart conference its reputation of one of the leading conferences worldwide in the research domains of digital/electronic, open, and smart government as well as electronic participation.

Unfortunately, due to the ongoing COVID-19 pandemic, this year's conference, held during September 7–9, 2021, at the University of Granada, Andalusia, Spain, was provided in a hybrid format of on-site and online attendances. All presentations and discussions, workshops keynotes, and panels were provided in this hybrid format. Despite this adjustment and a lower-than-normal on-site attendance, the conference was a great success.

The call for papers attracted completed research papers, work-in-progress papers on ongoing research (including doctoral papers), and project and case descriptions, as well as workshop and panel proposals. The submissions were assessed through a double-blind peer-review process, with at least three reviewers per submission, and the acceptance rate was 38%.

The conference tracks of the 2021 edition presented advances in the digital and socio-technological domain of the public sphere, demonstrating cutting-edge concepts, methods, and styles of investigation by multiple disciplines. The papers were distributed over the following tracks:

- General E-Government and E-Governance
- General E-Democracy and E-Participation
- Digital Society
- Digital and Social Media
- Open Data: Social and Technical Aspects
- Legal Informatics
- AI, Data Analytics, and Automated Decision Making
- Smart and Digital Cities (Government, Communities, and Regions)
- Emerging Issues and Innovation
- Social Innovation

Among the full research paper submissions, 23 papers (empirical and conceptual) were accepted for this year's Springer LNCS EGOV proceedings (vol. 12850) from the General E-Government track as well as from the tracks on Smart Cities, AI, and Open

Data. Another 16 completed research papers from the General E-Democracy and E-Participation track as well as from the tracks on Digital and Social Media, Legal Informatics, Digital Society, Social Innovation, and the Emerging Topics and Innovation went into this LNCS ePart proceedings (vol. 12849).

The papers included in this volume have been clustered under the following headings:

- Digital Participation
- Digital Society
- Digital Government
- Legal Issues

As in the previous years and per the recommendation of the Paper Awards Committee under the leadership of Noella Edelmann (Danube University Krems, Austria) and Evangelos Kalampokis (University of Macedonia, Greece), the IFIP EGOV-CeDEM-ePart 2021 Conference Organizing Committee granted outstanding paper awards in three distinct categories:

- The most interdisciplinary and innovative research contribution
- The most compelling critical research reflection
- The most promising practical concept

The winners in each category were announced during the obligatory awards ceremony at the conference.

Many people behind the scenes make large events like this conference happen. We would like to thank the members of the Program Committee and the reviewers for their great efforts in reviewing the submitted papers. We would also like to express our deep gratitude to Manuel Pedro Rodríguez Bolívar, Laura Alcaide Muñoz, and their local team at the University of Granada (UGR) for hosting the conference.

Voted the best institution of higher education in Spain by international students in 2014, the public UGR does not only reside on very famous historical premises, for example, the former Royal Hospital of Granada (1511-1526) and its unique Renaissance Courtyard, but it also was founded in historical times (1531) some forty years after the last Muslim rulers were forced to leave the Iberian Peninsula. Today, the university, with about 60,000 students, is the fourth largest in Spain with a large contingent of international students seeking and receiving their higher-education degrees at this extraordinary institution. UGR provides a wide range of studies organized in 5 schools, 22 faculties, and 116 departments.

The attendees who were able to make it to the conference in person were greatly reimbursed for their traveling efforts by finding themselves for a few days in a stunning environment of natural and architectural beauty, the latter of which spans many centuries with world-famous complexes such as the Alhambra, the famous palace city of the Muslim rulers, and the Cathedral, among other examples of outstanding architectural skill, taste, and ingenuity. Today, the quarter-million population City of Granada has remained a bustling Andalusian center of diverse culture, exquisite gastronomy, modern and traditional commerce, and great Mediterranean outdoor life surrounded by the august scenery of the Sierra Nevada and its snow-topped peaks. Granada and the UGR were unforgettable hosts of the 2021 conference.

September 2021

Noella Edelmann
Csaba Csáki
Sara Hofmann
Thomas Lampoltshammer
Laura Alcaide Muñoz
Peter Parycek
Gerhard Schwabe
Efthimios Tambouris

Organization

Conference Chairs

Noella Edelmann	Danube University Krems, Austria
Marijn Janssen	Delft University of Technology, The Netherlands
Ida Lindgren	Linköping University, Sweden
Laura Alcaide Muñoz	University of Granada, Spain
Peter Parycek	Fraunhofer Fokus, Germany/Danube University Krems, Austria
Gabriela Viale Pereira	Danube University Krems, Austria
Manuel Pedro Rodríguez Bolívar	University of Granada, Spain
Hans Jochen Scholl	University of Washington, USA
Gerhard Schwabe	University of Zürich, Switzerland
Efthimios Tambouris	University of Macedonia, Greece
Shefali Virkar	Danube University Krems, Austria

Program Committee Chairs

Karin Axelsson	Linköping University, Sweden
Csaba Csaki	Corvinus University of Budapest, Hungary
Noella Edelmann	Danube University Krems, Austria
J. Ramon Gil-Garcia	University at Albany, SUNY, USA
Sara Hofmann	University of Agder, Norway
Marijn Janssen	Delft University of Technology, The Netherlands
Evangelos Kalampokis	University of Macedonia, Greece
Robert Krimmer	University of Tartu, Estonia
Thomas Lampoltshammer	Danube University Krems, Austria
Habin Lee	Brunel University London, UK
Katarina Lindblad-Gidlund	Mid Sweden University, Sweden
Ida Lindgren	Linköping University, Sweden
Nuno Lopes	DTx - Digital Transformation CoLab, Portugal
Euripidis Loukis	University of the Aegean, Greece
Gianluca Misuraca	European Commission, Spain
Francesco Mureddu	Lisbon Council, Belgium
Anna-Sophie Novak	Danube University Krems, Austria
Panos Panagiotopoulos	Queen Mary University of London, UK
Peter Parycek	Danube University Krems, Austria
Manuel Pedro Rodríguez Bolívar	University of Granada, Spain
Marius Rohde Johannessen	University of South-Eastern Norway, Norway
Hans J. Scholl	University of Washington, USA

Efthimios Tambouris   University of Macedonia, Greece
Gabriela Viale Pereira   Danube University Krems, Austria
Shefali Virkar   Danube University Krems, Austria
Anneke Zuiderwijk   Delft University of Technology, The Netherlands

Outstanding Papers Awards Chairs

Noella Edelmann   Danube University Krems, Austria
Evangelos Kalampokis   University of Macedonia, Greece

PhD Colloquium Chairs

Gabriela Viale Pereira   Danube University Krems, Austria
J. Ramon Gil-Garcia   University at Albany, SUNY, USA
Ida Lindgren   Linköping University, Sweden

Webmaster

Sergei Zhilin   Delft University of Technology, The Netherlands

Program Committee

Karin Ahlin   Mid Sweden University, Sweden
Suha Alawadhi   Kuwait University, Kuwait
Valerie Albrecht   Danube University Krems, Austria
Laura Alcaide-Muñoz   University of Granada, Spain
Leonidas Anthopoulos   University of Thessaly, Greece
Wagner Araujo   UNU-EGOV, Portugal
Oscar Avila   University of the Andes, Columbia
Karin Axelsson   Linköping University, Sweden
Dian Balta   fortiss GmbH, Germany
Peter Bellström   Karlstad University, Sweden
Flavia Bernardini   Universidade Federal Fluminense, Brazil
Nitesh Bharosa   Delft University of Technology, The Netherlands
Radomir Bolgov   Saint Petersburg State University, Russia
Alessio Maria Braccini   University of Liechtenstein, Liechtenstein
Paul Brous   Delft University of Technology, The Netherlands
Matthias Buchinger   fortiss GmbH, Germany
Kelvin Bwalya   University of Johannesburg, South Africa
Edna Dias Canedo   Universidade de Brasília, Brazil
Jesus Cano   UNED, Spain
João Carvalho   University of Minho, Portugal
Youngseok Choi   University of Southampton, UK
Soon Chun   City University of New York, USA
Wichian Chutimaskul   King Mongkut's University of Technology Thonburi,
                               Thailand

Vincenzo Ciancia	Istituto di Scienza e Tecnologie dell'Informazione "Alessandro Faedo", Consiglio Nazionale delle Ricerche, Italy
Antoine Clarinval	Université de Namur, Belgium
Taiane Ritta Coelho	Federal University of Parana, Brazil
Andreiwid Sheffer Corrêa	Federal Institute of Sao Paulo, Brazil
Joep Crompvoets	Katholieke Universiteit Leuven, Belgium
Peter Cruickshank	Edinburgh Napier University, UK
Jonathan Crusoe	Linköpings University, Sweden
Csaba Csaki	Corvinus University of Budapest, Hungary
Alexandra Daikou	University of Macedonia, Greece
Frank Danielsen	University of Agder, Norway
Lieselot Danneels	Ghent University/Vlerick Business School, Belgium
Todd R. Davies	Stanford University, USA
Gabriele De Luca	Danube University Krems, Austria
Athanasios Deligiannis	International Hellenic University, Greece
Bettina Distel	Universität Münster, Germany
Ioanna Donti	International Hellenic University, Greece
Noella Edelmann	Danube University Krems, Austria
Gregor Eibl	Danube University Krems, Austria
Eiri Elvestad	University of Oslo, Norway
Gerhard Embacher-Köhle	Federal Computing Center of Austria, Austria
Montathar Faraon	Kristianstad University, Sweden
Shahid Farooq	Government of the Punjab, Pakistan
Marcelo Fornazin	FGV EBAPE, Brazil
Margarita Fourer	Danube University Krems, Austria
Mary Francoli	Carleton University, Canada
Gangadharan G. R.	IBM, USA
Jonas Gamalielsson	University of Skövde, Sweden
Luz Maria Garcia	Universidad de la Sierra Sur, Mexico
Francisco García Morán	European Commission, Luxembourg
Mila Gasco	University at Albany, SUNY, USA
Elisabeth Gebka	University of Namur, Belgium
J. Ramon Gil-Garcia	University at Albany, SUNY, USA
Dimitris Gouscos	University of Athens, Greece
Malin Granath	Linköping University, Sweden
Christina Grigoriou	International Hellenic University, Greece
Stefanos Gritzalis	University of Piraeus, Greece
Åke Grönlund	Örebro University, Sweden
Divya Kirti Gupta	Indus Business Academy, India
Mariana Gustafsson	Linköping University, Sweden
Sebastian Halsbenning	Universität Münster, Germany
Martijn Hartog	Delft University of Technology, The Netherlands
Marcus Heidlund	Mid Sweden University, Sweden
Moreen Heine	University of Lübeck, Germany
Marcia Hino	Universidade Positivo, Brazil

Edimara Luciano	Pontifical Catholic University of Rio Grande do Sul, Brazil
Luis F. Luna-Reyes	University at Albany, SUNY, USA
Bjorn Lundell	University of Skövde, Sweden
Ahmad Luthfi	Delft University of Technology, The Netherlands
Johan Magnusson	University of Gothenburg, Sweden
Michael Marti	Berner Fachhochschule, Switzerland
Flavia Marzano	Link Campus University, Italy
Ricardo Matheus	Delft University of Technology, The Netherlands
John McNutt	University of Delaware, USA
Keegan Mcbride	Hertie School, Germany
Fritz Meiners	Fraunhofer FOKUS, Germany
Ana Melro	University of Aveiro, Portugal
Tobias Mettler	University of Lausanne, Switzerland
Morten Meyerhoff Nielsen	UNU-EGOV, Portugal
Yuri Misnikov	University of Leeds, UK
Gianluca Misuraca	European Commission, Spain
Solange Mukamurenzi	University of Rwanda, Rwanda
Francesco Mureddu	Lisbon Council, Belgium
Galia Novakova Nedeltcheva	Sofia University, Bulgaria
Alessia Caterina Neuroni	Bern University of Applied Sciences, Switzerland
Mille Nielsen	IT University of Copenhagen, Denmark
Marco Niemann	European Research Center for Information Systems, Germany
Anna-Sophie Novak	Danube University Krems, Austria
Hannu Nurmi	University of Turku, Finland
Ann O'Brien	NUI Galway, Ireland
Monica Palmirani	CIRSFID, Italy
Panos Panagiotopoulos	Queen Mary University of London, UK
Peter Parycek	Danube University Krems, Austria
Samuli Pekkola	Tampere University, Finland
Sergio Picazo-Vela	Universidad de las Americas Puebla, Mexico
Luiz Pereira Pinheiro Junior	Universidade Positivo, Brazil
Athanasios Priftis	Ynternet.org, France
Luis Felipe M. Ramos	University of Minho, Portugal
Barbara Re	University of Camerino, Italy
Nicolau Reinhard	University of São Paulo, Brazil
Aya Rizk	Luleå University of Technology, Sweden
Manuel Pedro Rodríguez Bolívar	University of Granada, Spain
Alexander Ronzhyn	University of Koblenz-Landau, Germany
Athanasia Routzouni	University of the Aegean, Greece
Boriana Rukanova	Delft University of Technology, The Netherlands
Per Runeson	Lund University, Sweden

Saquib Saeed	Imam Abdulrahman Bin Faisal University, Saudi Arabia
Rodrigo Sandoval-Almazan	Universidad Autónoma del Estado de Mexico, Mexico
Hans J. Scholl	University of Washington, USA
Hendrik Scholta	Universität Münster, Germany
Harrie Scholtens	European Institute of Public Administration/PRIMO Europe, The Netherlands
Johannes Scholz	Graz University of Technology, Austria
Judith Schossböck	Danube University Krems, Austria
Luiza Schuch de Azambuja	Tallinn University of Technology, Estonia
Johanna Sefyrin	Linköping University, Sweden
Uwe Serdült	Ritsumeikan University
Masoud Shahmanzari	Brunel University London, UK
Kerley Silva	University of Porto, Portugal
Anthony Simonofski	Katholieke Universiteit Leuven, Belgium
Søren Skaarup	IT University of Copenhagen, Denmark
Ralf-Martin Soe	Tallinn University of Technology, Estonia
Karin Steiner	Danube University Krems, Austria
Leif Sundberg	Mid Sweden University, Sweden
Proscovia Svärd	Mid Sweden University, Sweden
Øystein Sæbø	University of Agder, Norway
Efthimios Tambouris	University of Macedonia, Greece
Ioanna Tamouridou	University of Macedonia, Greece
Luca Tangi	Politecnico di Milano, Italy
Lörinc Thurnay	Danube University Krems, Austria
Jean-Philippe Trabichet	HEG Genève, Switzerland
Andrea Trentini	University of Milano, Italy
Jolien Ubacht	Delft University of Technology, The Netherlands
Afe Vanveenstra	TNO, The Netherlands
Marco Velicogna	IRSiG-CNR, Italy
Gabriela Viale Pereira	Danube University Krems, Austria
Shefali Virkar	Danube University Krems, Austria
Gianluigi Viscusi	Imperial College London, UK
Felipe Vogas	Federal University of Rio de Janeiro, Brazil
Frederika Welle Donker	Knowledge Centre Open Data, The Netherlands
Guilherme Wiedenhöft	Federal University of Rio Grande, Brazil
Elin Wihlborg	Linköping University, Sweden
Peter Winstanley	Semantechs Consulting, UK
Stijn Wouters	Katholieke Universiteit Leuven, Belgium
Anja C. Wüst	Bern University of Applied Sciences, Switzerland
Maija Ylinen	Tampere University of Technology, Finland
Chien-Chih Yu	National Chengchi University, Taiwan
Mete Yıldız	Hacettepe Üniversitesi, Turkey
Qinfeng Zhu	University of Groningen, The Netherlands
Saleem Zoughbi	International Adviser
Anneke Zuiderwijk	Delft University of Technology, The Netherlands

Adelson de Araújo   University of Twente, The Netherlands
Ana Paula dos Santos   FGV EBAPE, Brazil
  Tavares
Sélinde van Engelenburg   Delft University of Technology, The Netherlands
Colin van Noordt   Tallinn University of Technology, Estonia
Jörn von Lucke   Zeppelin Universität, Germany
Anastasija Ņikiforova   University of Latvia, Latvia

Additional Reviewers

Nina Rizun   Gdansk University of Technology, Poland
Annika Hasselblad   Mid Sweden University, Sweden
  Hasseblad
Carsten Schmidtt   Tallinn University of Technology, Estonia
Dimitris Zeninis   Centre for Research Technology Hellas (CERTH),
                               Greece
Vera Spitzer   University of Koblenz, Germany
Christina Deutsch   Technische Universität München, Germany
Marissa Hoekstra   TNO, The Netherlands

Contents

Legal Issues

Digital Participation

Youths' Digital Participation in the Early Phases of COVID-19 Lockdown

Iikka Pietilä[1][✉], Jenni Kallio[2], Jari Varsaluoma[1], and Kaisa Väänänen[1]

[1] Human-Centered Technology, Unit of Computing, Tampere University, Tampere, Finland
{iikka.pietila,jari.varsaluoma,kaisa.vaananen}@tuni.fi
[2] Faculty of Social Sciences (SOC), Tampere University, Tampere, Finland
jenni.kallio@tuni.fi

Abstract. On 18 March 2020 the Finnish Government declared a state of emergency due to COVID-19 causing public services to limit their capacity or to close completely. Well-founded concerns have been raised on how the restrictions affect young people's well-being and their possibilities to get support. Youths use digital technologies in their everyday lives, and it can be assumed that the usage has increased during the COVID-19 pandemic, which can also be a benefit when coping with the situation. This paper explores young people's subjective experiences regarding digital services, digital societal participation, and social interactions in the early phases of COVID-19 pandemic. Moreover, the youths' backgrounds in relation to their utilisation of digital technologies and services are examined. A mixed-method survey including closed-ended and open-ended questions was conducted in spring 2020. The sample included 49 young Finnish people aged 15–26. Results suggest that digitality supports youths in their activities, such as work and school, societal participation, and social interactions. Also, problems, such as inadequate ICT skills and technical issues were identified. Furthermore, the ICT-savvy youths seem to benefit highly from digitality in comparison to their less ICT-savvy peers. This paper contributes to the discussions of digital divides, equal access to societal participation, and the activities that may support youths' coping in similar future lockdown situations.

Keywords: Digital participation · Societal participation · Youth · COVID-19

1 Introduction

The very first COVID-19 infection in Finland was diagnosed on 26 February 2020 and by the end of May, 6 859 people became infected (THL). On 12 March it was recommended that remote work should be favored as much as possible, and citizens should keep physical distance to avoid social contacts. On 18 March 2020, the Government declared a state of emergency causing libraries, museums, youth centers and other public services, also several welfare services, to limit their capacity or to close completely. Restaurants, cafés, and bars were ordered to be closed and public gatherings were limited to a maximum of 10 people. From 18 March to 14 May 2020 contact teaching in comprehensive schools,

© IFIP International Federation for Information Processing 2021
Published by Springer Nature Switzerland AG 2021
N. Edelmann et al. (Eds.): ePart 2021, LNCS 12849, pp. 3–14, 2021.
https://doi.org/10.1007/978-3-030-82824-0_1

secondary education institutions and higher education was suspended and replaced by remote teaching. On 19 March Finland's external borders were closed from passengers and goods traffic. From 28 March to 1 April traffic between the Region of Uusimaa, where the infection was most widely spread, and other regions, was restricted.

The Finnish Government's chosen COVID-19-strategy is called a hybrid strategy, in which the key principles are to prevent the virus from spreading but also to secure the capacity of the healthcare system and to protect people at special health risks. However, concerns have been raised in regard to the restrictions' effects on young people's well-being and COVID-19 fundamentally changing their lives and prospective futures. Moreover, the pandemic situation has put the youths in unequal positions in relation to for example their socioeconomic backgrounds and their possibilities to get adequate support.

Young people who had previously needed support have experienced the most difficulties (Herkama and Repo 2020), which can also be interpreted as an accumulation of inequality. Moreover, the crisis also appears to have had a detrimental effect on the mental well-being of youths (Wilska et al. 2020). Also, differences in coping strategies are affiliated with education (e.g., Mohammadzadeh et al. 2020) which implies further inequalities among youths. Additionally, Merry et al. (2020) express concerns on extending digital divides during COVID-19 as technologies provide access to services that support mental health. As information on COVID-19 is increasingly seeked digitally (Liu 2020), the concerns gain relevance.

Although general coping strategies during the COVID-19 pandemic have been studied to a degree, there seems to be a gap in research addressing the relationships between digital services, societal participation, social interactions, and coping responses among youths. This is an important research area as the various digital services enable societal participation and social activities that indeed support coping in hard circumstances.

According to Bandura (1977), the concept of self-efficacy is used to refer to people's internalised constructs concerning their preparedness to execute a task. These constructs can be for instance subjective beliefs and expectations of one's own abilities in regard to a goal that needs to be achieved (Ibid). The way that people experience their expertise in relation to an executable task, i.e., self-efficacy, is highly affiliated with motivations and commitment, and thus mediates behavior (Bandura 1995, 2006). Computer self-efficacy is used to refer to self-efficacy in ICT related contexts (Compeau and Higgins 1995). ICT skills and societal participation tend to fluctuate analogously (Meriläinen et al. 2018).

This paper aims to address these relationships through exploring the young people's experiences regarding digital technologies and services, digital societal participation, and social interactions in the early phases of COVID-19 pandemic. Moreover, this paper examines the youths' backgrounds (societal participation and computer self-efficacy) in relation to their utilisation of digital technologies and services for COVID-19 lockdown stress mitigation. This paper contributes to the discussions of digital divides, equal access to societal participation, and the activities that support coping.

2 Related Work

2.1 Societal Participation and Digital Participation

In the scope of this paper, by young people and youth we mean the people of ages between 15 and 26 (E.g., Pietilä et al. 2019; Finnish Youth Act 2017). Societal participation refers to various activities, such as taking part in decision-making instances (Checkoway 2011), involvement in societal processes, voting, or discussing political issues (Pietilä et al. 2019). Moreover, societal participation can be described to be affiliated with having an active role in sustainable societal development (UN 2018). As the various technologies have been developed and the wide audiences have adopted them, naturally societal participation activities are increasingly moving to digital and online settings (e.g., Xenos and Moy 2007; Auxer 2020). Furthermore, a majority of the youths may even prefer participation in digital and online surroundings in comparison to more traditional forms of societal participation (Weber et al. 2003; Omotayo and Folorunso 2020).

According to Youth Wiki (2020), eParticipation can be defined as the activities that aim to broaden the participation of the youth by using various ICT tools. Moreover, Albrecht et al. (2008) affiliate eParticipation with activities in digital realms among individuals, groups, and policymakers. Similarly, Panopoulou et al. (2014) describe eParticipation to make the societal participation available more broadly through the use of ICT. According to Nilsson et al. (2019) eParticipation services denote the plethora of digital online services that are intended to enhance societal participation, i.e., taking part in various democratic and decision-making processes.

While eParticipation consists of activities that take place in digital settings and are related to societal participation, digital participation in turn is seen as a wider frame of activities in digital realms. It is more common by the day that the youths take part in various of digital activities and some of these activities can be affiliated with societal participation (Xenos and Moy 2007; Auxer 2020; Van Kessel et al. 2020; Omotayo and Folorunso 2020) and thus be regarded as eParticipation. However, the digital activities that do not belong under the term eParticipation but still are participatory in their nature, constitute the concept of digital participation. In addition to that, in the context of this paper, we define digital participation as a sphere of activities, which can include discussing political or societal issues online, electronic voting (Sæbø et al. 2008), answering questionnaires online, and consuming digital contents (Meriläinen et al. 2018).

2.2 COVID and Coping

The most common human coping strategies during COVID-19 appear to be similar to general coping strategies. The coping strategies adopted during COVID-19 included seeking alternatives, self-preservation, seeking social support, and avoidance (Chew et al. 2020). However, young adults' strategies seem to associate especially with reduced distress, including keeping a daily routine, physical activities, and positive reappraisal/reframing (Shanahan et al. 2020).

To widely understand young people's coping strategies during COVID-19, and to foster their capacities of citizenship and societal participation, young people's individual capacities and skills, but also the societal environment and their possibilities to get social and emotional support from their family and peers, should be taken into account (Volk et al. 2020; see also Salin et al. 2021). Furthermore, abilities to cope in straining conditions, can be supported by experiences of communality, i.e., through social interactions (Blanc et al. 2021; Petzold et al. 2020). Experiencing significance and receiving and giving support through social interactions are mentioned as significant conditions in prevailing the encumbrance imposed by isolation (Polizzi et al. 2020).

3 The Survey Study

To explore the youth's perceptions on digital participation in the early phases of COVID-19 lockdown, we conducted a mixed-method survey study in Finland. A mixed-method approach was selected for this study as qualitative research enables acquisition of knowledge regarding detailed descriptive subjective experiences, and quantitative research enables the exploration of relationships between the youth's backgrounds and behavior amidst COVID-19 lockdown.

3.1 Research Questions

To explore the youths' backgrounds in relation to their utilisation of digital technologies and services for COVID-19 related lockdown stress mitigation, and more specifically, the relationships of ICT self-efficacy and previous experiences in societal participation with regard to digital technologies and services, the following research questions were formulated:

RQ1: How, if at all, have digital technologies and services supported societal participation of various youths in the early phases of COVID-19 lockdown?
RQ2: How are youths' backgrounds related to their digital participation in COVID-19 lockdown?

   A) How are previous experiences in societal participation related to digital participation in COVID-19 lockdown?
   B) How is computer self-efficacy related to digital participation in COVID-19 lockdown?

3.2 Variables and Operationalisation

To answer the research questions, five constructs were assembled. These constructs represent the digital technologies and services supporting coping (Coping support), consuming digital contents related to societal matters (Content consumption), participating actively in online and digital settings (Active participation), lockdown-anteceding societal participation (Societal participation), and lockdown-anteceding ICT skills and self-efficacy (Computer self-efficacy). The construct measuring societal participation was partly based on the questionnaires used by Pietilä et al. (2019) and Pajares et al. (2006) and the construct measuring computer self-efficacy was based on the work of Howard (2014). All of the formed constructs exhibited a moderate or strong internal consistency as they received more than .700 as their Cronbach's alpha value (E.g., Bland and Altman 1997). Although not an explicit measurement for reliability, higher Cronbach's alpha and higher internal consistency reflects higher reliability of a measurement (Cronbach 1951).

3.3 Methods: Data Acquisition, Processing Pipeline, and Analysis

Data Acquisition. The data was acquired through a digital questionnaire. The questionnaire was open from the 22nd of April until the 27th of May in 2020 and it was distributed on the research project [Removed for review] social media channels. Also, it was distributed on the channels of [Removed] University, and The Finnish National Youth Council Allianssi. The questionnaire consisted of four Likert scale sets, and four open-ended questions. Two of the Likert scale sets consisted of assertions regarding the usage of digital technologies and services during the lockdown. The other two Likert scale sets included assertions that concerned computer self-efficacy and societal participation. The four open-ended questions addressed experiences on how the digital technologies and services have provided support during the lockdown.

Data Processing and Analysis. To answer RQ1 the answers to the open ended questions were analysed. Grounded theory was applied as the data was subjected to categorizing that was led by concepts that were identified within the data (Glasser and Strauss 1967). More specifically, the formation of the categories was enabled by applying thematic content analysis (Braun and Clarke 2006). Analysis stages were structured similarly to analysis of Burnard (1991) and [Reference removed] followingly: 1. Forming an overview, 2. Systematic annotation, 3. Category creation by open coding (Malterud 2012), 4. Category iteration, 5. Juxtaposing the categories with theory and related literature.

In regard to research questions 2 A and B, the dependent variables are established by variables Coping support, Content consumption, and Active participation. In RQ2 A and B the independent variables are established by the variable Societal participation and the variable Computer self-efficacy, respectively. Due to small sample size, and to simplify the test setting, the independent variables were recoded into dichotomous variables by cutting the sample in half at each independent variables' median. Societal participation was aggregated followingly: if $0 < a_{old} \leq 4.50 \rightarrow a_{new} = 1$ and if $a_{old} > 4.50 \rightarrow a_{new} = 2$. Computer self-efficacy was aggregated in a similar manner as: if $0 < b_{old} \leq 5.64 \rightarrow b_{new} = 1$ and if $b_{old} > 5.64 \rightarrow b_{new} = 2$.

No strict alpha level was selected for the analyses due to the small sampling size. This was also supported by ethical consideration; A type II error could have more harmful repercussions than type I error (Trafimow et al. 2018). As there are two categorical independent variables and three continuous dependent variables, MANOVA was chosen as the testing method. The variables were considered to follow a normal distribution adequately after inspecting their QQ-plots. Variables multicollinearity did not violate MANOVA assumptions and the results of the Box's test of equality of covariance matrices suggests MANOVA suitability with $M = 25.811$ and $p = .536$. Thus, MANOVA was applied, and the results are reported in the Sect. 4, Results.

3.4 Participants

Altogether 49 young people from Finland participated in the study from 22 different municipalities. The youngest participant was 15 years old and the oldest was 26. Median age was 21 years. More than ¼ of the participants were under 18 (16/49). Seventeen of the participants were in the ages of between 18 and 24. Fifteen participants were 25 or 26 years of age. Twenty-six participants disclosed their gender as female, whereas 19 reported males. Two participants reported as else (Not male or female), and two of the participants did not want to answer the question regarding their gender.

4 Results

4.1 Digital Support for Societal Participation (RQ1)

As a result of the analysis, four categories were identified: Digitality supports regular non-freetime activities, Digitality supports connectedness, Digitality supports societal participation, and Recognised problems and needs.

Digitality Supports Regular Non-freetime Activities. Twenty participants connected the supportive aspect of the digital technologies and services with their regular free-time activities, such as school, work, rehabilitative activity, or work try-out. Online video lectures, work-related meetings and VOIP technologies were repeatedly mentioned as supportive activities. Also, one participant curiously phrased that "*Learning has completely migrated to online settings*" (Female, 25 years). Another participant experienced that the plethora of platforms and services they use had become more diverse.

Digitality Supports Connectedness. Twenty-three of the participants experienced that their social contacts and interactions were supported by digitality. Sixteen mentioned that they have used for instance video calls and instant messaging services notably more than normally to contact their close ones. One participant stated that "*I have taught myself to use Discord, so that I can keep in touch with my friends. [...] These services have supported me to stay in touch with my close ones.*" (F, 25) Another participant elaborated "*Digital services have enabled communications and a certain kind of sense of community*" (F, 26). Furthermore, it was said that "*Communality and sociality are preserved as it is possible to talk to friends*" (M, 25) by one participant highlighting the importance of these tools. Additionally, observations that conflicted with the mainstream trend were identified, as a participant stated that "*Use of social media and use of phone have decreased*" (M, 19). Interestingly one participant also mentioned that they had used Skype for "*Distant drunkenness*" (M, 23), which the authors interpret as a social gathering of two or more people that involves alcohol.

Digitality Supports Societal Participation. In the answers to the open-ended questions, altogether seventeen participants elaborated their experiences regarding the digital services supporting their societal participation. Seven of the participants stated that news and official content consumption has been supported by the various services. Moreover, the possibility to attend gatherings online has been experienced as a factor that has enabled societal participation. More specifically, Twitter, Discord, Zoom, and Google

Hangouts were mentioned separately. One participant described their sentiment on the relationship of digital technologies and services, and societal participation in the following way: *"Feeling of being part of something bigger. Being able to keep up to date and information from many sources enables forming knowledge."* (F, 26) Another participant elaborated: *"Organising meetings and events has been possible in services like Zoom and Hangouts. This has enabled us to keep up with societal participation. Supported so that activities don't stop."* (A 23-year-old) Furthermore, four participants highlighted that digitality has enabled them to participate in activities of a local youth council in the forms of discussions and voting. One participant said that *"All the info is available digitally."* (M, 23).

Recognised Problems and Needs. Eighteen participants separately mentioned technical issues that they had encountered. Issues such as services not functioning properly, connection problems, microphone and sound related challenges, and servers disconnecting were mentioned. Also, congestion and too many users in services were identified as problems. Three participants mentioned a surge in the amount of misinformation (but did not unfortunately elaborate in more detail). One of them wrote *"There is a huge amount of false and untruthful information"* (F, 26) and another participant described *"I run into misinformation in various social media services"*. (M, 25) Furthermore, three participants mentioned that some users lack the needed ICT skills and therefore there have been problems in communications. In relation to this, four participants elaborated that through educating the users and tackling usability issues in the services many problems could be avoided. In more detail, two participants mentioned that the school personnel should be more trained regarding these ICT tools. Additionally, three participants had experienced increased negative interactions and people deploring more than usually in digital services. A participant described that *"...People are more lazy. [...] Regarding local governing activities, moving from face to face interactions to mediated ones does cause the activity to paralyze."* (Did not disclose gender, 26 years) Another participant wrote *"The topics in all of the channels make me anxious"*. (F, 21) One participant described that they had *"...Overdosed on social media."* (F, 25).

Additionally, not appointed to any of the categories, one person mentioned that their online shopping had increased, and they had food delivered to their home more often than normally. Also, a participant was concerned that their Pornhub subscription had expired. Another participant pointed out physiological issues regarding their eyes getting tired due to excess screen time. Twenty participants (40%) explicitly stated that the ways they use digital technologies and services did indeed change. According to 18 participants, usage increased, however two participants reported that their overall usage actually had decreased from normal.

4.2 Youths' Backgrounds and Digital Participation (RQ2)

To answer the research questions RQ2 A and RQ2 B, a multivariate analysis of variance, MANOVA, was applied. First the 0-hypothesis "There are no differences in the dependent variables between the two categories of the independent variable Societal participation" is tested. The results suggest very weak or no evidence at all for rejecting it as $p = .125$. However, testing the 0-hypothesis "There are no differences in the dependent variables between the two categories of the independent variable Computer self-efficacy", the results suggest weak evidence advocating the rejection of 0-hypothesis, as $p = .073$.

Moreover, the MANOVA results are inspected at the dependent variable level in the two categories of the independent variable Computer self-efficacy, as weak evidence for rejecting the related 0-hypothesis was displayed in the previous step. Interpreting the test suggests that there is moderate evidence that supports rejecting 0-hypothesis "There is no difference in the dependent variable Content consumption between the two categories of the independent variable Computer self-efficacy" as $p = .036$. As visible in Fig. 1, there is evidence that the ICT-savvy participants consumed more digital contents than their less ICT-savvy peers during the early phases of the COVID-19 related lockdown.

In the same lines, weak evidence supporting the rejection of 0-hypothesis "There is no difference in the independent variable Coping support between the two categories of the independent variable Computer self-efficacy" can be observed as $p = .054$. Hence, the results suggest that there is weak evidence that supports considering H1 "There is a difference in the dependent variable Coping support between the two categories of the independent variable Computer self-efficacy". As described in Fig. 1, the ones that had more higher computer self-efficacy, gained more support to cope from digital technologies and services, than their peers with lower computer self-efficacy during the COVID-19 related lockdown.

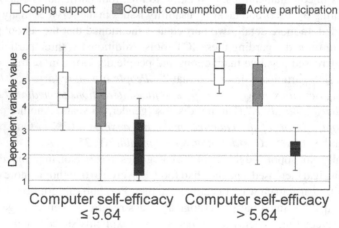

Fig. 1. A box plot describing the differences in the dependent variables between the two categories of the independent variable Computer self-efficacy

To conclude, the results suggest in regard to RQ2 A "How are previous experiences in societal participation related to digital participation in COVID-19 lockdown? that there is very weak or no evidence of differences in digital participation in the early phases of COVID-19 related lockdown between the youths that have more experience in societal participation and their less experienced peers. However, in regard to RQ2 B, "How is computer self-efficacy related to digital participation in COVID-19 lockdown?" The results suggest that there is evidence of differences between the youths with higher and lower computer self-efficacy. More specifically, the youths with greater computer self-efficacy gained more benefit in the coping support brought by digital technologies and services and consumed more (informative) digital contents than their peers with lower computer self-efficacy.

5 Discussion

Digital technologies and services have indeed supported the youths in the early phases of COVID-19 related lockdown in many ways. A substantial portion of the support has manifested in the domains of school, work, or other non-freetime regular activity, social contacting, and societal participation. However, the youths have identified a plethora of technical, competence-related, and content-related issues that have posed as obstacles for their participation at their work or school, communities or in the societal sphere. Moreover, for the majority of the youth, the nature of digital technologies and services usage has changed when society transitioned from normal to lockdown, although a significant minority experienced no change in their use of digital technologies or services. For most parts, the change meant an increase in the amount of use, albeit two participants did report a decrease in overall use of digital technologies and services.

The themes that emerged with the qualitative analysis can be thought to be interconnected through sociality. In addition to being a key function in participation, sociality is essential in regard to coping (Blanc et al. 2021; Petzold et al. 2020; Shanahan et al. 2020; Chew et al. 2020). In this sense, the social dimension of digitality cannot be left unaddressed as digitality does indeed provide access to sociality for many.

The finding that the youths that are more skilled in information and communication technologies gained more benefit from digital technologies and services in the domains of coping support and informative digital content consumption than their less skilled peers, reflect similar phenomena as the findings described by Meriläinen et al. (2018). This may be interpreted in the way that to enhance equal possibilities to societal participation, everyone should be equipped with the adequate competencies to navigate in the information intensive and technological environments. Thus, special attention should be placed on how the technological and content related skills, knowledge, and attitudes are taught to enable further utilisation of digitality to provide access to information and coping support. Otherwise, these digital and societal divides may grow under exceptional circumstances.

However, there are limitations to this study as the sample size is relatively small and thus the results generalisability is questionable. Moreover, the results are likely to vary between countries as various relevant attributes, such as prevalent ICT skills, infrastructures, access to activities that support coping, and family-centeredness differ. Also, the more specific mechanisms through which high computer self-efficacy enables benefitting from digitality in regard to coping support in isolation and informative content consumption, should be studied.

6 Conclusions

In this paper, we introduced a study regarding the changes in youths' use of digital technologies and services when the Finnish society transitioned from normal times to

COVID-19 lockdown. Furthermore, we explored how the digital technologies and services have supported the various youths in the early phases of COVID-19 lockdown in the domains of work, school, or other non-freetime regular activities, social interactions, and societal participation. Additionally, we reported the various problems that the youths have encountered in regard to digital technologies and services. Finally, the benefits gained from the digital technologies and services regarding coping support and digital societal participation are compared between the youths that had more or less experience in societal participation as well as between youths with higher or lower computer self-efficacy. Through enabling the acquisition of adequate technical, digital, and media competencies for all youths, their societal participation can be enhanced, and the formation of digital and societal divides can be mitigated even when transitioning from normal to exceptional times such as remote education and closing down societies due to pandemics.

Acknowledgements. This work was supported by Strategic Research Council of Finland: ALL-YOUTH grant (Decision no. 312693 and 326605). We thank the anonymous reviewers.

References

Albrecht, S., et al.: eParticipation – Electronic Participation of Citizens and the Business Community in eGovernment. Institut für Informationsmanagement Bremen GmbH (ifib) (2008)

Auxer, B.: Activism on Social Media Varies by Race and Ethnicity, Age, Political party. Pew Research Center, Washington, D.C. (2020)

Bandura, A.: Self-efficacy: toward a unifying theory of behavioral change. Psychol. Rev. **84**(2), 191–215 (1977). https://doi.org/10.1037/0033-295X.84.2.191

Bandura, A.: Self-efficacy in Changing Societies. Cambridge University Press, Cambridge (1995)

Bandura, A.: Guide for creating self-efficacy scales. In: Pajares, F., Urdan, T. (eds.) Self-efficacy Beliefs of Adolescents, pp. 307–337. Information Age Publishing, Greenwich (2006)

Blanc, J., Briggs, A.Q., Seixas, A.A., Reid, M., Jean-Louis, G., Pandi-Perumal, S.R.: Addressing psychological resilience during the coronavirus disease 2019 pandemic: a rapid review. Curr. Opin. Psychiatry **34**(1), 29–35 (2021)

Bland, J., Altman, D.: Statistics notes: cronbach's alpha. BMJ **314**, 275 (1997)

Braun, V., Clarke, V.: Using thematic analysis in psychology. Qual. Res. Psychol. **3**(2), 77–101 (2006)

Burnard, P.: A method of analysing interview transcripts in qualitative research. Nurse Educ. Today **11**(6), 461–466 (1991). https://doi.org/10.1016/0260-6917(91)90009-Y

Checkoway, B.: What is youth participation? Child Youth Serv. Rev. **33**(2), 340–345 (2011)

Chew, Q.H., Wei, K.C., Vasoo, S., Chua, H.C., Sim, K.: Narrative synthesis of psychological and coping responses towards emerging infectious disease outbreaks in the general population: practical considerations for the COVID-19 pandemic. Singapore Med. J. **61**(7), 350–356 (2020)

Compeau, D., Higgins, C.: Computer self-efficacy: development of a measure and initial test. MIS Q. **19**(2), 189–211 (1995). https://doi.org/10.2307/249688

Cronbach, L.J.: Coefficient alpha and the interval structure of tests. Psychometrika **16**, 297–334 (1951)

Finnish Government (2021). https://valtioneuvosto.fi/en/frontpage

Glaser, B.G., Strauss, A.L.: The Discovery of Grounded Theory. Aldine, New York (1967)

Hästbacka, E., Nygård, M., Nyqvist, F.: Barriers and facilitators to societal participation of people with disabilities: a scoping review of studies concerning European countries. Alter **10**(3), 201–220 (2016)

Herkama, S., Repo, J.: Valmistuitko koronakeväänä? Kyselytutkimus toisen asteen opinnoista valmistumassa olleille nuorille. University of Turku (2020). https://research.utu.fi/converis/por tal/Publication/51667985?lang=fi_FI

Howard, M.: Creation of a computer self-efficacy measure: analysis of internal consistency, psychometric properties, and validity. Cyberpsychol. Behav. Soc. Network. **17**(10), 677–681. 1089/cyber.2014.0255

Liu, P.L.: COVID-19 information seeking on digital media and preventive behaviors: the mediation role of worry. Cyberpsychol. Bch. Soc. Netw. **23**(10), 677–682 (2020). https://doi.org/10.1089/cyber.2020.0250

Malterud, K.: Systematic text condensation: a strategy for qualitative analysis. Scandinavian J. Public Health **40**(8), 2012 (2012)

Meriläinen, N., Pietilä, I., Varsaluoma, J.: Digital Services and Youth Participation in Processes of Social Change: World Café Workshops in Finland. Presented at 2018 ECPR General Conference, Universität Hamburg (2018)

Merry, S.N., et al.: Debate: Supporting the mental health of school students in the COVID-19 pandemic in New Zealand – a digital ecosystem approach. Child Adolescent Mental Health **25**(4), 267–269 (2020)

Mohammadzadeh, F., Noghabi, A.D., Khosravan, S., Bazeli, J., Armanmehr, V., Paykani, T.: Anxiety severity levels and coping strategies during the COVID-19 pandemic among people aged 15 years and above in gonabad, iran. Arch. Iran. Med. **23**(9), 633–638 (2020)

Montag, C., Elhai, J.D.: Discussing digital technology overuse in children and adolescents during the COVID-19 pandemic and beyond: on the importance of considering affective neuroscience theory. Add. Behav. Rep. **12**, 100313 (2020). https://doi.org/10.1016/j.abrep.2020.100313

Mushquash, A.R., Grassia, E.: Coping during COVID-19: examining student stress and depressive symptoms. J. Am. College Health 1–4 (2021). https://doi.org/10.1080/07448481.2020.1865379

National Institute for Health and Welfare (THL)

Nilsson, M., Barbutiu, S.M.: E-participation for increased citizen engagement? a case from Uganda. JeDEM – eJ. eDemocracy Open Govern. **11**(1), 14–36 (2019). https://doi.org/10.29379/jedem.v11i1.542

Panopoulou, E., Tambouris, E., Tarabanis, K.: Success factors in designing eParticipation initiatives. Inf. Organ. **24**(4), 195–213 (2014)

Omotayo, F., Folorunso, M.B.: Use of social media for political participation by youths. JeDEM - EJournal EDemocracy Open Govern. **12**(1), 132–157 (2020)

Pajares, F., Urdan, T.: Self-Efficacy Beliefs of Adolescents. Green-wich, Conn., IAP - Information Age Pub., Inc. (2006)

Pearman, A., Hughes, M.L., Smith, E.L., Neupert, S.D.: Age differences in risk and resilience factors in COVID-19-related stress. J. Gerontol. Ser. B, Psychol. Sci. Soc. Sci. **76**(2), e38–e44. https://doi.org/10.1093/geronb/gbaa120

Petzold, M.B., et al.: Risk, resilience, psychological distress, and anxiety at the beginning of the COVID-19 pandemic in Germany. Brain Behav. **10**(9) (2020). https://doi.org/10.1002/brb3. 1745

Pietilä, I., Varsaluoma, J., Väänänen, K.: Understanding the digital and non-digital participation by the gaming youth. In: Lamas, D., Loizides, F., Nacke, L., Petrie, H., Winckler, M., Zaphiris, P. (eds.) INTERACT 2019. LNCS, vol. 11747, pp. 453–471. Springer, Cham (2019). https://doi.org/10.1007/978-3-030-29384-0_28

Polizzi, C., Lynn, S., Perry, A.: Stress and coping in the time of COVID-19: pathways to resilience and recovery. Clin. Neuropsych. **17**(2), 59–62 (2020)

Salin, M., Kaittila, A., Hakovirta, M., Anttila, M.: Family coping strategies during Finland's COVID-19 lockdown. Sustainability **12**(21), 9133 (2020)

Sæbø, Ø., Rose, J., Skiftenes Flak, L.: The shape of eParticipation: characterizing an emerging research area. Gov. Inf. Q. **25**(3), 400–428 (2008)

Shanahan, L., et al.: Emotional distress in young adults during the COVID-19 pandemic: evidence of risk and resilience from a longitudinal cohort study. Psychol. Med. 1–10 (2020)

Tejedor, S., Cervi, L., Pérez-Escoda, A., Tusa, F.: Smartphone usage among students during COVID-19 pandemic in Spain, Italy and Ecuador. Paper presented at the ACM International Conference Proceeding Series, 571–576 (2020). https://doi.org/10.1145/3434780.3436587

The UN: Youth and the 2030 Agenda for Sustainable Development (2018). https://www.un.org/development/desa/youth/world-youth-report/wyr2018.html

Trafimow, D., et al.: Manipulating the alpha level cannot cure significance testing. Front. Psychol. **9**, 699 (2018)

Van Kessel, P., Widjaya, R., Shah, S., Smith, A., Hughes, A.: Congress Soars to New Heights on Social Media. Pew Research Center, Washington, D.C., July 16th, 2020. Retrieved February 27th from https://www.pewresearch.org/internet/2020/07/16/congress-soars-to-new-heights-on-socialmedia/

Discovering Sense of Community Enabling Factors for Public and Government Staff in Online Public Engagement

Ann O'Brien[(⊠)] [iD], William Golden, and Murray Scott

Department of Business Information Systems, J.E. Cairnes School of Business and Economics,
National University of Ireland Galway, Galway, Ireland
ann.obrien@nuigalway.ie

Abstract. eParticipation has largely not lived up to expectations and government responsiveness to public feedback, provided via eParticipation has proved challenging. In a new conceptualization of the theory of *Sense of Community* (SoC), this paper explores the dynamics of online government responsiveness, using dimensions of SoC to identify how those components *enable successful interaction* from both the perspective of government staff and public users. This study reports from two case studies designed to explore these interaction dynamics in online engagement initiatives in Ireland and the UK. The findings enabled the identification of important factors which facilitate successful SoC (for online public interaction) in this domain. Participation for government staff users was particularly associated with their perception of a safe online space. For public users, openness without responsiveness to public feedback was not valued, highlighting the importance of appropriate government responsiveness. The absence of social interactivity was identified as a negative for public users while the presence of social interactivity was identified as a positive for government staff users in the second case study. Overall, this study is the first empirical step to contribute to an understanding of successful social online processes in online public engagement. It highlights the utility of examining all four subconstructs of SoC and proposes factors to assist in the identification of critical SoC components in future studies.

Keywords: eParticipation · Responsiveness · Online social interaction · Sense of Community (SoC)

1 Introduction

Some have argued that government has largely chosen to ignore the implied value system of the social web [1] consisting of openness, participation and collaboration practiced by creative commons licences and open innovation [2]. The promise of the social web has been fulfilled to some extent in the business world via ecommerce where the utility of web social elements using SoC theory has been recognised [3, 4]. Much excitement has surrounded the potential of the internet for public engagement, yet it has largely not lived up to expectations [5, 6]. Challenges to achieving this promise come from

N. Edelmann et al. (Eds.): ePart 2021, LNCS 12849, pp. 15–26, 2021.
https://doi.org/10.1007/978-3-030-82824-0_2

governments' use of the internet for social interaction which has largely remained rooted in a bureaucratic and deeply formal mode. Other domains have recognised the value of web social tools [7] for interactivity, but governments have tended to pursue an unbalanced approach that favours the efficiency gains of using technology to disseminate information cheaply or to call on the public to contribute their opinion [8]. While there have been some successes [9] important barriers to government use of the social web include the worry of uncivil behaviour [10] and a lack of evidence regarding the impact of socially enabling internet technology on the success of government and public online interaction [11].

The term *Online Public Engagement* (OPE) [12] is used in this paper, as equal importance is placed on discovering elements of both staff and public participation, as 'public engagement' implies a two way interaction. This type of social interaction has proved to be challenging for many domains including eParticipation [13], Public Patient Involvement in health sciences research [14] and citizen science [15]. Common too are questions relating to the value of OPE [11] as the evaluation criteria often do not adequately accommodate understanding of the outcomes [6].

Challenges to successful OPE include a lack of understanding of the role of online interactivity in demonstrating government responsiveness to public feedback [1, 16] and the need to carefully consider the implications of the digital divide. This includes inequality of access due to cultural and material factors, the high costs of online participation for working class groups with regard to organisational resources, as well as individual differences in access, skills, empowerment and time [17].

Ireland where the study is based has been recently recognised as a leader in deliberative engagement, notably traditional citizen's assemblies [18]. Described here is the first attempt to identify *a type of online public interaction* that draws on the theory of SoC to help understand successful social online interaction between government staff and public users. Two case studies were investigated using an inductive approach to discover important components from both perspectives. This paper responds to the call for further research that goes beyond the technical challenges and examines the impact of social and physiological factors on the motivation of users of civic participation [12]. Recognising government responsiveness to public feedback as a key challenges to successful OPE, a broader conceptualisation of government responsiveness in the public sphere [16] is used. The approach taken to translate SoC theory for online public engagement is described below. The iterative data collection process of case studies referred back to SoC theory after each data gathering phase to help to identify SoC enabling factors specifically for online public engagement.

2   Sense of Community for Online Public Engagement

SoC is known as the cognitive component of social capital [19], and using all four subconstructs of SoC facilitates a more appropriate way to examine important social processes in online engagement compared to the network based approaches of the past [20]. Based on the foundational McMillan and Chavis framework [21]. The feeling of SoC has been defined as "a feeling that members have of belonging, a feeling that members matter to one another and to the group, and a shared faith that members' needs will be met through their commitment to be together" [21] 9). *SoC is built on interactions and this research identifies enabling factors of a SoC type of interaction for the purpose of identifying successful online public interaction.* SoC has a long empirical research history that is applicable to public engagement and has been found to strongly and positively correlate with important public values of trust and efficacy in traditional settings [22]. SoC has been found to positively influence important online behaviours such as information sharing and self-disclosure [23]. Linked to participation in social media communities [24] and in non-profit communities [25] SoC can also positively influence 'stickiness' (continued use, spending more time engaging with information) in eLearning [26].

The McMillan and Chavis original conceptualization of SoC in physically based communities consisted of four dimensions: *Sense of belonging, Shared emotional connection, Influence and Needs fulfilment*, and each have an important (interdependent) part to play in the theory of SoC. The concept of value that underpins SoC is a *shared value*, one that goes beyond individual value [21]. All four dimensions of SoC are introduced here to explore the utility of SoC to help understand social processes for both government staff and public participants of online public engagement.

A feeling of *Sense of belonging* is concerned with emotional safety and identification and more than the other SoC subconstructs has been identified by prior research as important to online participation in other domains; it has been used to represent the entire theory of SoC [27] and is often linked to usage or intention to use [28, 29].

In traditional communities the feeling of *Shared emotional connection* is associated with shared history, time together, contact and high-quality *interaction*; it has been identified as the subconstruct that best represents true SoC [21]. The impact of this subconstruct has not been explored adequately in online research and was not included in recent SoC research on participatory budgeting [30]. The potential of social interaction has been identified in public services in communities [31], yet little is known about the social processes involved regarding government responsiveness to public feedback.

The feeling of *Influence* refers to a bi-directional process where members are open to influence by the community and the community can influence members [21]. It is important in some influential SoC measures [32] yet it was dropped from an often-used measure of SoC online, in sense of virtual community SovC [33]. Existing indexes generally measure the SoC subconstruct Needs fulfilment in both traditional and online communities using a generic, non-specific measure of the extent that the community fulfils the individual's needs [23]. This study employs a comprehensive measure of SoC, extending SoC theory to describe a conceptualization of shared value, where successful online public engagement needs to create shared value and fulfil user's needs [21, 34].

SoC is conceptualized in this study uniquely as a type of *interaction suitable for government responsiveness to public feedback.* Here SoC reflects the foundational McMillan and Chavis framework [21, 33]. Enabling further exploration of the role of social interactivity as identified in public service communities [31].

3 Methodology

Using a novel re-conceptualization of SoC for online public engagement, this is the first time the entire SoC framework [21] has been used to explore social processes in online public engagement (OPE). Drawing on the extant literature from both online and offline public participation as a theoretical lens: scoping interviews (13) observations of relevant open group email (an **Open Government Partnership** (OGP) civil society group were used (179 discussions involving 43 participants)). Two case studies then explored public and staff user's perceptions of online interaction using a SoC lens. The first was a focus group of public users of the Irish OGP Development plan eConsultation platform. Initially the focus groups were planned to take place in a hotel in Dublin and moderated by an experienced moderator, no time was found that could suit a viable number of participants. Eventually an asynchronous online text focus group was used by 9 participants. This method overcame time and distance constraints and enabled as diverse and broadly representative group (of people who had submitted to the platform) as possible to participate. Interaction guidelines were developed to moderate the focus group using group methodology [35] and data analysis was conducted using content analysis [36].

It was not possible to discover a suitable example of government online interaction in Ireland instead the Knowledge Hub UK was used. Although somewhat culturally different, historically the English and Irish bureaucratic systems are similar. The second case study included a webinar/focus group with 17 participants, a survey with 13 respondents and interviews with the fulltime manager of the online facilitators' community on **Knowledge Hub** UK. A short SoC survey was circulated to all members of the online facilitators community as part of a larger survey undertaken by the management of Khub. Questions were drawn from SCI 2 [37] and [38] brief SoC scale (offline) using a five point Likert scale. Unfortunately, there was a technical difficulty saving responses to the questionnaire and only 13 responses were saved. While this was far from ideal, the aim of this part of the research was to gain an insight into the experiences of users, therefore, the responses to the questionnaire were analysed and reviewed with the KHub Manager and then used to examine the health of the online facilitators community and identify SoC enabling factors from the perspective of government staff users.

3.1 Case Study 1: Open Government Partnership – Public Users' Perspective

The OGP is a multi-stakeholder, trans-national collaboration initiative that began in 2011. The partnership is based on three principles of transparency, collaboration and participation and brings together government reformers and civil society leaders to create action plans. The aim is to make governments more inclusive, responsive and accountable [39]. Ireland joined in 2014 by endorsing a high-level Open Government Declaration and undertaking to develop a country level action plan with public consultation every two years [40]. The OGP e-Consultation portal was created to facilitate public input into the second Irish OGP development plan and was open in 2016 for public participation. There were 52 submissions on the OGP development plan platform which were reviewed as part of the case study. The contact details of 33 users were openly found on the platform from the 52 submissions. An asynchronous online text focus group was used to explore the participants' experience of value in online public engagement. Nine people took part in the focus group, which overcame time and distance constraints and enabled as diverse and broadly representative group (of people who had submitted to the platform) as possible to participate. SoC theory was distilled into the three concepts shown in Fig. 1 below as a more intuitive way to present to focus group members.

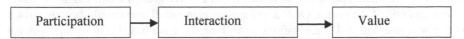

Fig. 1. The categories used to explore public users perception of value in online public engagement.

3.2 Case Study 2: Knowledge Hub – Government Staff Users' Perspective

As there was an absence of online participation perceived by government staff in case study 1, the second case study aimed to discover more about online interaction conducted by government staff. The **Knowledge Hub** (Khub) is the UK's largest public service collaboration platform (150,000 public service employees) it is an online networking platform and is free to use for public service professionals. Khub have been facilitating knowledge sharing between public service practitioners since 2006. Following an interview with the Digital Community Knowledge Manager, it was decided to discuss the utility of SoC from online communities in other domains with members. Members of the Online Facilitators Community on Khub (1,300 members) were invited to take part in a webinar/video focus group. SoC theory was discussed with reference to common community management challenges relating to participation, interaction and value with 17 members of this community. SoC subconstructs are outlined under the dashed line in Fig. 2 below.

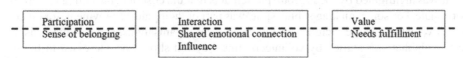

Fig. 2. Categories used to explore Staff users perception of value in an online public service community

4 Findings

Access to users was an issue in both case studies, the different approaches to the two case studies reflected the amount of access that was granted and the preferences of each group/platform management. Using SoC as a lens, each case study sought to discover users experience of participation, interaction and value. The first case study explores public user's perceptions of the value of online public engagement on the Irish OGP development plan portal with findings from the focus group. Reflecting these findings; the interviews with platform management of KHub, the webinar/focus group and questionnaire with the online community facilitators aimed to discover the government staff perspective of online engagement.

4.1   The Irish OGP Development Plan Portal – Public Users

The participants in the focus group were representative of the type of public users on the portal and contained representation from each of the five groups identified in the stakeholder analysis of the portal. OGP development plan portal users could be categorised as follows: International organisations describing the Irish based arm of international organisations whose primary concern was open government and transparency; interest groups describing sectoral and professional organisations who participated; social partnership organisations here describe unions, disability organisations and social advocacy organisations; local organisations describe those who identified themselves as from local networks (Public Participation Networks (PPN) attached to local councils); and finally, individuals (people who did not identify any affiliation). The portal enabled a diverse geographical spread of submissions which helped to enable one of the key aims of public participation: to gather a diverse range of views from as many people as possible for the development plan.

4.1.1   Participation

Many public users shared their identity and contact details; 33 out of 52 submissions. Respondents in the focus group mainly found the platform trustworthy and were willing to participate and share their names as shown by this quote from a participant of the focus group.

> "It was pretty easy to make a submission. It felt competent and trustworthy. It was a good idea because while it had some direction there was scope for plenty of freelance input. Seeing examples helped".

It was highlighted by focus group participants that the cost of contributing is disproportionate. For some, making submissions was part of their paid employment, for others it was voluntary. These included people from local organisations, some individuals or any group that was staffed by volunteers, this they felt should be addressed in future consultation processes.

4.1.2   Interaction

While the eConsultation portal had the potential to facilitate online interaction. Observation of the use of the platform confirmed that the platform was used almost exclusively for submitting contributions to the development plan replicating the traditional process. Despite the technical ability to interact informally on the platform, there was only formal statements/document drafts from government staff. A focus group participant stated.

> "I felt the platform had the ability to be interactive and responsive but was not used to its full potential by the participants, including myself!"

The effectiveness of the participatory process was questioned by participants of the focus group. They called for more clarity on the role of citizen input in the decision-making process regarding the proposals that were included or excluded in the draft development plan.

4.1.3 Value

The lack of responsiveness by government to the input of the public was highlighted as a key concern by public users. The formalised structures of responding with a draft document at the end of the consultation was not valued by the participants of the focus group. Public users were critical of the type of government responsiveness and unsure of the extent of process transparency in the development plan portal process.

"We did not consider that our opinions were well reflected in the plan...there was also no feedback that I could find on the final set of submissions".

The focus has traditionally been on how to engage with the public or increase public participation, very little is known about the government staff perception of interactivity in online public engagement. Case study 2 described below aimed to discover important elements of online participation from the perspective of government staff.

4.2 Knowledge Hub Online Facilitators Community – Government Staff Users

This case study was undertaken to discover factors that influence the online participation and interaction of public users/government staff. The findings from discussions with the Community Manager and webinar participants are outlined below with reference to SoC where all four subconstructs of SoC were evident.

4.2.1 Participation

The online facilitators community was a restricted group, which added an increased layer of *privacy* to the group. Each user created a profile of themselves on the Khub platform, (in some communities it was necessary to be a verified public sector employee). This enabled users to join groups and connect with other people on the platform and all of their participation on the platform was identified from this profile. The majority of staff answers to the survey *'agreed'* that they could trust other members and webinar/focus group participants recognised the concept sense of belonging. The Community Manager when interviewed felt that the closed nature of the community (including *verified identity*) helped to reassure users that the platform was a safe place to participate.

4.2.2 Interaction

In the Online Facilitators' Community two types of interactions could take place, private messaging, and open interaction. The latter was shared with email notifications from management of webinars and online events and comments in weekly updates. Most of the interactions were clustered around how to create and maintain an online group e.g., walk throughs of technical details of using the platform to facilitate a group. Much of the participation was receiving information from the expert community managers, supported by the private messaging system on the community.

Shared emotional connection was recognised by webinar participants and in the survey respondents *'agreed'* that users cared for each other. The Community Manager explained that there was a high level of support in this group. Private messaging was supported by the platform which is likely to an important additional support as users came to this community largely to receive support, but also 'agreed' it was important to participate.

Influence was recognised as challenging in practice, the Community Managers felt they could give more agenda setting control to members of the community in future as survey respondents felt unsure if they had influence in the community, but they mostly '*agreed*' that it was important to take all views into account when making decisions on the Khub.

4.2.3 Value

Along with interaction within the community, the fulltime Community Managers and other members of the community were available to provide additional support through private messaging. There was also the opportunity to network and find individuals working on similar projects or people who had similar challenges. Webinar participants and the Community Manager could recognise how the Khub fulfilled needs. Survey respondents '*agreed*' that they had needs met by participating on Khub but were unsure of the extent that Khub fulfilled their needs. They 'agreed' that their community could make decisions together for the good of the community.

This qualitative exploratory data collection indicated that the SoC as outlined above clearly had relevance for government employees who were online community facilitators. It created a framework for discussing the quality of online interactions and helped community managers to identify areas for improvement.

5   Discussion and Conclusions

In this initial empirical exploration of SoC for online public engagement, case study 1 focus group participants, who were users of the public portal, clearly showed a commitment to the public value principle of the citizens' role as a contributor and not just the receiver of public value [41]. A key finding of case study 1 corroborates earlier research findings [8], public participants found the type of government responsiveness used (formal documents) was insufficient. These public users expectations of responsiveness was closer to a broader conceptualisation of responsiveness [16]. The absence of government responsiveness (timely online interaction) more usually associated with social web interaction values [1] had a significantly negative affect on the participants' experience of value in online public engagement. The second case study extends the knowledge of conditions of online participation for government staff users, showing that the provision of a safe place to participate was a key element that enabled their participation and interaction online. Important too was the provision of timely and appropriate supports to facilitate that participation. Case study 2 shows the importance of providing a safe, supportive space to participate that fulfils the needs of users. The findings give an indication of the elements of SoC that are important for public and government staff users as shown in Table 1 below.

The following limitations to the study have been identified, it would have been preferable to conduct both case studies in one country only, but the special relationship

Table 1. Evidence of SoC in the case studies

Behaviour	Indication of Sense of community
OGP Ireland (Public) Some identity sharing and information sharing *Khub (Gov Staff)* Restricted groups, Verified ID, visible participation	*Sense of belonging* Some evidence of identity sharing Users highlighted the importance of feelings of safety on the platform
OGP Ireland Interaction possible but not displayed *Khub* Knowledge Exchange	*Influence* Only formal replies given by government, public influence not highlighted Shared agenda setting identified as challenging, but important
OGP Ireland No social interaction *Khub* Direct messaging/Manager support	*Shared emotional connection* No feelings of this type identified Feelings of support/care experienced
OGP Ireland Lack of responsiveness affected benefit *Khub* Webinars and online events and the availability of peer support	*Needs fulfilment* Openness, low cost of participation Knowledge exchange, learning, social interaction

and bureaucratic similarities in both countries helped to ameliorate this. It also would have been good to have more public uses take part in the focus groups, but care was taken that participants were representative of the types of stakeholders on the eConsultation platform. As an outsider to government, it was also difficult to gain access to their perspective, the focus group/webinar and interviews with the community manager helped to bridge the gaps in understanding from the small number of survey replies.

Until now social dimensions of online public engagement have received little attention [42], here new evidence and appropriate theory to support further examination of the importance of the social dimensions of online public engagement is described. Highlighting the separate challenges for both public and government staff users of online public engagement platforms. The paper builds on observations, interviews and case studies using the SoC lens to identify a type of online *interaction* for online public engagement. SoC is a highly desirable element for online engagement [24] and the SoC enabling factors described in Table 2 below can assist the identification of SoC in online public engagement for similar research endeavours.

The factors identified in Table 2 below were used to enable the next stage of this research to select a platform for qualitative and quantitative analysis of this conceptualisation of SoC interaction, confirming the effectiveness of these factors to indicate the presence of SoC in successful online public engagement.

Table 2. Enabling Sense of community factors for online public engagement

SoC	SoC enabling factors
Participation *Sense of belonging*	Moderation, Identity sharing/Verified identity
Interaction *Shared emotional connection* *Influence*	Social interactivity, Support Bi-directional influence
Value *Needs fulfilment*	Responsiveness, Learning, Peer support

Acknowledgements. This research was partially funded by an Enterprise Ireland Innovation Voucher.

References

1. Bryer, T.A.: The costs of democratization: Social media adaptation challenges within government agencies. Adm. Theory Praxis **33**, 341–361 (2011)
2. O'Reilly, T.: What is Web 2.0: design patterns and business models for the next generation of software. Commun. Strat. **17** (2007)
3. Tonteri, L., Kosonen, M., Ellonen, H.-K., Tarkiainen, A.: Antecedents of an experienced sense of virtual community. Comput. Hum. Behav. **27**, 2215–2223 (2011)
4. Gebauer, J., Füller, J., Pezzei, R.: The dark and the bright side of co-creation: triggers of member behavior in online innovation communities. J. Bus. Res. **66**, 1516–1527 (2013)
5. Bannister, F., Connolly, R.: Forward to the past: Lessons for the future of e-government from the story so far. Inf. Polity **17**, 211–226 (2012)
6. Toots, M.: Why E-participation systems fail: the case of Estonia's Osale. ee. Govern. Inf. Quar. **36**, 546–559 (2019)
7. Hajiheydari, N., Maskan, B.H.H., Ashkani, M.: Factors affecting loyalty of mobile social networks' users. Int. J. E-Bus. Res. **13**, 66–81 (2017)
8. Deschamps, R., McNutt, K., Zhu, W.: Environmental scan on social media use by the public sector. Graduate School of Public Policy, University of Saskatchewan. Retrieved April 11, 2014 (2012)
9. Royo, S., Pina, V., Garcia-Rayado, J.: Decide Madrid: a critical analysis of an award-winning e-participation initiative. Sustainability **12**, 1674 (2020)
10. Nabatchi, T., Farrar, C.: Bridging the gap between public officials and the public. A report of the Deliberative Democracy Consortium 1–64 (2011)
11. Panagiotopoulos, P., Bowen, F., Brooker, P.: The value of social media data: integrating crowd capabilities in evidence-based policy. Gov. Inf. Q. **34**, 601–612 (2017)
12. Epstein, D., Newhart, M., Vernon, R.: Not by technology alone: the "analog" aspects of online public engagement in policymaking. Gov. Inf. Q. **31**, 337–344 (2014)
13. Le Blanc, D.: E-participation: a quick overview of recent qualitative trends. United Nations (2020)
14. Wale, J.L., Thomas, S., Hamerlijnck, D., Hollander, R.: Patients and public are important stakeholders in health technology assessment but the level of involvement is low–a call to action. Res. Involve. Engage. **7**, 1–11 (2021)

15. Haklay, M.: Participatory citizen science. In: Haklay, M.H.S., Bowser, A., Makuch, Z., Vogel, J., Bonn, A. (eds.) Citizen Science: Innovation in Open Science, Society and Policy, pp. 52–62. UCL Press, London (2018)

16. Dekker, R., Bekkers, V.: The contingency of governments' responsiveness to the virtual public sphere: a systematic literature review and meta-synthesis. Gov. Inf. Q. **32**, 496–505 (2015)

17. Schradie, J.: The digital activism gap: how class and costs shape online collective action. Soc. Probl. **65**, 51–74 (2018)

18. Courant, D.: Citizens' Assemblies for referendums and constitutional reforms: is there an "Irish model" for deliberative democracy? Front. Polit. Sci. **2**, 14 (2020)

19. Perkins, D.D., Long, D.A.: Neighborhood sense of community and social capital, A multi-level analysis. In: Fisher, A.C.S., Bishop, B. (eds.) Psychological Sense of Community: Research, Applications, And Implications, pp. 291–318 Plenum, New York (2002)

20. Harris, J.K., Choucair, B., Maier, R.C., Jolani, N., Bernhardt, J.M.: Are public health organizations tweeting to the choir? Understanding local health department Twitter followership. J. Med. Internet Res. **16**, e31 (2014)

21. McMillan, D.W., Chavis, D.M.: Sense of community: a definition and theory. J. Community Psychol. **14**, 6–23 (1986)

22. Anderson, M.R.: community psychology, political efficacy, and trust. Polit. Psychol. **31**, 59–84 (2010)

23. Mamonov, S., Koufaris, M., Benbunan-Fich, R.: The role of the sense of community in the sustainability of social network sites. Int. J. Electron. Commer. **20**, 470–498 (2016)

24. Zhang, Z.: Feeling the sense of community in social networking usage. IEEE Trans. Eng. Manage. **57**, 225–239 (2010)

25. Yoo, W.-S., Suh, K.-S., Lee, M.-B.: Exploring the factors enhancing member participation in virtual communities. PACIS 2001 Proceedings, vol. 38 (2001)

26. Luo, N., Zhang, M., Qi, D.: Effects of different interactions on students' sense of community in e-learning environment. Comput. Educ. **115**, 153–160 (2017)

27. Zhao, L., Lu, Y., Wang, B., Chau, P.Y., Zhang, L.: Cultivating the sense of belonging and motivating user participation in virtual communities: a social capital perspective. Int. J. Inf. Manage. **32**, 574–588 (2012)

28. Lin, H.-F.: Determinants of successful virtual communities: contributions from system characteristics and social factors. Inf. Manage. **45**, 522–527 (2008)

29. Teo, H.-H., Oh, L.-B., Liu, C., Wei, K.-K.: An Empirical study of the effects of interactivity on web user attitude. Int. J. Hum Comput Stud. **58**, 281–305 (2003)

30. Naranjo-Zolotov, M., Oliveira, T., Casteleyn, S., Irani, Z.: Continuous usage of e-participation: the role of the sense of virtual community. Gov. Inf. Q. **36**, 536–545 (2019)

31. Meijer, A., Grimmelikhuijsen, S., Brandsma, G.J.: Communities of public service support: citizens engage in social learning in peer-to-peer networks. Gov. Inf. Q. **29**, 21–29 (2012)

32. Koh, J., Kim, Y.-G.: Sense of virtual community: a conceptual framework and empirical validation. Int. J. Electron. Commer. **8**, 75–94 (2003)

33. Blanchard, A.L., Markus, M.L.: The experienced "sense" of a virtual community: characteristics and processes. ACM Sigmis Database: Database Adv. Inf. Syst. **35**, 64–79 (2004)

34. Meynhardt, T.: Public value inside: what is public value creation? Int. J. Public Adm. **32**, 192–219 (2009)

35. Stewart, D.W., Shamdasani, P.: Online focus groups. J. Advert. **64**(1), 48–60 (2017)

36. Nili, A., Tate, M., Johnstone, D., Gable, G.: A Framework for Qualitative Analysis of Focus Group Data in Information Systems. ACIS (2014)

37. Chavis, D., Lee, K., Acosta, J.: The sense of community (SCI) revised: the reliability and validity of the SCI-2. In: 2nd international community psychology conference, Lisboa, Portugal (2008)

38. Peterson, N.A., Speer, P.W., McMillan, D.W.: Validation of a brief sense of community scale: confirmation of the principal theory of sense of community. J. Commun. Psychol. **36**, 61–73 (2008)
39. Lathrop, D., Ruma, L.: Open government: Collaboration, transparency, and participation in practice. O'Reilly Media Inc (2010)
40. Chari, R.: Ireland's Open Government Partnership National Action Plan 2016–2018, Draft End-term Self-Assessment Report. Department of Public Expenditure and Reform (2018)
41. Stoker, G.: Public value management a new narrative for networked governance? Am. Rev. Public Adm. **36**, 41–57 (2006)
42. McNutt, K.: Public engagement in the Web 2.0 era: Social collaborative technologies in a public sector context. Can. Public Adm. **57**, 49–70 (2014)

Understanding Civic Engagement on Social Media Based on Users' Motivation to Contribute

Sara Hofmann[1] (ID) and Ilias O. Pappas[1,2](✉) (ID)

[1] University of Agder, 4639 Kristiansand, Norway
{sara.hofmann,ilias.pappas}@uia.no
[2] Norwegian University of Science and Technology, 7491 Trondheim, Norway

Abstract. Social media offer various opportunities for civic engagement by, e.g., liking, sharing, or posting relevant content. Users' motivation to contribute to relevant topics is quite divers and can stem from an intrinsic motivation to do good or external incentives such as being recognised and rewarded by other users. In our study, we adopt self-determination theory, which defines motivation as broad continuum ranging from intrinsic motivation to external regulation. We conducted a quantitative survey with 667 Facebook users to identify how the different kinds of motivation impact the users' behaviour in terms of reading, liking, sharing, commenting, and posting topics relevant to civic engagement. Our results suggest that social media users are mainly driven by intrinsic motivation while different forms of extrinsic motivation play a less important role.

Keywords: Civic engagement · Social media · Self-determination theory · Survey

1 Introduction

Civic engagement refers to "individual and collective actions designed to identify and address issues of public concern" [1]. These actions can take various forms, ranging from individual voluntarism to organisational involvement or participating in elections. Civic engagement involves working directly to solving an issue of public concern such as offering meals to homeless people, being organised in a group with others such as being part of a neighbourhood association or a political party, to interacting with political decision makers by e.g., writing them a letter.

With the rise of social media, taking part in civic engagement activities has become easier and more convenient. Social media enable simple and cheap opportunities to express opinions, organise actions or acquire knowledge about a topic of public concern [1–3].

While these technological affordances that social media offer for civic engagement have been well explored, people's motives for contributing to civic engagement activities on social media are still opaque. There are, for example, conflicting believes as to whether the driving force is to express oneself in terms of sharing opinions or whether the use

© IFIP International Federation for Information Processing 2021
Published by Springer Nature Switzerland AG 2021
N. Edelmann et al. (Eds.): ePart 2021, LNCS 12849, pp. 27–39, 2021.
https://doi.org/10.1007/978-3-030-82824-0_3

of social media is mainly seen as an instrument for reaching a higher civic engagement goal [1]. The individual motivation, which is the driving force for all kinds of action [4], has hardly been investigated when it comes to contributing to issues of public concern on social media. Therefore, the aim of our study is to answer the question:

RQ: What motivates users to contribute to civic engagement activities on social media?

To answer this question, we have conducted a survey that builds on the self-determination theory (SDT). SDT is a well-established theoretical approach to human motivation and differentiates motivation among a spectrum ranging from intrinsic motivation that is characterised by the will to do good to extrinsic motivation, where people are driven by external incentives such as receiving recognition from others [4, 5]. We have conceptualised civic engagement on social media using a multi-dimensional construct, consisting of reading, liking, sharing, commenting, and posting topics of civic engagement on social media. Our results suggest that social media users are mainly driven by intrinsic motivation while different forms of extrinsic motivation play a less important role.

The remainder of the paper is organised as follows. In the next section, we present related work on civic engagement on social media and self-determination theory and develop our research model. In Sect. 3, we describe our methodological approach. Afterwards in Sect. 4, we present our findings, which we discuss in Sect. 5. Finally, in Sect. 6, we conclude our paper, explain limitations, and point out directions for future research.

2   Related Work and Research Model

2.1   Civic Engagement on Social Media

There is no unified definition as to what civic engagement entails. Adler and Goggin have identified four different, partly contradicting perspectives on civic engagement in the literature [6]. First, civic engagement is understood as community service where citizens contribute alone or in cooperation with others to the wellbeing of their local community. Second, it refers to collective action, i.e., it only encompasses activities that are pursued jointly with other individuals. Third, civic engagement is seen as political involvement, which excludes all activities that are not explicitly targeted towards political processes. Finally, it is perceived as social change, i.e., not the activities but rather the goal of shaping the future and creating social change are in the focus of civic engagement. In this paper, we refer to the rather broad definition by the American Psychological Association (APA), which understands civic engagement as all "individual and collective actions designed to identify and address issues of public concern" [7]. Just like the forms of civic engagement, also the issues of public concern that are addressed by civic engagement cover a broad variety of different topics. They include, among many others, the areas of health (e.g., by donating blood), education and learning (e.g., by serving as a tutor or mentor for a young person), and politics (e.g., by voting or being member of a political party) [6]. Civic engagement activities can, on the one hand, be organised top-down where public institutions actively seek for citizen participation. On the other hand, they can be bottom-up initiatives that are organised by actors of the civil society [8].

The Internet is assumed to have promoted civic engagement since it offers convenient and manifold opportunities to gather up-to-date information, gain knowledge, connect with others and organise actions [3]. While the goals of traditional offline and online civic engagement are the same, expressing opinions and sharing believes can be done with little effort and at a low cost on the Internet, especially on social media [1, 9]. Civic engagement activities on social media such as liking a post that deals with a topic of public concern, require as little effort as one click [1, 2]. In addition, social media offers even individuals who are not members of a specific community the opportunity to engage in activities they deem important.

Social media offer different interaction functions for contributing to issues of public concern such as sharing information, exchanging views and opinions by liking, sharing, and commenting posts, becoming a fan, joining or following a profile or group, adding hashtags, posting status updates, or adding profile pictures [1]. Datyev et al. have developed a conceptual model for analysing civic engagement on social media [10]. They have identified five types of interaction, i.e., views, likes, comments, re-posts, and posts. These interaction types are the basis for our conceptualisation of civic engagement on social media in our study where we use the dependent variables (a) *reading*, (b) *liking*, (c) *sharing*, (d) *commenting*, and (e) *posting* civic engagement topics.

2.2 Motivation for Civic Engagement on Social Media: Self-determination Theory

Motivations to contribute to civic engagement activities online can differ from civic engagement in the offline world [11]. Hong et al. found that the motives for civic engagement on social media were first and foremost to express their opinion as well as to connect with other users that share similar viewpoints. The idea that their engagement would actually have an impact outside the world of social media seemed less important, though [1].

Motivation as such is no singular concept but can be differentiated according to different types of factors. These can range from being motivated because people value a certain activity to being externally pressured. The external pressure, in turn, can range from external incentives such as financial stimulation to being forced or bribed to perform a certain behaviour [4]. A renowned approach to human motivation is the self-determination theory (SDT). SDT offers a differentiated description of motivation and distinguishes between self-motivation or intrinsic motivation and differing degrees of extrinsic motivation [4, 5, 12]. Later on, SDT was expended by three basic psychological needs, i.e., the need for autonomy, relatedness, and competence, that moderate the motivation to perform a certain behaviour.

SDT distinguishes between the three basic types of motivation *amotivation, extrinsic motivation*, and *intrinsic motivation* (cf. Fig. 1). *Amotivation* refers to not being interested in performing an activity, not feeling competent enough, or not expecting a result. On the other side of the motivational spectrum, *intrinsic motivation* describes "the doing of an activity for its inherent satisfaction" [4]. Conducting an activity due to intrinsic motivation is a source of enjoyment and pleasure. According to SDT, intrinsic motivation is the prototypical form of self-determination. In between the continuum ranging from amotivation to intrinsic motivation, *extrinsic motivation* is located. Extrinsic motivation can be further distinguished into four types, depending on how autonomous the regulation is. *External regulation* refers to the least autonomous behaviour and covers activities that are performed to satisfy an external demand or receive a reward. *Introjected regulation* takes in regulation to a higher degree but does not fully perceive it as one's own. People often perform activities to avoid feeling guilty or in order to feel proud. Actions that are characterised by *identified regulation*, which is a more autonomous form of extrinsic motivation, are accepted as personally important. The most self-determined or autonomous form of extrinsic motivation is represented by *integrated regulation*. Although activities characterised by this form of motivation are not pursued for inherent enjoyment, integrated regulation shares many characteristics with intrinsic motivation. Here the regulations have been fully assimilated and overlap with people's values and believes.

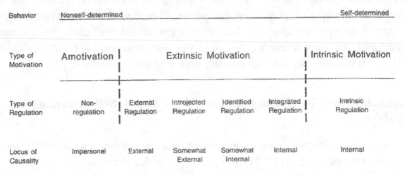

Fig. 1. The self-determination continuum [5]

SDT has been applied to a variety of contexts where motivation plays an important role such as work motivation [12], environmental-friendly behaviour [13], or dental treatment [14]. Recently, it has also found its way into understanding what motivates people's behaviour in civic engagement (cf. e.g. [11, 15]). Zhao and Zhu applied SDT to participation in crowdsourcing contests and hypothesise that both extrinsic and intrinsic motivation positively relate to participation efforts in crowdsourcing contests [16]. Schmidthuber et al. used SDT for analysing citizens' motivation to participate in ideation platforms initiated by government agencies [17]. They differentiated participation in terms of number of posted ideas, number of comments and responses, as well as number of likes and dislikes a user gave.

2.3 Research Model

Our aim in this study was to identify what motivates users to contribute to civic engagement activities on social media. We conceptualised civic engagement as a multidimensional construct consisting of (a) reading, (b) liking, (c) sharing, (d) commenting, (e) posting civic engagement topics on social media, in our case Facebook. Based on self-determination literature and its application to the context of political and civic participation, we developed the following research model and hypotheses (Fig. 2).

H1:   External regulation positively influences the intention to (a) read, (b) like, (c) share, (d) comment, (e) post civic engagement activities on Facebook.
H2:   Introjected regulation positively influences the intention to (a) read, (b) like, (c) share, (d) comment, (e) post civic engagement activities on Facebook.
H3:   Identified regulation positively influences the intention to (a) read, (b) like, (c) share, (d) comment, (e) post civic engagement activities on Facebook.
H4:   Integrated regulation positively influences the intention to (a) read, (b) like, (c) share, (d) comment, (e) post civic engagement activities on Facebook.
H5:   Intrinsic regulation positively influences the intention to (a) read, (b) like, (c) share, (d) comment, (e) post civic engagement activities on Facebook.

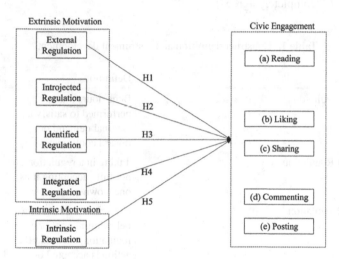

Fig. 2. Research model

3   Research Method

3.1   Sample

Our research model deals with experienced users in social media. The respondents were given a definition of social media, followed by a few examples, and they were asked to keep this in mind, while answering the questions based on their previous experience. We received 978 responses and we removed those who did not have experience with civic engagement activities on Facebook. This left us with a sample of 667 users of social media that had participated in civic engagement activities on Facebook. Participation in the survey was voluntary and no reward was given.

The sample is balanced in terms of gender and consists of 49% women and 51% of men. The average age for the respondents was 37 years, with a range between 16 to 69 years of age. The sample has a normal distribution with the majority being between 24–50 years old, while having representation in all age groups.

In terms of the educational status, the majority (31%) were university graduates, 30% were junior high school graduates, 26% were high school graduates, and 10% had left school after 9 years.

3.2 Measures

The questionnaire was divided into two parts. The first part included questions on the demographics of the sample (age, gender, education). The second part included measures of the constructs as they were identified in the literature review section. Table 1 lists the operational definitions of the constructs in our theoretical model along with their source in the literature. We employed a 7-point Likert scale anchored from 1 ("completely disagree") to 7 ("completely agree").

Table 1. Construct definition and instrument development

Construct	Definition	Source
1. External Regulation	Behaviours that are performed to satisfy an external demand or reward contingency	[4]
2. Introjected Regulation	Taking in a regulation but not fully accepting it as one's own	[4]
3. Identified Regulation	Conscious valuing of a behavioural goal or regulation, such that the action is accepted or owned as personally important	[4]
4. Integrated Regulation	Fully assimilating identified regulations to the self, i.e., having evaluated and brought into congruence with one's other values and needs	[4]
5. Intrinsic Regulation	Doing an activity for the inherent satisfaction of the activity itself	[4]
6. Reading/7. Liking/8. Sharing/9. Commenting/10. Posting	Reading, liking, sharing, commenting, or posting civic engagement topics on Facebook	[10]

4 Results

4.1 Measurements

To test our model, we applied partial least squares-based structural equation modeling (PLS-SEM), using SmartPLS version 3.0 software [18]. PLS-SEM allows to estimate multiple relations between multiple dependent and independent variables. First, a measurement model was created to test for construct reliability and validity, and then the structural model was built in order to test the hypothesised relationships.

The constructs are assessed for reliability based on the Cronbach alpha and Composite Reliability indicators, that show acceptable indices of internal consistency as all constructs exceed the cut-off threshold of .70. For validity, the average variance extracted (AVE) needs to be larger than .50, correlations among variables should be lower than .80 points, and the square root of each factor's AVE should be higher than its correlations with the other factors (Fornell-Larcker criterion) [19].

The AVE ranges between 0.74 and 0.88, all correlations are lower than 0.80, and square root AVEs are larger than corresponding correlations. The findings are presented in Table 2. Multicollinearity [20] is examined along with the potential common method bias by utilizing Harman's single factor test, an acceptable assessment tool for common methods variance [21]. Variance inflation factor (VIF) for all factors is lower than the recommended value (<5), thus multicollinearity is not an issue. Common method bias is not a problem, as variance of the first factor accounts for less than 50% of the variance among variables, based on Harman's single factor test.

Table 2. Descriptive statistics and correlations of latent variables

Construct	CR	AVE	1	2	3	4	5	6	7	8	9	10
1. External regulation	.96	.87	**.92**									
2. Introjected regulation	.96	.86	.69	**.87**								
3. Identified regulation	.89	.74	−.09	.19	**.91**							
4. Integrated regulation	.92	.75	.60	.65	.29	**.86**						
5. Intrinsic regulation	.93	.77	.38	.43	.45	.63	**.86**					
6. Reading	.94	.83	−.02	.11	.46	.21	.32	**.88**				
7. Liking	.93	.83	.23	.32	.33	.41	.45	.59	**.90**			
8. Sharing	.95	.88	.34	.42	.31	.49	.46	.48	.74	**.93**		
9. Commenting	.92	.79	.45	.43	.23	.48	.48	.40	.61	.69	**.93**	
10. Posting	.95	.87	.40	.42	.25	.50	.47	.41	.65	.80	.78	**.93**

Note: Diagonal elements (in bold) are the square root of the average variance extracted (AVE). Off-diagonal elements are the correlations among constructs. For discriminant validity, diagonal elements should be larger than off-diagonal elements

The estimated path coefficients of the structural model were examined in order to evaluate our hypotheses. Figure 3 presents the analysis of the research model.

Specifically, external regulation has a positive effect on commenting and posting, while it has no effect on reading, liking, and sharing. Thus, H1d-e are supported, while H1a-c are rejected. Next, regarding the dimensions of intrinsic motivation, introjected regulation has a positive effect on sharing, while it has no effect on reading, liking, commenting, and posting. Thus, H2c is supported, while H2a, b, d, e are rejected. Next, the results show that identified regulation has a positive effect on all dimensions of civic engagement, that are reading, liking, sharing, comment, posting, thus H3a–e are supported. Next, integrated regulation has a positive effect on liking, sharing, commenting, and posting, while it has no effect on reading. Thus, H4b–e are supported, while H4a is rejected. Finally, intrinsic regulation has a positive effect on all dimensions of civic engagement (i.e., reading, liking, sharing, comment, posting), thus H5a–e are supported.

Square multiple correlations (R^2) for the five dimensions of civic engagement are presented on Fig. 2 as well. The R^2 for reading is 0.24, for liking is 0.26, for sharing is 0.31, for commenting is 0.34, and for posting is 0.32. Values higher than 0.26 imply relatively high effects of the predictors of civic engagement.

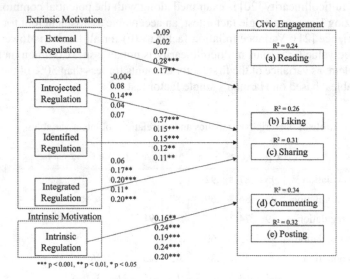

Fig. 3. SEM analysis of the research model

5   Discussion

Our study has shed light on civic engagement on social media and has analysed how different types of motivation influence people's civic engagement behaviour. We have based our study on the well-established SDT that differentiates between external, introjected, identified, integrated regulation, and intrinsic motivation.

We have developed a new construct for our dependent variable civic engagement. Civic engagement has been measured as a multi-dimensional construct, consisting of reading, liking, sharing, commenting, and posting civic engagement topics on Facebook. In doing so, we built on the framework developed by [10]. To the best of our knowledge, we are the first ones to have conceptualised civic engagement on social media in such breadth. The results of the hypothesis testing reveal several significant relations.

First, *intrinsic regulation* has a significant positive influence on all five dimensions of civic engagement (5a–e). This indicates that contributing to issues of public concern on social media is driven by inherent satisfaction and joy of doing good for society. Our findings are in line with related studies that have also found a merely positive impact of intrinsic motivation on participation [16, 17].

Second, a different picture shows for the different types of extrinsic motivation. Only *identified regulation* has a significant positive influence on all dimensions of civic engagement (3a–e). This indicates that after consciously valuing the goal of civic engagement on social media, the actions are accepted as personally important [4]. In contrast to this, *integrated regulation*, which refers to having brought civic engagement on social media into congruence with one's own value system, has a significant positive impact on liking, sharing, commenting, and posting civic engagement activities on social media (4b–e), while it does not have a significant impact on reading. *Introjected regulation* only has a significant impact on sharing civic engagement topics on social media (2c). Since introjected regulation refers to conducting a behaviour but not fully accepting it as one's own, this result is not surprising. Still, it is in contrast to the findings by Zhao and Zhu [16], who have identified a significant impact on participation effort. *External regulation* has a positive impact on commenting and posting civic engagement activities on social media (1d–e). Since this type of motivation refers to behaviours that are performed to satisfy an external demand or reward contingency, it is understandable that this motivation triggers the two most 'visible' civic engagement activities on social media.

Regarding the different dimensions of civic engagement on social media, it is striking that four out of five hypotheses postulating an influence on commenting and posting were confirmed in contrast to only two hypotheses suggesting an impact on reading. This suggests that reading, which is a rather passive activity, often preferred by citizens when it comes to interacting with government on social media [22], is especially not important when the motivation is extrinsic, that is, to show others that one is contributing to issues of public concern.

6 Conclusions

In our study, we have raised the question "What motivates users to contribute to civic engagement activities on social media?" To answer this, we have conducted a quantitative survey with Facebook users, building on SDT. The findings suggest that especially intrinsic motivation is very important for civic engagement activities while different types of extrinsic motivation play a less important role. Our results are not totally congruent with previous findings from literature, which might be explained by our multi-dimensional conceptualisation of civic engagement.

Our findings have implications for both research and practice. As for the first, we have contributed to the research body of knowledge by applying SDT to the area of civic engagement on social media. In addition, we have developed and applied a new, multi-dimensional construct of civic engagement on social media, consisting of reading, liking, sharing, commenting, and posting activities. As for implications for practice, our results suggest that, at least to a certain degree, civic organisations can strengthen people's motivation to contributing to issues of public concern on social media. This also applies for public sector organisations with the goal of reaching a higher level of participation.

Our research comes with several limitations and calls for further research. First, we have not differentiated between different topics of civic engagement such as political, environmental, or societal issues. Also, we did not distinguish between top-down initiatives (i.e., initiatives initiated by public organisations) and bottom-up actions. Further, future studies may examine how the required skills for citizen-public official interaction that changed due to digitalization [23] impact civic engagement. Second, the findings are based on self-reported data; other methods such as in-depth interviews could provide a complementary picture of the findings. Third, our data stem from a German-speaking context, thus probably including cultural biases. Therefore, our study should be extended to further national contexts. As a future step, we additionally plan to examine civic engagement as a third order construct, in which the related categories sharing/liking and commenting/posting are summarised as second-order construct. Finally, we plan to apply fuzzy-set Qualitative Comparative Analysis (fsQCA) [24], which enables us to identify the necessary and sufficient conditions for an outcome to occur [25, 26] and get more in-depth insights into the relationships between the concepts.

Appendix

Scale items with mean, standard deviation and standardized loading.

Construct and scale items	Mean	S.D	Loading
I read, like, share, comment, or post topics relevant to civic engagement on Facebook…			
Extrinsic Motivation: *External Regulation*			
1… because other people will be upset if I don't	2.50	1.75	0.918
2… because I get recognition from others in doing so	2.62	1.69	0.911
3… because my friends expect me to do so	2.49	1.73	0.944
4… to avoid being criticised	2.33	1.70	0.941
Extrinsic Motivation: *Introjected Regulation*			
1… because I feel bad about myself if I don't	2.70	1.78	0.856
2… because I feel dissatisfied with myself if I don't	3.11	1.79	0.883
3… because I feel internal pressure that compels me to	3.67	1.82	0.790
4… because I feel uncomfortable if I don't	3.14	1.84	0.915

(continued)

(*continued*)

Construct and scale items	Mean	S.D	Loading
5... because I regret it if I don't	2.98	1.77	0.899
6... to calm my consciousness	2.87	1.81	0.859
Extrinsic Motivation: *Identified Regulation*			
1... because I feel it is important for me personally to do it	5.18	1.48	0.914
2... because it has great personal significance for me	4.77	1.59	0.908
3... because I experience it as personally important	5.06	1.55	0.916
Extrinsic Motivation: *Integrated Regulation*			
1... because it is a well-established habit of mine	3.07	1.76	0.885
2... because it is now quite natural for me	4.08	1.76	0.801
3... because it is now an entrenched habit of mine	3.12	1.75	0.891
Intrinsic Motivation: *Intrinsic Regulation*			
1... because I enjoy doing it	3.78	1.76	0.865
2... because I find that it is a pleasurable experience	3.95	1.75	0.892
3... because I like the feeling when contributing to civic engagement	4.00	1.72	0.869
4... because I experience pleasure in contributing to civic engagement	4.43	1.66	0.835
Reading			
1 Whenever I see a post relevant to civic engagement on Facebook, I read it	5.32	1.21	0.927
2 It is likely that I read a post relevant to civic engagement when it is displayed in my newsfeed on Facebook	5.34	1.24	0.899
3 I read all posts relevant to civic engagement that I see on Facebook	4.68	1.53	0.833
Liking			
1 Whenever I see a post relevant to civic engagement on Facebook, I like it	4.54	1.30	0.926
2 It is likely that I like a post relevant to civic engagement when it is displayed in my newsfeed on Facebook	4.61	1.33	0.915
3 I like all posts relevant to civic engagement that I see on Facebook	3.86	1.73	0.883
Sharing			
1 Whenever I see a post relevant to civic engagement on Facebook, I share it	4.06	1.50	0.945
2 It is likely that I share a post relevant to civic engagement when it is displayed in my newsfeed on Facebook	4.03	1.52	0.945
3 I share all posts relevant to civic engagement that I see on Facebook	3.52	1.79	0.909

(*continued*)

(*continued*)

Construct and scale items	Mean	S.D	Loading
Commenting			
1 Whenever I see a post relevant to civic engagement on Facebook, I comment on it	3.75	1.47	0.942
2 It is likely that I comment on a post relevant to civic engagement when it is displayed in my newsfeed on Facebook	3.75	1.51	0.946
3 I comment on all posts relevant to civic engagement that I see on Facebook	3.30	1.73	0.919
Posting			
1 Whenever I see a contribution relevant to civic engagement on the Internet, I post it on Facebook	3.77	1.54	0.942
2 It is likely that I post a contribution relevant to civic engagement on Facebook when I see it on the Internet	3.72	1.56	0.954
3 I post all contributions relevant to civic engagement that I see on the Internet	3.25	1.78	0.915

References

1. Hong, H., Kim, Y.: What makes people engage in civic activism on social media? Online Inf. Rev. **45**, 3 (2021)
2. Vicente, M.R., Novo, A.: An empirical analysis of e-participation. The role of social networks and e-government over citizens' online engagement. Gov. Inf. Q. **31**(3), 379–387 (2014)
3. Shah, D.V., Nojin, K., Lance Holbe, R.: 'Connecting' and 'disconnecting' with civic life: patterns of internet use and the production of social capital. Polit. Commun. **18**(2), 141–162 (2001)
4. Ryan, R.M., Deci, E.L.: Self-determination theory and the facilitation of intrinsic motivation, social development, and well-being. Am. Psychol. **55**(1), 68–78 (2000)
5. Deci, E.L., Ryan, R.M.: The 'What' and 'Why' of goal pursuits: human needs and the self-determination of behavior. Psychol. Inq. **11**(4), 227–268 (2000)
6. Adler, R.P., Goggin, J.: What do we mean by 'civic engagement'? J. Transform. Educ. **3**(3), 236–253 (2005)
7. American Psychological Association: Civic Engagement (2009). https://www.apa.org/educat ion/undergrad/civic-engagement
8. Radtke, J., et al.: Energy transition and civic engagement. In: The Role of Public Participation in Energy Transitions, pp. 81–91. Elsevier (2020)
9. Kushin, M.J., Yamamoto, M.: Did social media really matter? college students' use of online media and political decision making in the 2008 election. Mass Commun. Soc. **13**(5), 608–630 (2010)
10. Datyev, I.O., Fedorov, A.M., Shchur, A.L.: Framework for Civic Engagement Analysis Based on Open Social Media Data. CSOC 2020, AISC 1225, pp. 586–597 (2020)
11. Lilleker, D.G., Koc-Michalska, K.: What drives political participation? motivations and mobilization in a digital age. Polit. Commun. **34**(1), 21–43 (2017)
12. Gagné, M., Deci, E.L.: Self-determination theory and work motivation. J. Organ. Behav. **26**(4), 331–362 (2005)

13. Pelletier, L.G., Nortel, N.T., Beaton, A.N.N.M.: Why Are You Doing Things for the Environment ? The Motivation Toward the Environment Scale (MTES), pp. 437–468 (1998)
14. Mu, A.E., Bjørnebekk, G., Deci, E.L.: Motivation and anxiety for dental treatment: testing a self-determination theory model of oral self-care behaviour and dental clinic attendance, pp. 15–33 (2010)
15. Hassan, L.: Governments should play games. Simul. Gaming **48**(2), 249–267 (2017)
16. Zhao, Y.C., Zhu, Q.: Effects of extrinsic and intrinsic motivation on participation in crowd-sourcing contest a perspective of self-determination theory. Online Inf. Rev. **38**(7), 896–917 (2014)
17. Schmidthuber, L., Piller, F., Bogers, M., Hilgers, D.: Citizen participation in public administration: investigating open government for social innovation. R D Manag. **49**(3), 343–355 (2019)
18. Ringle, C.M., Wende, S., Becker, J.M.: SmartPLS 3. SmartPLS GmbH, Boenningstedt (2015)
19. Fornell, C., Larcker, D.F.: Structural equation models with unobservable variables and measurement error: algebra and statistics. J. Mark. Res. **18**(3), 382 (1981)
20. O'brien, R.M.: A caution regarding rules of thumb for variance inflation factors. Qual. Quant. **41**(5), 673–690 (2007)
21. Hair, J., Hollingsworth, C.L., Randolph, A.B., Chong, A.Y.L.: An updated and expanded assessment of PLS-SEM in information systems research. Ind. Manag. Data Syst. **117**(3), 442–458 (2017)
22. Hofmann, S.: Becoming friends with the government–a qualitative analysis of citizens' decision to 'like' government profiles on Facebook. In: 24th European Conference on Information Systems. Istanbul, Turkey (2016)
23. Lindgren, I., Madsen, C.Ø., Hofmann, S., Melin, U.: Close encounters of the digital kind: a research agenda for the digitalization of public services. Gov. Inf. Q. **36**(3), 427–436 (2019)
24. Ragin, C.C.: Redesigning Social Inquiry: Fuzzy Sets and Beyond. Wiley Online Library (2008)
25. Pappas, I.O., Woodside, A.G.: Fuzzy-set Qualitative Comparative Analysis (fsQCA): Guidelines for research practice in Information Systems and marketing. Int. J. Inf. Manage. **58**, 102310 (2021)
26. Kourouthanassis, P.E., Pappas, I.O., Bardaki, C., Giannakos, M.N.: A matter of trust and emotions: a complexity theory approach to explain the adoption of e-government services. In: European Conference on Information Systems (ECIS) (2016)

Digital Society

Researching Digital Society: Using Data-Mining to Identify Relevant Themes from an Open Access Journal

Judith Schoßböck[1] ⓘ, Noella Edelmann[1](✉) ⓘ, and Nina Rizun[2] ⓘ

[1] Danube University Krems, Krems an der Donau, Austria
{judith.schossboeck,Noella.edelmann}@donau-uni.ac.at
[2] Gdansk University of Technology, Gdańsk, Poland
nina.rizun@pg.edu.pl

Abstract. Open Access scholarly literature is scientific output free from economic barriers and copyright restrictions. Using a case study approach, data mining methods and qualitative analysis, the scholarly output and the meta-data of the Open Access eJournal of e-Democracy and Open Government during the time interval 2009–2020 was analysed. Our study was able to identify the most prominent research topics (defined as thematic clusters) of the journal, their evolution over time and how these were influenced by journal management factors. This kind of analysis helps editors to develop an editorial strategy, decide on the thematic development of the journal and address the expectations of future authors of the journal. It further can provide insights about research themes and trends within a scholarly community and their development over time.

Keywords: Scholarly-led publishing · Open access · Data analysis · Journals · Data mining · Research topics

1 Introduction

Open access (OA) publications play an important role for different stakeholders, such as academia, policy-makers, and practitioners [1]. Apart from the objective of OA to free scientific output from economic barriers and copyright restrictions, ensuring accessibility to high-quality research output in the form of open publication, the access to openly available data and metadata allows an analysis of research topical trends, methods, or "scientific turns" [2], by editors, industry and practitioners [3]. Trends are often noticeable across disciplines, and demonstrate the interaction of research and sociological, historical or political developments [4]. Publication foci are created in accordance with societal issues, specific research trends, methodological turns, or dominant theoretical frameworks, but also policy, "politics" of academia and publishing cultures [5]. For instance, "Plan S" [6], a dedicated radical open access initiative, is often referenced to both as a turning point towards more open science and as an important policy that explains shifts in the nature of research publications [7]. Similarly, topical trends or

© IFIP International Federation for Information Processing 2021
Published by Springer Nature Switzerland AG 2021
N. Edelmann et al. (Eds.): ePart 2021, LNCS 12849, pp. 43–54, 2021.
https://doi.org/10.1007/978-3-030-82824-0_4

thematic turns in research can indicate, reflect, but also influence socio-political change or action [8].

There are several ways to analyse the development of a field, research agendas, and their relation to societal and technological developments, such as literature reviews, meta-analysis, or data-based approaches. For this contribution, our work demonstrates how the computational and analytics-driven methods can be used in scholarly-led research to adjust its thematic scope, and to guide journal development. Hence, the objective of this study concerns the strategic choices of journal editors and managers, as well as the reserach community. First, it aims to provide an approach that can be used by journal editors to identify topical trends in scholarly-led publishing and to derive important clues regarding thematic clusters within a research community (RQ1), and second, we investigate what factors might impact the trends, research topics and research cooperation evolution over time (RQ2). The rest of the paper is organized as follows: Sect. 2 provides a review of topical trends within research communities and scholarly-led publishing from an editorial perspective. Section 3 describes the research methods in detail. Our results are provided in Sect. 4. Section 5 contains a discussion on consistent themes and the utility of our method. Finally, the limitations and recommendations for future research are addressed in Sect. 6.

2 Literature Review

The review covers exemplary research themes investigated in a scholarly community and reflects on the journal management and scholarly-led perspective relevant to the case study.

2.1 Topical Trends and Agendas Within Research Communities

The "open society" has been framed as a watchword of liberal democracy and the market system in the modern globalised world, and "openness" stands for both bottom-up empowerment and top-down transparency [9]. The emergence of research areas such as "open data" [10], "open science", "open access" [3], "open government" [11], and "open access" [12] reflects this trend across many disciplines and locations. On the policy level, the *Open Government Directive* in the US is often cited as important influence for the trend towards more "openness" in e-government research [13]. Another example is the development of the field of e-participation research, fostered by technology innovations and research programs, and was later characterised and recognised as "emerging research area" [14, p.415]. Understanding the field was, particularly in the beginning, complex, as there was no generally agreed upon definition and no clear overview of disciplines or methods to draw upon. As Sæbø et al. [14] note, their initital analysis provided a starting point for the development of a modelused to define e-participation activities such as e-voting, online discourse, online decision-making, e-activism, e-consultation, e-campaigning, and e-petitioning. Such work helps to better understand emerging fields, the role of related disciplines, and provides the basis for developing research agendas in the future [14]. Another study [8] analysed a total of 150 publications during a timeframe of 10 years related to this research field and a conference series, showed how the agenda has changed over a decade of research. This data-based approach, in contrast to literature reviews, offers insights on the development of a field over time.

Thus, it is critically important to study the intellectual core and the dynamics of knowledge development over time [15]. Many scholars have paid attention to evolution within different research fields, using several research methods: exploratory content analysis, to investigate the progress and development of e-government research [15], Natural Language Processing (NLP) techniques, in order to extract key terms or their co-occurrence, to discover the underlying knowledge structure and evolution of the Journal of Knowledge Management [16], topic modeling (LDA) or Structural Topic Modelling (STM) to profile the research hotspots, exploring annual topic proportion trends and topic correlations, potential future research directions in information management [17] and transportation engineering [18] research.

2.2 Scholarly-led Publishing: Managing a Diamond OA Journal

Journal editors face various issues and choices in order to support the development of the journals they lead and manage. One issue are the strategic choices that are to enhance the visibility, accessibility and impact of research published in their journal. Another issue is how to provide potential authors of the journal with useful information that will support them with their publication choice [19]. This is important as scholarly-led publishing is increasingly connected to academic metric systems such as journal indexes, e.g. Scopus or Web of Science, as well as authors' citation scores and academic evaluation such as Publish-or-Perish, h-index, or Google Scholar.

In order to define their scope and strategy, editors of scholarly-led (or academic-lead) journals [20] have to know the scientific trends, common themes and research methods within their publishing communities. Journal establishment and maintenance might be motivated by offering an independent arena for specific topics and the research community, but also by strategic or political reasons, such as offering open access publication venues. Editors must offer continuity and stability to authors when establishing their brand and choosing their thematic scope throughout the years. Further, research trends can lead to the development and coining of new disciplines, such as gender studies, once considered a niche discipline (e.g. the OA journal Aspasia). Journal editors must react to research trends within their field, and need to have knowledge of current research agendas [21]. They will also have to consider the different action domains across disciplines that are typical for inter- and transdisciplinary science and learning processes [22]. This is reflected in the journal's name, strategy, and the submission guidelines: while catering to different disciplines, editors need to be aware of common research cultures and long-standing research areas, methodological consensus, or emerging themes within their chosen scope [8]. While informal processes undoubtedly occur, there is only little research that reflects on such strategies for editors. Hence, it is important to investigate the emerging topics trends and thematic clusters within research communities and to understand how they might change and evolve over time. Our study offers an opportunity (i) to ground such reflections in empirical data and to relate the strategy to the output dimension, and (ii) to demonstrate that deep insights can be extracted from open access articles' content and metadata to improve our comprehension and to derive influential factors and drivers for journal development. Based on the above observations, our research questions for this study are: RQ1: What are the research topics of papers and their evolution over time? RQ2: What factors influence the research cooperations and research topics from a journal management and editorial perspective?

3 Methods

A threefold approach to study the topic was applied: a case study of a scholarly community represented by the platinum OA scholarly-led eJournal of e-Democracy and Open Government (JeDEM, www.jedem.org), data mining algorithms applied to the content and metadata of all articles published in JeDEM since 2009, and qualitative analysis.

3.1 Case Study

The case study approach allows the investigation of a phenomenon within its real-life context and the use of multiple sources of evidence [23], such as publication data and the reflexive perspective of different editors. The case further defines the scholarly field the results are applicable to: an inter- and transdisciplinary field of technology and social studies.

The investigated journal, JeDEM, is published by the Department for E-Governance and Administration (Danube University Krems) and has an acceptance rate of 50% on average. Publication frequency is twice a year, and the journal is indexed in Scopus, EBSCO, DOAJ, Google scholar, and the Public knowledge project (PKP) metadata harvester. Articles are referenced with a digital object identifier (DOIs).

3.2 Data Mining

Methods, techniques and algorithms for data-mining have already been successfully applied to such scholarly studies [20]. Text mining scholarly research refers to the extraction of implicit, potentially valuable information and patterns from natural language texts by identifying promising topics that characterize the document collections, document classifications based on predetermined keywords set, or the detection of a group of semantically close documents [24]. In our study, we apply the set of data mining and text mining algorithms to realize the following methodological steps. *First*, we pre-processed the scientific papers (title, abstract and content), including word normalization, stemming, removal of stop words, punctuations, and numbers. *Second*, each subset of the paper collections was pre-ordered over time (years) and divided into a disjoint set, then the top 30 keywords (and bigrams) were extracted. We consider these keywords sets as a thematic context parameter, characterizing a particular epoch of research field development. *Third*, to derive the insights regarding thematic clusters within the analyzed paper collection, unsupervised k-means clustering algorithm was applied. Cosine similarity was adapted as a measure of thematic semantic closeness for clusters building [25]. The resulting thematic cluster (TC) were manually labelled based on their keywords set. *Fourth*, to deeper investigate the contextual structure of each TC, the LDA [26] topic model was used. To determine the optimal number of sub-topics for each cluster, the perplexity of a held-out set of papers has been calculated. As a result, 3 sub-topics were identified for cluster 1, and 4 each for clusters 2 and 3. The topics labels were determined based on a set of keywords describing them according to the LDA algorithm results.

3.3 Qualitative Analysis

Qualitative methodologies seek to portray a world in which reality is socially constructed, complex and ever changing [27]. The qualitative interpretation was conducted from a journal management and editorial perspective and represents the reflexivity inherent to auto-ethnographic methods [28]. An interpretative approach focuses on the analysis of meanings ascribed to data and the perceptions of a phenomenon, whist reflexivity enabled us to relate the trends in the data to experience and knowledge about cooperations, events, or advertising strategies that impact strategic decisions and publication.

4 Results

We focus on the main insights from the data on publications, namely: (1) the prominent research topics (and sub-topics) and their evolution over time and (2) the reflection on potentially influential factors from a journal management and editorial perspective.

4.1 Research Topics, Thematic Clusters and Sub-topics

Research Topics and Evolution Over Time
We identified 3 clusters of prominent thematic trends emerging in the collection of scientific papers. Table 1. Research topics clusters presents the thematic clusters' (TC) labels, cluster proportion (CP, %) over articles collection, cluster description, and word clouds for the research topic clusters.

Table 1. Research topics clusters

Cluster 1	CP, %	Cluster 2	CP, %	Cluster 3	CP, %
Citizen engagement	24.49	Disruptive technology	47.96	Smart governance	27.55
Cluster Description					
Electronic petitions, e-participation initiative & citizen participation		Open data, social media & social networking, disruptive technologies & digital transformation		Open data-driven government, smart city & co-creation	
Cluster Wordcloud					

Figure 1 below shows the thematic evolution the research publihsed, where the identified clusters are highlighted by colours and their contextual evolution is represented by a set of major keywords (bigrams). The results enable us to define some "scientific turns" such as "disruptive technology" and "smart governance": (1) while the thematic citizen engagement (cluster 1) was present during the start-up phase of the journal (2009–2010), there is a trend towards disruptive technologies (cluster 2) as from 2011. Cluster 2 concerns many different innovations and disruptions, e.g. social media, parliamentary informatics and open data. From 2014, we also notice the emergence of the theme of smart governance (cluster 3), which became a more established cluster from 2016 onwards. Drawing on this kind of data can help determine the emergence of certain research foci and its representation in publications (such as 2014 for "smart" and 2011 for "open"). For example, following the Open Government Directive in 2009 [29] the investigated research community was quick to publish on this subject within a timeframe of two years.

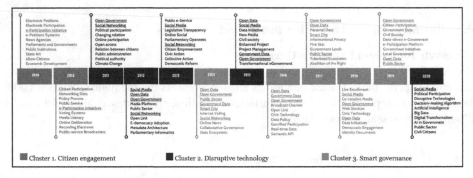

Cluster 1. Citizen engagement   Cluster 2. Disruptive technology   Cluster 3. Smart governance

Fig. 1. Thematic clusters throughout the years

Regarding the main factors influencing the thematic development of the journal, our study noted: (1) Specific research topics addressing the call for papers, demonstrating a strong correlation relationship with identified thematic clusters in the corresponding year. Thus, in our case-study, Cramer's V statistic, calculated based on the data about correspondence between thematic clusters associated with the period and special issue topics, is equal to 8.75 and is statistically significant (p-value = 0.0377); (2) Special offline events (mainly conferences) and the related materials, which are annually published in one of the journal issues, contribute to the continual evolution of e-democracy and e-government as a research domain in JeDEM.

The following main factors influencing article quantity were defined: (1) Offline events such as conference series, connected to the publishing community, could be an additional initiator of an increase in article quantity; (2) changing the journal title, as well as the title of the related community conference. In our case study, when the E-Democracy Conference (EDEM) changed its title to Conference for E-Democracy (CeDEM) in May 2011, this led to the disappearance of citizen engagement topics and, at the same time, led to the emergence of a new large thematic cluster named disruptive technology with "open government" as one of the most significant contextual bigrams.

Research topics in calls for papers impact the regional dimension of the articles' authors, if the title of the calls mentions the regional focus. In our case-study, from the years 2013 and 2015 onwards, the journal had special issues addressing Asian experiences, which led to a natural influx of articles from authors based in Asia.

Sub-topics and Word Co-occurrence in Papers Over Time

For a deeper understanding of the nature of thematic trends, the Topic Modelling app-roach was used to identify the sets of subtopics for each of the clusters (Fig. 2). The following insights were identified: (1) the subtopic of data openness undergoes a trans-formation stage from the Open Data concept in cluster 2 to Open Linked Data (or linked open data) in cluster 3; (2) the same phenomena can be noticed for the Open Government subtopic in cluster 2, which in cluster 3 evolved into an Open Data-driven Government concept; (3) there is a large predominance of subtopic such as Online Deliberation, E-Petitions, Open Linked Data in the context of Smart Cities, and Decision-making and Social Media.

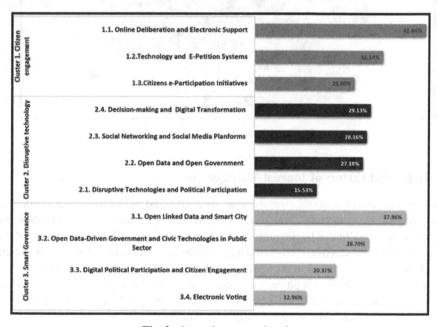

Fig. 2. Journal papers subtopics

To define a contextual profile of the research development of the scholarly community over the past 11 years, the analysis of the co-occurrence of words (Fig. 3) hinted at the anchoring of research themes within specific contexts, such as (1) governance and the public sector, as well as open, data and technology; but also (2) the context of participation and politics was more visible than the context of democracy or collaboration.

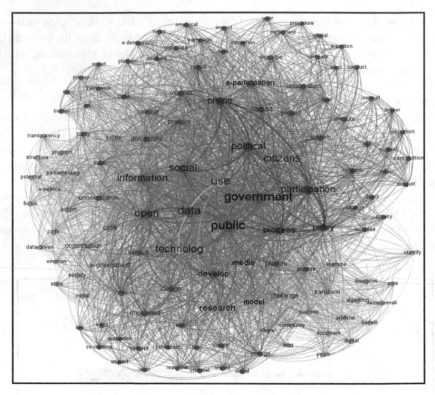

Fig. 3. Contextual profile of the scholarly community

4.2 Influential Factors of Journal Management

Based on our above analysis, we are able to derive and summarise four influential factors of journal development, related to its thematic focus, research cooperations and other challenges addressed by the journal on the visibility, accessibility and impact of the journal. Table 2 gives an overview on the most important factors, their description and the area of influence as detected in the analysis and evaluated by managing editors. Topical influence refers to the development of research areas and thematic clusters over time; regional influence to spatial ties of research cooperations; quantitative to the number of publications; and qualitative to the quality of submissions.

Table 2. Influential factors of journal development

Influential factors	Description	Area/Nature of influence
Research cooperations: guest editors	Guest editors work on special issues and call for papers addressing specific research topics	Topical, regional
Research cooperations: offline events	Mainly international scientific conferences	Topical, quantitative
Editorial strategy: title	The title and naming of the journal, including strategic decisions regarding name change	Topical
Editorial strategy: indexing*	Listing of the journal in indexing systems such as Scopus, EBSCO, DOAJ, Google scholar, and the Public knowledge project (PKP) metadata harvester	Quantitative, qualitative

*Indexing systems were strongly perceived as one of the biggest factors enhancing the number of publications (e.g. with Scopus, in 2019) [30]

5 Discussion

Using data mining methods, editors can analyse whether the topics included in their call for papers match the topics the journal aims to publish or whether adaptations need to be made to better manage the expectations of future journal authors. The results gained help authors' publication choices by tracing the evolutionary stages of the study of scientific problems, and using a conscious analysis in the shaping of research agendas (f.i. what is involved, what is not). It offers the advantage to tie such activities to data gained from the publishing communities, and to reflect on scholarly developments, research trends and setting the agendas. On one hand, the research cooperations detected in this study seem to be tied to certain economic privileges of specific countries and showcase a certain hegemonic bias with expectable domination and lack of representation of some countries. One the other hand, we could identify specific research realities or interests. Journal editors can therefore use this approach to better target their managing and advertising efforts and include a spatial dimension in calls for papers, for instance by adapting the call or advertisement according to the themes and cooperations identified. We were able to confirm trends in research agendas and related connotations and timestamps, such as the use of "smart" (2014) or "open" (2011) as reflected in the publications of the investigated scholarly community. For editors, this can provide a starting point for reflecting on emerging trends, which influence journal strategies, such as the name of a journal, the scope of the calls for papers and announcements to the scholarly community. As evident in our data, consistent themes within the thematic clusters could be taken more into account in calls for papers and special issues in order to enhance the identification and reach of targeted authors.

The data mining method offers a fresh perspective and specific weighting of the editor evaluations, as, without this approach, journal editors might think that their topics are represented mostly equally throughout the call, or they might miss important topical developments or long-term emphases. The topic modelling algorithm can be used for the formulation of specific sub-topics, f.i. for calls for papers for special issues, and confirm or contest the general topical orientation of a journal. For instance, for the editors, the strong prevalence of the topic e-petitions in publications was surprising, made visible by the data mining. This also points towards a potentially crucial development regarding the definition of research agendas, as strategic decisions can be supported by publication-based data.

6 Conclusion and Outlook

Our study was able to identify research cooperations, the most prominent research topics (defined as thematic clusters) of the studied journal, as well as their evolution over time. The most important influential factors were identified. From the methodological side, we demonstrated that deep and valuable insights can be extracted from freely available open access journal content and article metadata in order to improve the whole publishing community's comprehension of research themes, influential factors and drivers of journal development. This approach was found to be useful for gaining insights concerning the influence of research cooperations and editorial decisions and might also be used by editors of all other types of journals to determine their strategy as well as consider the readers' demands for articles on particular research topics. Our next steps concern (1) the analysis of further data points such as regions, methods, rejection rate, or factors of openness (f.i. whether research data underlying the studies is made openly available), and (2) the validation of our results by comparison to the prominent topics emerging in the scientific papers published in other OA digital society journals. The limitations of this study lie in its focus on one case as well as the reflexive aspects of data interpretation. As this is partly a qualitative endeavour, there are always other means of interpretation and defining umbrella terms, f.i. for thematic clusters.

References

1. Edelmann, N., Schoßböck, J.: Open access perceptions, strategies, and digital literacies: a case study of a scholarly-led journal. Publications, vol. 8 (2020)
2. Alperin, J.P., Gomez, C.J., Haustein, S.: Identifying diffusion patterns of research articles on Twitter: a case study of online engagement with open access articles. Public Understanding of Science (2018)
3. Bach, T.A., Ray-Sannerud, B.: Benefits of open access articles for industry. Nordic Perspectives on Open Science, vol. 1 (2017)
4. Shehata, A., Ellis, D., Foster, A.: Scholarly communication trends in the digital age. The Electronic Library (2015)
5. Agate, N.: From Evaluated Outputs to Values-Embedded Practices. Septentrio Conference Series (2020)
6. European Science Foundation. www.coalition-s.org. Accessed on 01 June 2020

7. International Science Council. https://council.science/current/blog/could-plan-s-be-a-tur ning-point-for-global-open-science-interview-with-robert-jan-smits/. Accessed on 23 Jan 2019
8. Johannessen, M., Berntzen, L.: A decade of eParticipation research: an overview of the ePart conference 2009–2018. In: Panagiotopoulos, P., et al. (eds.) Electronic Participation: 11th IFIP WG 8.5 International Conference, ePart 2019, San Benedetto Del Tronto, Italy, September 2–4, 2019, Proceedings, pp. 3–14. Springer International Publishing, Cham (2019). https://doi.org/10.1007/978-3-030-27397-2_1
9. Götz, N., Marklund, C.: The Paradox of Openness: Transparency and Participation in Nordic Cultures of Consensus. BRILL (2015). https://doi.org/10.1163/9789004281196
10. Sveinsdottir, T., Wessels, B., Finn, R., Wadhwa, K.: Open Data and the Knowledge Society. Amsterdam University Press (2017). https://doi.org/10.1515/9789048529360
11. Parycek, P., Schossböck, J.: Adopting a new political culture: obstacles and opportunities for open government in Austria. In: Book Adopting a New Political Culture: Obstacles and Opportunities for Open Government in Austria, pp. 210–236 (2014)
12. Chesbrough, H.W.: The era of open access. Managing Innovation and Change, 127 pp. (2016)
13. Sachs, M., Parycek, P.: Open government - information flow in Web 2.0. Euro. J. ePractice 9, 1–70 (2010)
14. Sæbø, Ø., Rose, J., Flak, L.S.: The shape of eParticipation: characterizing an emerging research area. Gov. Inf. Q. 25(3), 400–428 (2008)
15. Rodríguez Bolívar, M.P., Alcaide Muñoz, L., López Hernández, A.M.: Scientometric study of the progress and development of e-government research during the period 2000–2012. Inf. Technol. Dev. 22, 36–74 (2016)
16. Chaudhuri, R., Chavan, G., Vadalkar, S., Vrontis, D., Pereira, V.: Two-decade bibliometric overview of publications in the journal of knowledge management. In: Book Two-decade bibliometric overview of publications in the Journal of Knowledge Management (2020)
17. Sharma, A., Rana, N.P., Nunkoo, R.: Fifty years of information management research: a conceptual structure analysis using structural topic modeling. Int. J. Inf. Manage. 58, 102316 (2021)
18. Das, S., Dixon, K., Sun, X., Dutta, A., Zupancich, M.: Trends in transportation research exploring content analysis in topics. In: Book Trends in transportation research exploring content analysis in topics, pp. 27–38 (2017)
19. Schoßböck, J., Edelmann, N., Rizun, N., Zuiderwijk, A.: Scholarly research and publications over time: identifying trends for an open access journal by applying data-mining methods. In: Book Scholarly Research and Publications Over Time: Identifying Trends for an Open Access Journal by Applying Data-Mining Methods (2020)
20. Dridi, A., Gaber, M.M., Azad, R.M.A., Bhogal, J.: Scholarly data mining: a systematic review of its applications. Wiley Interdisciplinary Reviews: Data Mining and Knowledge Discovery, pp. 1–23 (2020)
21. Teixeira Da Silva, J.A.: Conflicts of Interest Arising from Simultaneous Service by Editors of Competing Journals or Publishers. Publications 2021, vol. 9 (2021)
22. Viale Pereira, G., et al.: South American expert roundtable: increasing adaptive governance capacity for coping with unintended side effects of digital transformation 12(2), 718 (2020)
23. Yin, R.K.: Case Study Research: Design and Methods, 5th edn. SAGE Publications (2014)
24. Hassani, H., Beneki, C., Unger, S., Mazinani, M.T., Yeganegi, M.R.: Text mining in big data analytics. Big Data Cogn. Comput. 4, 1–34 (2020)
25. Qayyum, F., Afzal, M.T.: Identification of important citations by exploiting research articles' metadata and cue-terms from content. Scientometrics 118(1), 21–43 (2018). https://doi.org/10.1007/s11192-018-2961-x
26. Blei, D.M., Ng, A.Y., Edu, J.: Latent dirichlet allocation. In: Book Latent Dirichlet Allocation, pp. 993–1022 (2003)

27. Sloan, A., Bowe, B.: Phenomenology and hermeneutic phenomenology: the philosophy, the methodologies, and using hermeneutic phenomenology to investigate lecturers' experiences of curriculum design. Qual. Quant. **48**, 1291–1303 (2014)

28. Guillemin, M., Gillam, L.: Ethics, reflexivity, and "ethically important moments" in research. Qual. Inq. **10**, 261–280 (2004)

29. Lathrop, D., Ruma, L.: Open Government. Collaboration, Transparency, and Participation in Practice (2010)

30. Pranckutė, R.: Web of Science (WoS) and scopus: The titans of bibliographic information in Today's Academic World. Publications **9**(1), 12 (2021)

Whose Agenda Is It Anyway? The Effect of Disinformation on COVID-19 Vaccination Hesitancy in the Netherlands

Natalia I. Kadenko[1]([✉]) [iD], J. M. van der Boon[1] [iD], J. van der Kaaij[1,2] [iD],
W. J. Kobes[1,2] [iD], A. T. Mulder[1] [iD], and J. J. Sonneveld[1,2] [iD]

[1] Delft University of Technology, Delft, The Netherlands
n.i.kadenko@tudelft.nl
[2] University of Twente, Enschede, The Netherlands

Abstract. With the problem of disinformation becoming more apparent, one of the current topics for disinformation campaigns is the COVID-19 vaccine, which has broad implications for public health. This research was conducted to investigate a possible connection between the amount of vaccination-related disinformation and the willingness among the Dutch population to get vaccinated. The contribution of this research is 1) developing a tool-supported approach to identify words and bigrams used in alternative news outlet, 2) classifying disinformation-related vocabulary, 3) applying the approach that relates disinformation and vaccination willingness in the context of the COVID pandemic, highlighting its strengths and limitations. We conceptualised vaccination disinformation, expressed it in certain 'trigger terms' and plotted the popularity of those terms amongst Dutch Internet users over time, using Google Trends and Twitter data. Using a linear regression model, we combined this with vaccination willingness studies of June through December of 2020 to investigate a possible correlation. Our results, while not statistically significant, did point towards a negative relationship between disinformation spread and willingness to vaccinate. Further research, utilizing similar approach and additional available information on vaccination willingness, may provide more insight on disinformation spread and vaccination willingness across the world.

Keywords: Disinformation · Social media · Vaccine hesitancy

1 Introduction

With the rise of social media and ease of website hosting, almost every message can get amplified and reach a large audience. This has enabled diverse actors to spread disinformation and influence a broad range of issues, from democratic processes to public health. Spreading disinformation can plant the 'seed of doubt' leading to the vaccination hesitancy [1]. In case of COVID-19 vaccination, the existing narratives of vaccine scepticism have been enhanced by obscure web of relationships between

N. Edelmann et al. (Eds.): ePart 2021, LNCS 12849, pp. 55–65, 2021.
https://doi.org/10.1007/978-3-030-82824-0_5

vaccines, 5G, microchips, Great Reset, and Bill Gates. Narratives of a secret government entity which uses or has fabricated the virus to get control of the population [2], or the QAnon movement [3] have been spread predominantly via social media.

The number of adults that indicate to be willing to vaccinate themselves against COVID has steadily decreased in the Netherlands in the last few months of 2020 [4]. Understanding the causes of vaccination hesitancy can help address this issue. This paper sets out to investigate whether there is a correlation between the amount of disinformation related to the COVID-19 vaccines in the Netherlands and the population's willingness to vaccinate themselves against this virus. We focus on the Netherlands, as, to the best of our knowledge, no similar research has been conducted for this country. Furthermore, while the country has known relatively low vaccine hesitancy, the data from 2018 and 2020 shows decrease in confidence in the safety and effectiveness of vaccines in general, and the reasons for this are not clear [5]. This paper will attempt to answer the following research question:

RQ: To what extent does disinformation spread affect the willingness to vaccinate against COVID-19 among the Dutch population?

We conceptualised vaccination disinformation, expressed it in certain 'trigger terms' and plotted the popularity of those terms among the Dutch Internet users over time, using Google Trends and Twitter data. Using a linear regression model, we combined this with vaccination willingness studies of June through December of 2020 to investigate a possible correlation. We used a mixed method approach to explore how the discourse changed over time, and subsequently related this evolution to the estimated vaccination willingness of the Dutch population. First, we used an automated approach to isolate commonly used terms (words or bigrams) in both mainstream and alternative media, where a bigram is a sequence of two adjacent elements from a string of words. This list of bigrams was then manually classified into categories using a qualitative approach. Subsequently we used a second automated tool to measure how the usage of those terms on Twitter and Google Trends evolved. Finally, we used survey data to quantify vaccination willingness and to compare it to the evolution of the usage of those terms.

The key contributions of this paper are: 1) developing a tool-supported approach to identify words and bigrams used in alternative news outlet, 2) classifying disinformation-related vocabulary, 3) applying the approach that relates disinformation and vaccination willingness in the context of the COVID pandemic, highlighting its strengths and limitations.

All the supporting materials referenced in the paper are available in the research data repository[1].

2   Literature Review

According to UNESCO handbook [6], misinformation and disinformation mean explicitly false information. Misinformation may result from honest mistakes, negligence, or unconscious biases [7] including possibly outdated or incomplete information that

---

[1] https://doi.org/10.4121/14714031 - dataset in the 4TU.Research Data repository, containing supporting material, (non-copyrighted) data and code used for this study, with its documentation.

could still be misleading [8]. Disinformation "entails the distribution, assertion, or dissemination of false, mistaken, or misleading information in an intentional, deliberate, or purposeful effort to mislead, deceive, or confuse" [9, p. 228]. It may hold the same properties as misinformation, adding an intent to deceive. Studies on the effect of disinformation on individuals' attitudes and actions indicate that we need better understanding on the relationship between social media usage, disinformation spread, and polarization [10]. A recent study suggests that even short exposure to fake news could significantly modify the unconscious behaviour of individuals [11]. Finally, Pizzagate and QAnon conspiracies have resulted in real-life violence.

The interaction between vaccination hesitancy and disinformation has been studied before COVID-19 [12]. The studies from Italy and Denmark identified negative influence of a landmark event (a court ruling confirming a link between a specific vaccine and autism in Italy [13] and a documentary about the complications related to HPV vaccine in Denmark [14]) on the vaccination uptake. Other studies focused on information diffusion concerning the debate on vaccines in Brazil [15, 16] relating disinformation websites and their low Google search result ranking. A study [17] found that the vaccine discourse on the social media (namely, Twitter) has become increasingly polarized in the period between 2011–2019: the percentage of both negative and positive tweets has increased, while the percentage of the neutral ones decreased. The study used hybrid models combining lexicon-based and supervised machine-learning approaches to study the tweets containing vaccination-related keywords. Loomba et al. [18] measured the impact of COVID-19 misinformation on vaccination intent in the UK and USA by conducting a survey on the vaccination readiness before and after exposing the respondents to factual information and misinformation. In both countries they identified a misinformation-induced decline in intent to vaccinate. Kurten and Beullens [19] examine the COVID-related public discourse on Twitter by looking at the change of number of tweets with time and in relation to the landmark events, as well as at the changes in the (emotional) content. They computed the network of bigrams and showed that landmark events correlated with immediate increase in related tweeting.

In light of this related research, we 1) assume that vaccination-related disinformation can potentially have real-life consequences; 2) apply innovative combination of methods in underexplored setting to investigate the possible connection between the amount of disinformation and the vaccination willingness against COVID-19 among Dutch population; 3) expect to observe a negative relationship.

3 Methodology

This approach is designed to relate the influence of alternative media on the Dutch population with their willingness to vaccinate against COVID-19 (see Fig. 1). We consider that the influence of alternative media grows if the Dutch population uses terms that are specific to alternative media in the Google search engine (the most popular search engine in the Netherlands [20]) or rely on such vocabulary in messages shared on Twitter (2.8 million Dutch users).

We start by selecting news outlet relevant to our research goal. Our list includes four of the most popular newspapers in the Netherlands (NOS, NRC, FD, NU) and

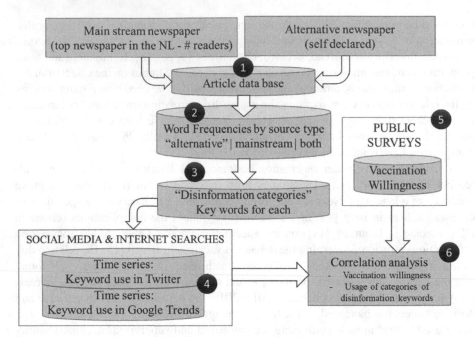

Fig. 1. Methodology overview

eight alternative media sites (*corona-nuchterheid, oervaccin, xanderniews, dagelijkses-tandaard, transitieweb, stichtingvaccinvrij, viruswaarheid, and staopvoorvrijheid*). For selecting the alternative media, we used snowballing technique, starting with the media mentioned in the mainstream news (e.g., due to organized protests) and compiling a list of the other alternative media referenced by these media until the point of saturation has been reached. In all cases, accessibility of the articles was a key criterion, as well as permission from the website's maintainers where appropriate.

From all those media outlets, we isolate all articles mentioning "CORONA" and covering the studied period (January to December 2020), from which we remove HTML tags, and stop-words (step 1), and store the output in the database, relating the text, the source, and its classification ("mainstream"/ "alternative"). From this database, we extract words and combination of words (bigrams) from each source to identify which words/bigrams are specific to mainstream media, alternative media, and those present in both (step 2). This allows us to isolate words/bigrams specific to alternative media, which were manually analyzed and classified by four independent coders in iterative process (step 3). In these steps, we found 7 categories of "alternative" information: people referred to in conspiracy theories (e.g. "Bill Gates"), people involved in alternative media, alternative media's name, other diseases (e.g. "Ebola"), vaccine discouraging terms (e.g. "DNA damage"), accusatory terms for corona's protagonists (e.g. "Big Pharma"), other (partly) complot theories (e.g. "Big brother"). Subsequently we use those categories, and their associated keywords, to identify usage of terms from alternative media in Dutch messages on Twitter, and queries on Google (step 4). We obtain, for the given time frame, the number of tweets and trends of searches containing keywords.

The next step was to collect data regarding COVID vaccination willingness in the Netherlands (step 5) from the reports by the two research institutes (IPSOS and I&O Research). We selected five studies conducted in June, July, August, September, November and December 2020. Four studies were conducted by research institute I&O Research [4, 21–23] and the fifth one by research institute IPSOS [24]. For comparability in our analysis, the results were recoded into a dichotomous variable. The option "Don't know" from the IPSOS questionnaire was regarded as a "no, as doubt could also lead to vaccination refusal. The availability of information regarding vaccination willingness limited the time frame of the study – reducing it to June to December 2020. As the final step (step 6), we use linear regression analysis to relate the usage of alternative media terms on Twitter and Google (dependent variables), indicating appropriation of the vocabulary, with vaccination willingness over time (independent variable).

All this data was in ratio scale, allowing us to create such a model.

$$y_i = a_0 + a_i x_{1i} + \cdots + a_n x_{ni}$$

The formula above represents a linear regression model, where x are the categories of disinformation, y is the willingness and i are the months.

4 Results and Analysis

4.1 Distinguishing Disinformation from Regular Information

A total of four mainstream media and eight alternative media websites were scraped for their articles. The repository lists the sites and the number of articles which were scraped per site. Notably, more articles from the mainstream media (17301) have been used, compared to the alternative media (2652). The difference can be explained by the mainstream media producing considerably more content related to coronavirus from the different categories. After extracting the words and bigrams which are significantly more popular among alternative media, we had a list of over 1300 terms. These trigger words and bigrams were coded as mentioned in the Methodology section. The final list of coding categories and their description is available in our repository. Category 1, "person referred to in conspiracy theories" was populated not only by the internationally renowned names like Bill Gates and Klaus Schwab, but included several Dutch politicians who hadn't been closely associated with conspiracy theories before. Categories 2 and 3, "Person involved in alternative media production" and "Name of alternative media" mostly included specific Dutch content. Category 4, "Other disease" was used to try and nuance the severity of COVID-19, or was mentioned as a part of government immunisation programs (i.e., capitalizing on the pre-existing vaccine hesitancy narratives) – similarly to category 5, "Vaccine discourage term", which included both old and new terms. Category 6 "Accusatory term for corona protagonists" was created to include a broad range of terms, from Big Pharm, tyranny and elite to slave mentality and risk obsession. An interesting find was that category 8, "Other (partly) conspiracy theories" included 5G and microchips narratives, but the relation between COVID-19 and QAnon-related conspiracy theories did not come forward from the data. A possible explanation could be that, despite their growing popularity, QAnon theories have been less popular on Dutch media.

4.2 Measuring the Amount of Disinformation Over Time

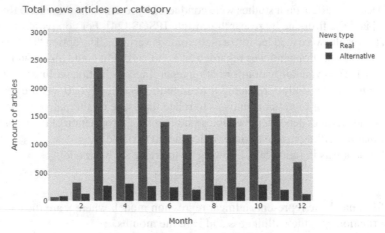

Fig. 2. Publication date of articles

Figure 2 shows the number of alternative and mainstream media articles over the studied period. We can see that the mainstream (blue) and alternative (red) media numbers follow the same curve and do not show considerably different numbers. However, the number of mainstream media articles demonstrates a peak in March and April, when the lockdown was introduced, and a lower valley in July and August, when the number of cases was lower, while the alternative media show an increase in content, possibly due to the protests and lawsuits (more on that below).

The number of tweets (7719 in total) that included words and/or bigrams from a category is visualized in Fig. 3. We observe a peak in vaccine discourage terms in July. One possible explanation is that we are seeing an example of increased inauthentic activity [25], with bots tweeting to discourage vaccination willingness. Publications from alternative news sources could lead to such a peak in tweets, such as the reports about a mass protest against corona measures that took place at the end of June. Another explanation could be news publication, such as the reports on the lawsuit started by the action group "Viruswaarheid" against the Dutch state with the demand to lift all corona measures, which the group lost in July. Simultaneously, there is a small peak for category 8 ("Other (partly) conspiracy theories"). After the peak in July, the "vaccine discourage term" category has an upwards trend, which could be related to the news about vaccine development and approval starting the public debate. Category 3 has a peak starting in August, characterized by more protest activity, and ending around November, when the above-mentioned group lost another lawsuit against the Dutch State.

Figure 4 shows the number of searches done per category between June and December, relative to our normalisation factor that was used to combine all the terms. A value above 100 indicates that the term was more popular than our normalisation factor. What is clear is that most categories have a more or less constant search value with no clear peaks for any category. There are, however, several categories which demonstrate an increase

Usage of keywords, by category, on the Twitter platform

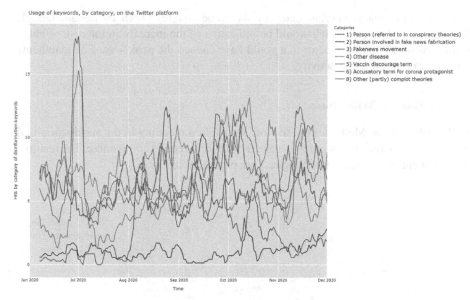

Fig. 3. Tweet count over time per category

Hits on Google Trends for terms in each categories

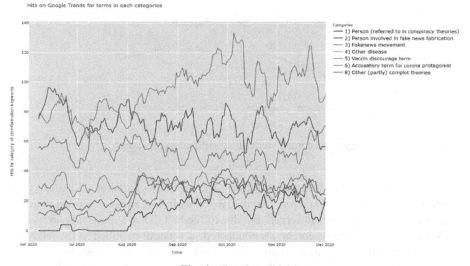

Fig. 4. Google trends

in searches, such as category 2 ("Person involved in alternative media production"), categories 3 ("Name of alternative media") and 4 ("Other (partly) conspiracy theories"). This might indicate the interest in both the content and the concept of alternative news outlets and their main public figures. Notably, category 5 ("Vaccine discourage term") does not see an increase in any period. This does not correspond with the clear Twitter peak in July 2020, and the increase after that period. One could argue that the rising of a general interest in a certain category should be visible in both Twitter and Google. This lack of alignment, which would be indicative of the increase in interest, might be accounted for by another factor that could have caused the peak – such as inauthentic behaviour or coordinated activity.

4.3 Vaccination Willingness

As described in the Methodology section, we applied recoding to the vaccination willingness from the research reports to make the different reports comparable. The resulting measurement of vaccination willingness are presented in Fig. 5.

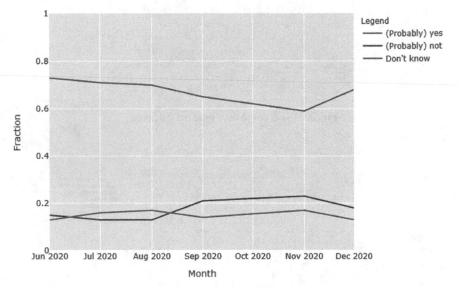

Fig. 5. Recorded vaccination willingness per month

The main observation is that we see a steady decrease of vaccination willingness over the period June till November, from about 75%–60%. In December a sudden increase in vaccination willingness is observed, but due to the fact that we only had partial data for December at the time research was conducted, it was not included in the analysis. Another observation is that the fraction of the respondents indicating to not be willing to vaccinate is approximately equal to the fraction of respondents still unsure about their stance against the vaccine. Both these fractions fluctuate between 15 and 25%.

With the vaccination willingness operationalised, we are now able to execute the analysis where vaccination willingness is used as the dependent variable.

4.4 Analysis

The model created during this research set out to predict the willingness of the Dutch public to get vaccinated. Unfortunately, we were not able to create a model that provided significant results for both the Twitter data ($F(3.1) = 0.53$, $p = 0.73$, $R^2_{adjusted} = -0.54$) and the Google trends data ($F(3,1) = 104.2$, $p = 0.072$, $R^2_{adjusted} = 0.987$). The biggest obstacle in this quantitative analysis was the low number of predictor values. Only five points were available to use at the time of creation. Due to this the degrees of freedom were significantly restrained and it was not even possible to fit a model using all categories at the same time. The significance of the factors could also not be found due to the high standard error.

Table 1. Correlation factors of the categories with the willingness to vaccinate per model

	Twitter	Google
1) Person (referred to in conspiracy theories)	0.119	0.849
2) Person involved in alternative media production	-0.387	-0.753
3) Name of alternative media	-0.145	-0.540
4) Other disease	-0.395	-0.790
5) Vaccine discourage term	-0.686	0.194
6) Accusatory term for corona protagonist	-0.146	-0.120
8) Other (partly) conspiracy theories	-0.447	-0.630

The models did not prove a significant relationship with the willingness to get vaccinated. However, in the process of building the models the correlation of the categories with the willingness has been calculated. We can make an interesting observation: as can be seen in Table 1, in accordance with our expectations, the direction of the relationship is correct and for some categories a high correlation is present. This may indicate that there might be a relationship between the categories and the willingness to get vaccinated, but our dataset is insufficient to draw conclusion.[2]

5 Discussion

This research investigated the possible effect of disinformation spread on the vaccination willingness against COVID-19 in the Netherlands and attempts to bring into picture broader context of disinformation spread and its implications for the real world. By distinguishing different categories of disinformation terms identified in newspapers, we have been able to nuance both the spread of disinformation (in Google searches and social media) and its possible real-life effect (vaccination willingness). Using the calculated correlations between the different disinformation categories and vaccination willingness, we observed negative correlations in line with our expectations. While there is no statistically significant relationship between willingness to vaccinate and search for or use of the category "derogatory terms for actors in the pandemic management", we observed a slight correlation between searches for the category "people involved in

---

[2] Recently, the Dutch government released a dataset on vaccination willingness, which is not compatible with the data set initially used in this study, as the questions asked to members of the public differed, and the time coverage was not suitable for our research: https://coronadas hboard.government.nl/verantwoording#willingness-to-be-vaccinated.

alternative media production" and lack of willingness to vaccinate. We attribute the lack of significance to the very low number of available points for predictor values, of which more may be available in the future.

Our results are to be a stepping stone for the similar research, and an illustration of what could be achieved with our method combination. Taking into consideration the lack of statistical significance, we would still like to argue that disinformation has had a negative effect on the vaccination willingness against COVID-19 among Dutch population for the observed period of time. We found some indication for several categories of disinformation negatively influencing vaccination readiness, with relatively high correlation present. This may indicate a relationship between the certain disinformation categories and the willingness to get vaccinated, which could be proved by further research using our disinformation categorization approach.

The study contributes to the developing body of literature on the possible relationship between the disinformation spread and the real-word effects in general, and the possible effect of the vaccination disinformation in particular. The contribution of this research is 1) developing a tool-supported approach to identify words and bigrams used in alternative news outlet, 2) classifying disinformation-related vocabulary in Dutch, 3) applying the approach that relates disinformation and vaccination willingness in the context of the COVID pandemic, highlighting its strengths and limitations. Further work needs to extend this exploratory study to more media outlets. A more detailed qualitative analysis would be beneficial to investigate the possible links between the changes in usage patterns and the diverse worldwide and national current events. Finally, the tweet count used was objective, i.e., the tweets could have originated both from the supporters or opponents of a certain viewpoint or movement. All these limitations can and should be addressed by future research.

Acknowledgements. The authors would like to thank Nicolas Dintzner for his assistance with the data management, proofreading, and general support, Digital Competence Centre of TU Delft for their help with making code F.A.I.R., and the reviewers for their valuable comments. This work has been supported by the European Commission through the H2020 program in project CyberSec4Europe (Grant No. #830929). Any opinions, findings, and conclusions or recommendations in this paper are those of the authors and do not necessarily reflect the views of their host institutions or the European Commission.

References

1. Steffens, M.S., Dunn, A.G., Wiley, K.E., Leask, J.: How organisations promoting vaccination respond to misinformation on social media: a qualitative investigation. BMC Public Health **19**(1), 1–12 (2019)
2. Reuters: Fact check: Video makes multiple false claims about COVID-19 pandemic. https://www.reuters.com/article/uk-factcheck-pandemic-video/fact-check-video-makes-multiple-false-claims-about-covid-19-pandemic-idUSKBN27J2HM. Accessed on 18 March 2021
3. BBC News: QAnon: What is it and where did it come from. https://www.bbc.com/news/53498434. Accessed on 18 March 2021
4. Kanne, P., Driessen, M.: Coronabeleid: bereidheid tot vaccineren. I&O Research, Amsterdam, Tech. Rep. (2020)

5. De Figueiredo, A., Karafillakis, E., Larson H.J.: State of Vaccine Confidence in the EU and the UK A Report for the European Commission (2020)
6. Cherilyn, I., Julie, P.: Journalism, Fake News and Disinformation: Handbook for Journalism Education and Training. UNESCO Publishing (2018)
7. Fallis, D.: What is disinformation? Libr. Trends **63**(3), 401–426 (2015)
8. Karlova, A., Fisher, K.E.: A social diffusion model of misinformation and disinformation for understanding human information behaviour. Inf. Res. **18**(1), 1–17 (2013)
9. Fetzer, J.H.: Information: does it Have To Be True? Mind. Mach. **14**(2), 223–229 (2004)
10. Tucker, J.A., et al.: Social media, political polarization, and political disinformation: a review of the scientific literature (2018). https://dx-doi-org.tudelft.idm.oclc.org/10.2139/ssrn.314 4139. Accessed on 1 June 2021
11. Bastick, Z.: Would you notice if fake news changed your behavior? an experiment on the unconscious effects of disinformation. Comput. Hum. Behav. **116**, 106633 (2021)
12. Gostin, L.O.: Global polio eradication: Espionage, disinformation, and the politics of vaccination. Milbank Q. **92**(3), 413–417 (2014)
13. Carrieri, V., Madio, L., Principe, F.: Vaccine hesitancy and (fake) news: quasi-experimental evidence from Italy. Health Econ. (United Kingdom) **28**(11), 1377–1382 (2019)
14. Suppli, C.H., Hansen, N.D., Rasmussen, M., Valentiner-Branth, P., Krause, T.G., Mølbak, K.: Decline in HPV-vaccination uptake in Denmark–the association between HPV-related media coverage and HPV-vaccination. BMC Public Health **18**(1), 1–8 (2018)
15. Massarani, L., Leal, T., Waltz, I.: The debate on vaccines in social networks: an exploratory analysis of links with the heaviest traffic, Cadernos de Saude Publica, vol. 36 (2020)
16. Arif, N., et al.: Fake news or weak science? Visibility and characterization of antivaccine webpages returned by google in different languages and countries. Front. Immunol. **9**(June), 1–12 (2018)
17. Piedrahita-Valdés. H., et al.: Vaccine hesitancy on social media: sentiment analysis from June 2011 to April 2019. Vaccines **9**(1), 28 (2021). https://doi.org/10.3390/vaccines9010028
18. Loomba, S., de Figueiredo, A., Piatek, S.J., de Graaf, K., Larson, H.J.: Measuring the impact of COVID-19 vaccine misinformation on vaccination intent in the UK and USA. Nat. Hum. Behav. 1–12 (2021)
19. Kurten, S., Beullens, K.: #Coronavirus: monitoring the belgian twitter discourse on the severe acute respiratory syndrome coronavirus 2 pandemic behavior, and social networking. Cyberpsychology 117–122 (2021). http://doi.org.tudelft.idm.oclc.org/https://doi.org/10.1089/cyber.2020.0341
20. Marktaandelen zoekmachines Q2 2020. https: //www.pure-im.nl/blog/marktaandelen-zoe kmachines-q2-2020/. Accessed on 18 March 2021
21. Kanne, P., Driessen, M.: Coronabeleid: draagvlak september 2020. I&O Research, Amsterdam, Tech. Rep. (2020)
22. Bereidheid tot vaccineren (onder publiek en zorgpersoneel). I&O Research, Amsterdam, Tech. Rep. December (2020)
23. Kanne. P.: De coronamaatregelen: draagvlak en gedrag. I&O Research, Amsterdam, Tech. Rep. (2020)
24. IPSOS: Bereidheidtotvaccinatietegencorona (2020)
25. Allyn, B: Researchers: Nearly Half of Accounts Tweeting About Coronavirus are Likely Bots. https://www.npr.org/sections/coronavirus-live-updates/2020/05/20/859814085/res earchers-nearly-half-of-accounts-tweeting-about-coronavirus-are-likely-bots?t=161609870 7209. Accessed on 18 June 2021

A Conceptual Model for Approaching the Design of Anti-disinformation Tools

Mattias Svahn[1]([⊠]) [iD] and Serena Coppolino Perfumi[1,2] [iD]

[1] eGovlab Stockholm University, Stockholm, Sweden
svahn@dsv.su.se, serena.perfumi@sociology.su.se
[2] Department of Sociology, Stockholm University, Stockholm, Sweden

Abstract. With the increasing amounts of mis- and disinformation circulating online, the demand for tools to combat and contain the phenomenon has also increased. The multifaceted nature of the phenomenon requires a set of tools that can respond effectively, and can deal with the different ways in which disinformation can present itself, such as text, images, and videos, the agents responsible for spreading it, and the various platforms on which incorrect information is prevalent. In this paper, after consulting independent fact-checkers to create a list, we map the landscape of the most known tools that are available to combat different typologies of mis and disinformation on the basis of three levels of analysis: the employment of policy-regulated strategies, the use of co-creation, and the preference for manual or automated processes of detection. We then create a model in which we position the different tools across three axes of analysis, and show how the tools distribute across different market positions. The most crowded positions are characterized by tools that employ automated processes of detection, varying degrees of policy implementation, and low levels of co-creation, but there is an opening for newly developed tools that score high across all three axes. The interest in co-creative efforts in the challenge towards addressing mis- and disinformation could indeed be an effective solution to cater to the need of the users, and respond effectively to the amounts and variety of mis and disinformation spreading online.

Keywords: Disinformation · Misinformation · Anti-disinformation tools · Fact-checking · Co-creation · Policy

1 Introduction and Problem Discussion

The issue of misinformation in social media is currently attracting a lot of attention, especially for the effects that it has on health-related and political behaviour, among other realms of interest [3]. Structural evidence of scientific research on misinformation phenomena can, for instance, be found in studies like the one conducted by Allport and Postman [1], in which they identified "the basic law of rumour", demonstrating that the strength of a rumour is dependent on the importance of the subject and individual concerns regarding this as well as of the time and ambiguity of the evidence on the topic. While misinformation in itself is not a new phenomenon, as the Allport and Postman

© IFIP International Federation for Information Processing 2021
Published by Springer Nature Switzerland AG 2021
N. Edelmann et al. (Eds.): ePart 2021, LNCS 12849, pp. 66–76, 2021.
https://doi.org/10.1007/978-3-030-82824-0_6

study from 1946 shows [1], the social media era has made it more pervasive. The 2000s has witnessed a rapid development of social media that has facilitated a spread of both information and misinformation regarding everything from local neighbourhoods to global issues. Studies analysing misinformation on social media platforms, have found that misinformation and disinformation travel faster than trustworthy information [20]. That has put social media platforms and their architecture at the centre of discussion on the spread of misinformation. While platforms like Facebook, Twitter and Instagram have started collaborating with fact-checkers to flag incorrect information, and giving users the possibility to report items for fact-checking, the tools provided by these platforms do not yet responding effectively to the demands. Furthermore, the echo-chamber-like structure of the networks within social media platforms [8, 17], and the personalization process carried out by algorithms, reinforce existing biases within the users [18], who tend to be exposed mostly to information that reinforces their pre-existing beliefs. Research on misinformation in the media has been progressing rapidly, with studied contextualizing misinformation within different realms and events, such as within journalism [5], and in the context of elections [21], and also trying to predict and identify future challenges [7].

Other studies have focused on taxonomizing the phenomenon [4]. The taxonomy of Giglietto et al. [9] is based on factors such as perceptions of the source, the story, the context, and the decisions of the audience and the propagator. The authors propose a taxonomy of "pure disinformation" where both the original author and the propagator are aware of the "false" nature of information, but they nevertheless decide to share it. A different situation is the one called "misinformation propagated through disinformation" where information is originally produced as "true" and then shared by a propagator who believes it is "false". Finally, "disinformation propagated through misinformation" is the situation in which information is devised as "false" by a creator but is perceived as "true" by a propagator.

On the ground the fact-checking work, i.e. the act of taking up published information, examining it for factualness and veracity and the re-publishing it, has also been carried out intensively in the past years. Given the demand for fact-checking, several tools have been developed to help the users navigate the information landscape within social media. It is these tools that are the object of research for this paper.

2 Aim

The aim for the proposed model in this paper, is to map the current anti-disinformation tools landscape, by analysing the architectural choices that govern the tools' functioning and response to disinformation. We see tools as software developed with the intention to detect and in some way judge and give the user a notice of mis/disinformation. In this way, we provide a framework for understanding what is available to the users, what is missing within the current landscape, and in which direction the tools should evolve in order to provide diversified options catering to the users' needs, as well as to effectively address different typologies of disinformation in different online environments.

3   Literature Review on the Qualities of Anti-disinformation Tools

The work on combating disinformation can take on many shapes, at least as many as dis-information itself. Farrell and colleagues [6] outlined some of the specific problems that misinformation detection has to address. The authors also explain some different models of how misinformation spreads that are relevant for detection, and provide a typology of anti-misinformation tools such as style-based, knowledge-based, propagation-based or credibility-based tools. They position tools within the misinformation ecosystem, with regard to how, when and what kinds of misinformation they handle. However, the study does not focus on the users' perspective, a gap that is taken up by the work of Komendatova et al. [11]. The authors reviewed disinformation tools in the perspective of design approaches, putting them into a perspective of value driven design. They found that design qualities of a lean back character i.e. not favouring active engagement are preferred by stakeholders, if compared to approaches favouring user engagement. This multitude of shapes and qualities that anti-disinformation tools can assume, shapes the ontology of the theoretical model we propose.

Still some qualities seem to be present across many of the tools, and refer to how they are constructed, how they function, and what they allow. Within the main qualities that have been identified, the tools we examined in this study can rely on either automated or manual fact-checking, which means that the veracity of the information is assessed either by algorithms who rely on the existing databases of fact-checked information, or by humans who check the claims against other verified sources of information. They can be either proactive or reactive (i.e., what we will call "policy" versus "ad hoc"), meaning that they either set up strategies to prevent the circulation of misinformation, *ex ante* or they react to misinformation at the point when it is detected in the system, *ex post*. Or finally, the tools can to varying degrees rely on collaborative, co-creative efforts. This means that some tools allow the broader community of users to provide information in different forms, such as flagging, fact-checking or feedback on the fact-checking process.

Our object of research is the ontology of design qualities, that make up the con-ceptualization space of anti-disinformation tools. We do that by organising a theoretical model of the conceptualization space. With this we take a perspective of critical realism and constructionism [15].

3.1   Aspects of Anti-disinformation Tools

As highlighted in the previous paragraph, three main qualities of the existing anti-disinformation tools indicate how these approaches disinformation (proactively or reac-tively, namely establishing policies a priori, or establishing ad-hoc strategies to respond to specific cases), which modality they use to analyse it (manual or automated) and to what extent they allow joint efforts (degree of co-creation). We have also found Babakar [2] inspiring, as they postulate that fact-checking exists in a triangular trade off where the angles are; Speed: how quickly the task can be done; complexity, and how difficult the task is to perform. Babakar [2] can be seen as a precursor to the model of this study. Their triangle corner of Speed versus Difficulty relates to this study's axis of AI/Handicraft and their third angle of Complexity can relate to this study's axis of policy. Their notion of how a systems designer can only optimise for two of these at a time relates to how our studies' cube model postulates and illustrates inherently opposed trade-offs. On the basis of all these identified qualities, we proceed to build our model.

Degree of Policy. One of the axes of our model is dedicated to assessing to what extent a tool is driven by policy. The degree of policy is measured in high and low, where "policy" represents the high end of the spectrum, and "ad-hoc" represents the opposite, low end. With the "degree of policy" we measure to what extent the various anti-disinformation tools on one hand establish rules that regulate the definition and circulation of misinformation *"ex ante"*, and an instance of misinformation detected according to these policies triggers the tool. Or on the other hand tools that evaluate circumstantially the single cases. Hence a high-end place on the spectrum represents a tool design based on an *ex ante* policy that drives the judgements of the tool, a low end is a situation of a more flexible character that evaluates instances of misinformation *sui generis, post facto*. Research in the area of policy has shown that policy work is crucial in a user-focused conceptualization of anti-disinformation tools [10, 19] Furthermore, the many and varied taxonomies of disinformation contribute to showing that an awareness of policies, may be advantageous when devising a user centred approach.

Degree of AI. The second axis of our model is dedicated to the assessment of the extent to which the misinformation detection process is carried out by means of manual or automated fact-checking, applying AI and machine-learning. The amount of information that requires fact-checking produces an increasing demand for a number of tools and fact-checking services that rely on the use of AI to assess the veracity of the information. This approach can either be used as the sole method of information scanning, or in conjunction with manual fact-checking. Therefore, in our model we measure the degree of AI, where "AI/Machine learning" represents the high end of the spectrum, and "manual" represents the opposite, low end of the spectrum.

Degree of Co-creation. In the last few years co-creation has spread rapidly in the business sector as a way of engaging with stakeholders and building knowledge. The application of co-creation methods is more recent in the public sector, particularly for policy development, and multiple challenges still need to be overcome [16]. It has been suggested that co-creation of anti-misinformation work in the public sector can be a way of meeting the multifaceted complexity of the task of anti-misinformation work [12]. Therefore, in our model, we measure the level of co-creation, where "high degree of co-creation" represents the high end of our third axis, and "low degree of co-creation (solo)" represents the opposite, low end of the same spectrum. In our model co-creation is intended as the extent to which the tools allow contributions and inputs from larger communities of users while carrying out the fact-checking work.

4   A Model for Evaluating Anti Disinformation Tools for Conceptual Purposes

The presented qualities can be imagined as axes and presented as a model in the form of a cube. This form of model also illustrates how we postulate the three qualities to be communicating buckets. We apply the examples that follow below as a means of validation (Fig. 1).

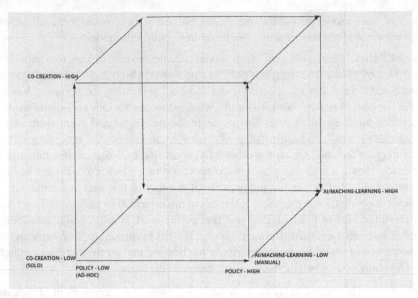

Fig. 1. Organization of the axes in the cube

5   Review of Anti-disinformation Tools

In the past few years, several tools that rely on both automated and "manual" fact-checking, or on a combination of the two modalities have been developed to help users navigate the information encountered online.

The overarching aim of these tools is to fact-check different aspects of the disinformation content, such as the information architecture (e.g. the claims, the sources, the authors and the platforms), and aspects related to the typology of content (e.g., images, headlines). These tools can be employed as a way to prevent the spread of disinformation, or as a way for a user to react to it.

Among the tools that more generally assess the content are; NewsGuard[1] [14], ClaimBuster,[2] The Factual,[3] CredEye,[4] Public Editor,[5] and Newstrition.[6] Within these, tools like Cyabra[7] employ more advanced technologies to detect deep-fakes, and the Co-Inform Dashboard[8] is designed to help professionals such as journalists, fact-checkers and policy-makers in their everyday job.

Some social media platforms have developed their own fact-checking systems, often in collaboration with external fact-checking organizations. Examples of these are

---

[1] https://www.newsguardtech.com/.

[2] https://idir.uta.edu/claimbuster/.

[3] https://www.thefactual.com/.

[4] https://gate.d5.mpi-inf.mpg.de/credeye/.

[5] https://www.publiceditor.io/.

[6] https://our.news/.

[7] https://cyabra.com/.

[8] https://coinform.eu/.

the Facebook Fact Checking Program,[9] Twitter Birdwatch,[10] and the Whatsapp IFCN chatbot.[11]

Besides the tools developed in collaboration with the platforms, there are also platform-specific tools developed externally, like CaptainFact,[12] designed for YouTube, Foller.me,[13] the Co-Inform plug-in[14] and Hoaxy,[15] designed for Twitter, FakeSpot,[16] specific for e-commerce platforms, and tools like Botometer[17] that are not only platform-specific, but also agent-specific: Botometer provides information about the probability that a Twitter account is a bot. Other tools are content-specific, for example Tin-Eye[18] focuses on detecting fake and decontextualized images, and the WeVerify/InVID plug-in[19] is created for the assessment of videos.

Finally, tools are being developed not only to detect, signal and correct misinformation, but also to work on the critical thinking and analytical abilities of the users, and one of these is Fiskkit.[20] To make sure that fact-checking work is carried out transparently and to counter the rise of counter-fact-checking initiatives, the International Fact-Checking Network[21] provides information and assessments on the credibility of the various fact-checkers and fact-checking initiatives [14].

6 A Model for Evaluating the Concept Space of Anti-disinformation Tools

We have proposed a model to be used to categorize and define anti-misinformation tools from the perspective of the functionalities encountered by the user. Here we map a number of chosen examples to the cubic model. We made a theoretical sample and in February 2021 we tested the content validity of the choice against a panel of nine experts from the IFCN network.[21] The chosen tools are placed within the cube in a place that represents their position in relation to the three axes. The bottom horizontal axis represents the degree of policy, moving from left (lowest degree) to right (highest degree). The vertical left axis represents the degree of co-creation, moving from the bottom (lowest degree) upwards (highest degree). Finally, the third and last dimension, which indicates the degree of AI/Machine-learning, is placed at the conjunction point with the policy axis and is visualized as the "cube depth axis", which moves starting

---

[9] https://www.facebook.com/journalismproject/programs/third-party-fact-checking.

[10] https://twitter.github.io/birdwatch/about/overview/.

[11] https://faq.whatsapp.com/general/ifcn-fact-checking-organizations-on-whatsapp/?lang=en.

[12] https://captainfact.io/.

[13] https://foller.me/.

[14] www.coinform.eu.

[15] https://hoaxy.osome.iu.edu/.

[16] https://www.fakespot.com/.

[17] https://botometer.osome.iu.edu/.

[18] https://tineye.com/.

[19] https://www.invid-project.eu/.

[20] https://fiskkit.com/.

[21] https://ifcncodeofprinciples.poynter.org/.

from the conjunction point with the policy axis (lowest degree), and runs alongside the bottom of the right cube face until the next conjunction point (highest degree).

In the previous section we proposed a model to be used to categorize, define and evaluate converging media to be considered for use when approaching anti disinformation tools. The cubic structure of the model, based on the three aspects or dimensions discussed above and shown in Fig. 2, makes it salient how the axes are connected vessels. To be evaluated, a disinformation tool is measured with a design analysis and positioned in the cube with respect to the three dimensions, and then evaluated from its position. In the following final section of the chapter we apply the proposed model to a number of examples in order to show whether it can be used as intended.

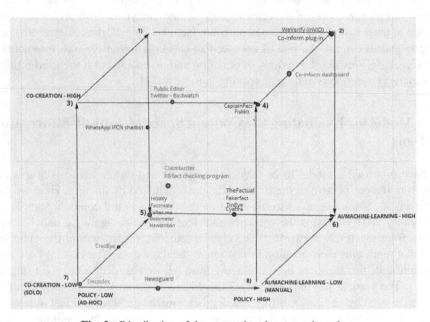

Fig. 2. Distribution of the mapped tools across the cube

7 Application of the Proposed Model on Anti-disinformation Tools

The model presented above, whilst being theoretical, presents several practical implications. We can see a crowded market position in the fifth corner with Hoaxy, Factmata Foller.me, Botometer, and Newstrition. These are all characterized by high degrees of AI/Machine-learning, and low degrees of policy and co-creation.

The second most-crowded market position we find in the middle between the fifth and the sixth corners, it is represented by tools like The Factual, FakerFact, Tin-Eye and Cyabra. These tools score similarly across our axes, and they are characterized by a high degree of AI/Machine-learning, a medium degree of policy, meaning that they use a mixed approach, and a low degree of co-creation.

We can observe that the third corner is empty. It is defined by a high degree of co-creation, a low degree of policy and a mostly manual process. However, it would be unlikely to see an anti-disinformation tool in that market position, as the functioning and usability of such a tool would be impaired by these very characteristics. To provide an example, a platform that perhaps represents this position is Reddit, but it is not within the realm of anti-disinformation tools. The other tools appear to be more diversified across the various axes, with the exception of WeVerify (InVID), the Co-inform plug-in, and the Co-inform dashboard, which are roughly grouped in the same area round the second corner: the Co-inform plug-in and WeVerify are both characterized by high degrees in all the axes (AI/Machine-learning, policy and co-creation), while the Co-Inform dashboard also has high degrees of policy and co-creation, but medium degrees of AI/Machine-learning. These are among the few that meet up to the idea of applying co-creation to meet the demands of combatting disinformation (cf. 3.2.3). It is unlikely that the tools in the crowded fifth corner defined by being high in AI, low in policy and low in co-creation will develop away from that corner. This is due to them being designed as stand-alone tools that are not part of any ecosystem, and that is an intrinsic design quality in these that is unlikely to change in the short term.

Birdwatch is an interesting case, it occupies a unique position with being high in human processing and co-creation while being highly dependent on policy. Its future position is dependent on the way it manages to over time keep and implement policy, we can right now in March 2021 see that the design qualities of Birdwatch may be moving it towards the empty corner of a high degree of co-creation, a low degree of policy and a mostly manual process.

This is a conceptual study, a natural next step would be to bring users into the picture, and examine their perceptions exploring e.g. how design qualities are categorized into product definitions, c.f. e.g. [19, 20], to deeper explore user needs.

Acknowledgements. This work has been partially funded by the Co-Inform project (770302), under the Horizon 2020 call "H2020-SC6-CO-CREATION-2016–2017 (CO-CREATION FOR GROWTH AND INCLUSION)" of the European Commission. We would also like to express our special thanks and gratitude to Allan Leonard and Orna Young from FactCheckNI for their valuable contribution in identifying and analyzing the chosen tools, and for their help in reaching out to the broader community of fact-checkers within the International Fact Checking Network and also to Myrsini Glinos of egovlab at Stockholm University.

Appendix

Here follows a table that lists tools onto the three axes that make up the model. Some tools of these are in competition some are complementary (Table 1).

Table 1. Selected tools and axes evaluation

Tool	*Policy:* (reactive vs proactive) **(low/medium/high)**	*Process:* (manual vs AI/machine learning) **(low/medium/high)**	*Creation:* (solo vs co-creation) **(low/medium/high)**	Notes
Public editor	Medium	Low	Community/high	
Botometer (by OSoMe)	Low	High	Low	
CaptainFact (France) (plugin)	High	Low	High	Focus on inserting fact checks in videos
Claimbuster (human input)	Medium	Medium	Medium	Human assisted matching learning to identify potential claims
Co-Inform (plugin)	High	High	High	
Co-Inform (dashboard)	High	Medium	High	
Cyabra	Medium	High	Low	
Decodex (Le Monde) (France) (plugin); run by journalists) (how) (why)	Low	Low	Low	Focus on source credibility
Facebook fact-checking program	Medium	Medium	Medium	Facebook Third-Party Fact Checking Program with IFCN-verified partners
Factmata	Low	High	Low	
FakerFact (plugin)	Medium	High	Low	
Fiskkit	High	Low	High	Works on the critical thinking and analysis skills
Foller.me	Low	High	Low	Similar to MisinfoMe

(continued)

Table 1. (*continued*)

Tool	Policy: (reactive vs proactive) (low/medium/high)	Process: (manual vs AI/machine learning) (low/medium/high)	Creation: (solo vs co-creation) (low/medium/high)	Notes
Hoaxy (by OSoMe)	Low	High	Low	Similar to MisinfoMe
NewsGuard (plugin)	Medium	Low	Low	Focus on source credibility; run by journalists
Newstrition	Low	High	Low	
TheFactual (plugin) (how) (who)	Medium	High	Low?	Focus on article credibility
TinEye replace AI and crowdsourcing as opposites	Medium	High	Low	Reverse image search
Twitter Birdwatch	Medium	Low	High	Crowd-sourced fact checking
WeVerify (InVID) (plugin)	High	HIGH	High	Focused on videos
Whatsapp IFCN Chatbot	Low	HIGH	Medium	
CredEye	Low	Medium	Low	Web page. Produces *credibility* score of a given text

References

1. Allport, G.W., Postman, L.: An analysis of rumor. Publ. Opin. Q. **10**(4), 501–517 (1946). https://doi.org/10.1093/poq/10.4.501
2. Babakar, M.: Crowdsourced fact checking (2018). https://medium.com/@meandvan/crowds ourced-factchecking-4c5168ea5ac3. Accessed Feb 2021
3. Bergmann, E.: Populism and the politics of misinformation. Safundi **21**(3), 251–265 (2020). https://doi.org/10.1080/17533171.2020.1783086
4. Choy, M., Chong, M.: Seeing through misinformation: a framework for identifying fake online news. arXiv preprint arXiv:1804.03508 (2018)
5. Ekström, M., Lewis, S.C., Westlund, O.: Epistemologies of digital journalism and the study of misinformation. New Media Soc. **22**(2), 205–212 (2020). https://doi.org/10.1177/146144 4819856914
6. Farrell, J., McConnell, K., Brulle, R.: Evidence-based strategies to combat scientific misinformation. Nat. Clim. Chang. **9**(3), 191–195 (2019). https://doi.org/10.1038/s41558-018-0368-6

7. Fernandez, M., Alani, H.: Online misinformation: challenges and future directions. In: Companion Proceedings of the Web Conference 2018, pp. 595–602, April 2018. https://doi.org/10.1145/3184558.3188730

8. Ford, E.: What's in your filter bubble? Or, how has the internet censored you today? (2012). http://pdxscholar.library.pdx.edu/cgi/viewcontent.cgi?article=1078&context=ulib_fac. Accessed Jan 2021

9. Giglietto, F., Iannelli, L., Rossi, L., Valeriani, A.: Fakes, news and the election: a new taxonomy for the study of misleading information within the hybrid media system (2016). https://papers.ssrn.com/sol3/papers.cfm?abstract_id=2878774

10. Jaursch, J., Lenoir, T., Schafe, B., Soula, E.: Tackling disinformation: going beyond content moderation, November 2019. https://www.institutmontaigne.org/en/blog/tackling-disinformation-going-beyond-content-moderation. Accessed 10 Nov 2020

11. Komendantova, N., et al.: A value-driven approach to addressing misinformation in social media. Human. Soc. Sci. Commun. 8(1), 1–12 (2021). https://doi.org/10.1057/s41599-020-00702-9

12. Koulolias, V., Jonathan, G.M., Fernandez, M., Sotirchos, D.: Combating Misinformation: An Ecosystem in Co-creation. OECD Publishing, Paris (2018)

13. Alex, M.: Twitters crowdsourced fact-checking experiment reveals problems. https://www.poynter.org/fact-checking/2021/analysis-twitters-crowdsourced-fact-checking-experiment-reveals-problems/. Accessed 17 Mar 2021

14. Mensio, M., Alani, H.: News source credibility in the eyes of different assessors. In: Conference for Truth and Trust Online, 4–5 October 2019, London, UK (2019, in press)

15. Moon, K., Blackman, D.: A guide to ontology, epistemology, and philosophical perspectives for interdisciplinary researchers. Integration and Implementation Insights (2017)

16. Osborne, P.S.: From public service-dominant logic to public service logic: are public service organizations capable of co-production and value co-creation? Publ. Manag. Rev. 20(2), 225–231 (2018). https://doi.org/10.1080/14719037.2017.1350461

17. Parisier, E.: The Filter Bubble: What the Internet is Hiding from You. Penguin, London (2011)

18. Pennycook, G., Cannon, T.D., Rand, D.G.: Prior exposure increases perceived accuracy of fake news. J. Exp. Psychol. Gen. 147(12), 1865 (2018). https://doi.org/10.1037/xge0000465

19. Seo, B., Park, D.: The effective type of information categorization in online curation service depending on psychological ownership. Sustainability 12(8), 3321 (2020)

20. Svahn, M., Lange, F.: Marketing the category of pervasive games. In: Montola, M., Stenros, J., Waern, A. (eds.) Pervasive Games; Theory and Design. Morgan Kaufman, Burlington (2009)

21. Tenove, C.: Protecting democracy from disinformation: normative threats and policy responses. Int. J. Press/Polit. 25(3), 517–537 (2020). https://doi.org/10.1177/1940161220918740

22. Vosoughi, S., Roy, D., Aral, S.: The spread of true and false news online. Science 359(6380), 1146–1151 (2018). https://doi.org/10.1126/science.aap9559

23. Wardle, C., Derakhshan, H.: Thinking about 'information disorder': formats of misinformation, disinformation, and mal-information. In: Ireton, Cherilyn; Posetti, Julie. Journalism, 'fake news' & disinformation, pp. 43–54. Unesco, Paris (2018)

User Needs for a Mobility App to Support Living in Rural Areas

Vera Spitzer$^{(\boxtimes)}$ ⓘ and Maria A. Wimmer ⓘ

Institute for IS Research, University of Koblenz-Landau, Koblenz, Germany
{vesp91,wimmer}@uni-koblenz.de

Abstract. Among the biggest challenges rural areas currently face are the impact of demographic change and limited mobility offers. While younger people tend to either move to urban areas or have their own car at hand for satisfying everyday needs, elderly or people with compromised health suffer most from these challenges. They prefer to live in their habitual and familiar environment and remain mobile for as long as possible. To enable self-determined living in rural areas and to make rural areas more attractive as places to live, municipalities and regions with substantial rural character need to develop concepts and modern digital solutions to achieve these objectives. In this paper, we introduce stakeholder-driven requirements elicitation for a mobility platform, which supports local communities and citizens in remaining autonomous in their living. The aim of the mobile app is to intelligently match offers of different mobility providers (e.g. voluntary drivers, public transportation services, taxis drivers etc.) with citizens' mobility demands in rural areas. Citizens needing a ride can find, book and pay the best offer for their journeys through the app. They can also rate the mobility service after its use. In the paper, we present the findings from 60 semi-structured face-to-face interviews with elderly in rural areas, thereby applying qualitative and quantitative content analysis. The empirical results were transcribed, categorized and analyzed quantitatively and qualitatively. We conclude with recommendations for the design and implementation of the mobility app.

Keywords: Digital transformation · Mobility · Rural areas · User needs · Mobility app

1 Introduction

Demographic change is noticeable throughout Germany and represents a challenge for public administrations, especially for municipalities in rural areas due to the low population and settlement density [1]. Over the years, the population in urban cities increased, while the rural population declined [2]. According to a recent comparison by [3], the figures of Germans living in rural regions vary between 23% and 66%. The German Federal Statistical Office estimates a decreasing and aging population in Germany in the next 20 years[1]. In addition, more and more younger people decide to move to the

---

[1] Statistisches Bundesamt (2021): Bevölkerungsvorausberechnung. https://www.destatis.de/DE/Themen/Gesellschaft-Umwelt/Bevoelkerung/Bevoelkerungsvorausberechnung/_inhalt.html.

© IFIP International Federation for Information Processing 2021
Published by Springer Nature Switzerland AG 2021
N. Edelmann et al. (Eds.): ePart 2021, LNCS 12849, pp. 77–89, 2021.
https://doi.org/10.1007/978-3-030-82824-0_7

cities due to the still poorly developed infrastructure and public transportation or partly non-existent internet connection in rural areas [3]. Elderly or those with limited mobility are often no longer able to reach groceries, doctors or sports clubs themselves, so they have to rely on carpooling with family or neighbors [4]. In order to guarantee citizens a high quality and self-determined life in familiar surroundings for as long as possible, the municipalities are challenged to develop and offer new solutions by the use of ICT [5, 6] to meet the expectations and needs of people living in rural areas. While people in cities and urban areas benefit from fast internet connection and smart city solutions to use digital tools in daily life, citizens in rural regions suffer from limited broadband access and lack of high-speed internet. The deployment of broadband access develops very slowly, and only 50% of rural areas can offer broadband with a bandwidth of 50 Mbits/s.[2] Therefore, the German federal state currently funds digital transformation with programs like "Ländliche Entwicklung" and pilot projects like "LandZukunft" and "SmarteLandRegionen".[3]

Among the projects co-funded in one of the aforementioned programs is SWiA of the district Cochem-Zell Germany. The aims of SWiA are to conceptualize and implement a digital solution, which offers mobility on demand based on the needs of the citizens in the rural part of the district. The objective of the mobile app is to match the most appropriate offers of mobility service providers (such as public transportation, taxi or voluntary drivers) and the mobility needs of citizens. The project applies a co-creation approach [7], involving the citizens in the analysis of needs, in the conceptual design, and the evaluation of the solution.

The paper at hand focuses on the analysis of the user needs of such a mobile app that supports mobility on demand in rural areas. The ultimate goal is therefore to investigate the user needs – especially those of elderly that seek sustained self-determined living in rural areas – for a mobile app that supports citizens in finding, booking and rating the most suitable mobility service that meets their needs. The re-search aims to answer the following two research questions:

1. What are the needs of citizens living in rural areas for a digital mobility app?
2. What motivates users, especially elderly, in using a digital application for finding and booking mobility services to meet their needs in rural areas?

To answer these research questions, we apply qualitative content analysis according to Mayring [8]. Section 2 reviews the situation of mobility in rural regions. Section 3 provides an overview of digital transformation in society through a review of existing literature, followed by a summary of the co-creation and co-production approach in Sect. 4. The methodology of qualitative content analysis and the category system applied thereby are presented in Sect. 5. Subsequently, Sect. 6 presents the results and interpretation of

---

[2] BMVI—Bundesministerium für Verkehr und digitale Infrastruktur (2018) Breitbandatlas https://www.bmvi.de/SharedDocs/DE/Publikationen/DG/breitband-verfuegbarkeit-ende-2018.html.

[3] Bundesministerium für Ernährung und Landwirtschaft (2019). Modell- und Demonstrationsvorhaben. https://www.bmel.de/DE/Laendliche-Raeume/BULE/zukunftsfelder/zukunftsf elder_node.html.

the user needs based on the qualitative and quantitative analysis. Section 7 concludes with a discussion of the findings and with further research planned.

2 Mobility in Rural Regions

Rural regions offer beautiful opportunities to live, which includes strong communities, affordable housing prices and many open and green spaces [9]. In the European Union (EU), 28% of the population lives in the countryside. However, depopulation and social exclusion have led to an aging population in many rural areas, and mainly elderly choose to stay and live in these regions [10, 11]. Therefore, for the elderly population, mobility is a crucial asset in maintaining autonomy and independence in their self-determined lives. This particularly includes car ownership, which plays a significant role in enabling social inclusion, employment as well as the completion of everyday affairs [12]. Consequently, sustainable mobility management calls for a flexible transport system (which goes beyond the traditional ownership of a car to get around) to improve transport services in rural areas, which allows for a wider choice in mobility services such as public transportation, taxi or car sharing [13–16]. Beyond that, environmentally friendly and sustainable alternative mobility services like public transportation and car sharing or voluntary driving support municipalities in reducing the local pollutant and CO_2 emissions. To realize this transition, municipalities seek new strategies that embark on digital services to improve mobility and quality of life for citizens while reducing the mass of car use.

In the past decade, society started to support new models of a sharing economy and of utility services such as Airbnb and Uber. In the transport sector, the concept of the sharing economy is also evolving into the transport paradigm of "Mobility as a Service" (MaaS) [17, 18]. The idea of MaaS is to assemble all potential mobility providers (e.g. public transport, bike sharing, car sharing, taxi etc.) and bundle them into a single service [19], with a digital platform to manage the mobility services. The plat-form enables users to book and pay for the mobility services through a single account. Nevertheless, bundling is not a new concept, but it is used to increase consumer acceptance of underutilized products and services. Less popular transport systems, like car sharing could be bundled to increase and drive demand for them. The use of MaaS can be seen as a soft mobility management tool to reshape the face of the existing travel services and the way services are perceived by individuals [20]. In rural areas, different public transport services and different user groups with their particular needs could be managed with intelligent digital solutions [15]. For this purpose, the SWiA project investigates user needs and develops a MaaS that matches the mobility needs of the users with the offers of mobility providers in rural environments based on a co-creation approach.

By applying qualitative content analysis of Mayring (2000), the first step is to review relevant literature, which is outlined in the next two sections.

3 Digital Transformation in Society

Digital transformation is one of the key contemporary terms characterizing the change and implementation of digital technologies in organizational structures. In the public sector, the term was coined along digital government and e-government. Advances in ICT are leading to an increasingly digitized world in which data, information and knowledge need to be made more and more available for citizen, companies and sub-ordinate agencies. Digital landscapes are emerging in which society finds various media platforms and intelligent technologies so that digital services and processes can be demanded and used [21, 22]. Through the use of ICT, public facilities and digital services become more accessible to society and customer-oriented solutions can be offered [23]. This should improve the quality of public services and the relationship and trust of citizens [24, 25].

According to Charalabidis et al., e-government has evolved from Government 1.0 to Government 3.0, with Government 1.0 referring to ICT mainly used as a tool to improve communication of citizen with most common methods like local, national or one-stop portals as well as internal digitalization efforts [26]. The same authors characterize Government 2.0 as the use of Web 2.0 technologies e.g. social media, social networks, blogs, wikis and RSS feeds to strengthen participation and collaboration in society. Government 2.0 also encompasses Open Government, as the use of social media enables the transformation of services. Furthermore, public information and Open Government Data can be provided through social media channels [21, 27]. In contrast to Government 1.0, Government 2.0 is characterized by bidirectional communication as different stakeholders are able to contribute in decision making and policy modelling processes in public issues [28]. With Government 3.0, disruptive technologies such as artificial intelligence, machine learning, big data analytics, inter-net of things or blockchain are employed to offer customized solutions, governance as well as data-driven applications and evidence-based decision and policy making are realized [26, 29]. The challenge of using disruptive technologies in context of public services is to strengthen society's trust in the use of smart ICT while at the same time meeting ethical standards such as data protection, inclusion and accountability [30]. Especially in e-government, projects are challenging in the implementation due to legal, technical or organizational issues [31]. On a legal level, the protection of personal data plays a crucial role as concerns about data protection can lead to a loss of user trust in the acceptance and use of public services. Society's trust and understanding are essential to the success and adoption of new processes and technologies in public sector [32]. Security concerns about information systems and web applications often lead to unused digital services [33]. On the technical level, the implementation of e-government projects often lacks IT-experts in combination with a lack of knowledge about e-government in general or the use of outdated infrastructure in public organizations. Organizational challenges include a lack of support of political or administrative staff, or insufficient collaboration between administrative bodies [34].

Successful implementation of digital services in the public sector depends on the collaboration of users. In case of the SWiA project, the acceptance and trust is necessary for the success and sustainable use of the application. Therefore, the concept of co-creation is applied for the mobile app development. Co-creation is explained in the following section.

4 Co-creation and Co-production

The development of the SWiA application is driven by a co-creative approach and the contribution of users' expectations and requirements in order to ensure citizens' acceptance of such a smart technology in the long term.

According to the European Commission (2013), co-production is generally understood as improved, more user-friendly and innovative public services which can be offered to meet users' needs. Definitions of co-production vary between "the mix of public services agents and citizens who contribute to provision of public services" to "a partnership between citizens and public service providers" [35]. Stakeholders can assume different roles and profiles in a co-production context: Public authorities, citizens, businesses or NGOs can take part and provide information, knowledge, data or services to solve and improve a social challenge [36].

Co-creation is seen as another concept for user participation in the design of public services [7]. Governments should provide incentives to ensure processes in co-creation to integrate citizens in the design of e-government services [37, 38]. Especially the field of Smart Governance as key dimension of a smart city development emphasizes the importance of stakeholder collaboration to increase public value and to adapt more innovative users' requirements [39, 40]. The method of co-creation has its origin in the software development and has been implemented in the form of three main practices: Participatory design, user-centered design and user innovation [38]. In participatory design, users can act as assessors of prototypes or they represent a specific user group. In this process, users are seen as equal partners. On the other hand, user-centered design describes the influence of user needs in the user interface. In user innovation, the problem identification and the design solution are done by the users. In a federal system, co-creation can contribute public services on all levels, especially on local government level. Preferred methods for the use of co-creation are questionnaires, interviews, workshops, test of a prototype or crowd-based requirements engineering. In the context of e-government projects, stakeholder participation is much more difficult than in traditional software development projects, as services have to be developed for large, homogeneous user groups. In this case, individual requirements and ideas must be considered and analyzed for the holistic project design [25]. In [35] co-creation is also referred to as co-governance, as people from the third sector are involved in the development public service. Older people in particular pose a special challenge due to a lack in ICT and a lack of acceptance in the use of digital public services. With co-creation, these citizens can be involved in the process at the beginning and strengthen their trust in public administrations. Moreover, co-creation does not only consider citizens as users, as social and democratic rights in particular are considered [39].

The SWiA project adapts the co-creation approach to involve citizens in every step of the application development – from the elicitation of user requirements to the matching of mock-ups to the prototypical implementation and piloting of the SWiA-application. The next section outlines the methodological approach for determining the user requirements of a mobility application and thus clarifies the first stage of the co-creation approach.

5   Methodological Approach and Category System

In order to analyze the user needs and to involve the users directly in the co-creation process, qualitative content analysis was conducted according to the approach of Mayring [41] to study initial material from the project scope and to develop a structured interview, which was used for the investigation of the user needs. The stepwise approach applied is as follows:

1. Selection of the material to be analyzed e.g. the whole text or text passages to be studied. In this research, literature and project material were analyzed. The deductive approach is based on previously developed research questions and aspects which need to be connected with the text. Along this, the initial category system was specified for the deductive analysis as well.
2. Based on the initial deductive analysis, a structured interview was constructed with open and closed questions. The structured interview included 17 questions and was developed along the objective of the project scope and mobility app to identify the needs of the users. For example, users were asked if they need a walker or wheelchair for mobility services; if they use mobile devices or if they need help and introduction into IT services etc.
3. The target group (older people aged 60 and beyond) was interviewed in person by project members. The participants received materials about the project in advance and were informed about the survey context. The actual interview took place in the home environment of the users and was documented by written notes and recordings. In total, 60 interviews with citizens from 6 villages in the district Cochem-Zell were collected. Supplementary notes were also taken during the interview process.
4. The recordings of the interviews were transcribed and analyzed along the category system. Following the procedure, the material was looped through, by reducing categories into main and sub-categories. Besides qualitative aspects, quantitative results were also taken to answer the research questions, by analyzing frequencies or categories in the transcript [41–43].

Table 1 presents the category system derived from the project material to examine the transcriptions of the empirical research [8]. The first two columns spot the main categories deduced from the project material and the evaluation criteria to highlight whether the qualitative results are to be evaluated as a benefit, barrier, challenge, need or a requirement. The last column provides a short explanation of the categories or sub-categories.

The categories roughly reflect the structure of the interviews and were entered into the MAXQDA program. A category includes all components of the transcripts that represent a requirement or need for the app as well as aspects that could influence the success of the app. The results could then be classified using the evaluation mechanism described above. Subsequently, the findings from the structured interviews are presented.

Table 1. Category system

Category (evaluation criteria)	Sub-category (evaluation criteria)	Definition
1. Self-determined life in old age/social participation	1.1 Living in your own flat or house (benefit)	Citizen want to live at home as long as possible
	1.2 Decreasing own mobility (challenge)	Citizen want to use their own car for as longs as possible
	1.3 Mobility offers from others (need and challenge)	Use of alternatives such as public transport, carpooling etc.
	1.4 Leisure activities/activities that are regularly pursued (benefit) or not used (challenge)	Leisure activities such as club activities fire department, carnival, choir etc. and how those activities are reached
2.Conditions (need)	2.1 Deteriorated conditions in rural areas/higher dependencies on existing structures (challenge)	Organizations or small shops close because the catchment area in rural areas is too small
	2.2 Disintegration of traditional rural family communities (challenge)	Migration of children from rural communities to urban centers
	2.3 Demographic change (challenge)	Need for mobility services for the elderly that meet their needs
3. Enabler (requirements)	3.1 Broadband infrastructure (requirements)	Supportive building blocks; digital services require a stable internet connection
4. Project requirements (need, benefit	/	Targets for user needs of elderlies e.g. doctors, pharmacy, shopping; development of smart applications
5. App requirements (need, benefit)	/	Easy-to-use virtual platform considers all defined needs of customers
6. Requirement for Social change/digital transformation (requirements, need, challenge, benefit)	/	Supporting technical aids; use of digital devices; use of the internet, operating experiences in the use of digital devices

6   Findings from the Structured Interviews

Below, the main results of the interviews are presented and explained along the established categories. They are grouped along the defined evaluation criteria (see Table 1).
Due to limited space, only those questions and answers are summarized that reflect the
needs of the users in relation to the mobile app. As indicated before, sample size is 60.

Category 1.1 and 2.2, Question 1: *"You live in a relatively rural community. Do you
have family members living in your immediate vicinity and do they support you when
needed?"*

43 citizens indicated that family members either live in the house or in the same
place or in neighboring communities. 17 citizens rely on the support of family members.

Challenge: Differences could be found between the places considered: In villages with
poor public transport connections, lack of internet connections and the remoteness of
the regions, more family members move away.

Category 1.2, Question 2: *"What basic means of transport do you use to reach e.g.
a supermarket or a doctor?"*

At the time of the interviews in autumn 2019 to spring 2020, 51 citizens still use
their own car. 13 people rely on private carpooling e.g. by the husband, family members
or neighbors, 8 use taxi or public transport and 17 people us other options (bike, on
foot...).

Need and Benefit: The respondents predominantly use their own car, but they have
realized that such a smart solution could help meet future mobility needs. By connecting
many voluntary mobility providers, more individual mobility needs can be met.

Category 1.3 and 2.3; Question 3: *"Are there any barriers to the use of the means of
transport and if so, what are they"*

26 citizens out of 60 stated that they face barriers using transportation. Barriers:
Public transport in rural regions is not geared to the needs of elderly, even though their
population will be the majority in the long run due to demographic change. The user
interface of digital services is not geared towards older people.

Category 1.4 and 2.1, Question 4: *"What [leisure time] activities do you regularly
engage in and how do you achieve them?"*

50 citizens reach their leisure activities on foot, 35 by own car, 9 each by bike or
carpooling, 5 via public transport and 2 use other opportunities.

Benefit: Major activities the citizens engage with are club activities in the immediate
vicinity such as hiking, church, voluntary fire brigade etc. These are reached on foot or
by own car or carpool.

Barriers and challenges: Activities such as church or club activities were found to
be limited by closures in the vicinity in the future. Carpooling is the most frequently
chosen option next to using a car to reach such activities at more distant locations. While
communities already exist in rural areas, they however lack efficient communication
networks to organize themselves in the communities.

Category 1.4, Question 5: *"Are there any activities you would like to do but cannot
achieve?"*

Barrier: Elderly do no more want to drive longer distances on their own. Frequent public transport connections are not available in many villages.

Need: Public transport systems need adaption to the challenges of demographic change and rural structures.

Category 4, Question 6 and 7: *"Which digital device do you use and how easy do you find it to use?"*

11 citizens do not own a smartphone, tablet, laptop or computer. The majority, however, have such a device, some of the respondents even own several devices. Of these 48 citizens, 40 use their smartphones daily and 30 users have no difficulties in using a digital device. When asked if they like to try new apps, 20 of these 48 respondents denied. The users argued that they only use apps that are absolutely necessary for their daily needs. The majority of citizens that use a digital device answered that it is not cumbersome (37 of 48). Overall, 48 of 54 people said that they needed help in operating new digital devices.

Challenge: Elderly only use the functionalities and apps of the devices that are taught to them by other people.

Need: Users need training on the use of additional functionalities of the devices.

Need: Training in IT should be offered free of charge in villages. This is the only way to overcome tentativeness in dealing with digital applications in the long run and to take individual needs into account, e.g. online banking, online public services, etc.

Category 4, Question 9: *To what extent do you use the devices and how easy is it for you to operate them?*

50 citizens use digital devices for private contacts and 37 for obtaining information. 21 of the respondents use them for online shopping and 19 for online banking. Just 4 people do not use such devices at all.

Challenge: Lack of understanding the potentials and social networking possibilities of devices and infrastructures in the personal environment.

Category 6, Question 16 *"What recommendations would you give the project team?"* and 17 *"Could you imagine using an app like this beyond organizing mobility?"*

Need: Additional mobility offers are needed and there is a demand for citizen buses in the municipalities.

Barrier: Digital solutions (timetables and bookings) of public transport are too cumbersome for elderly.

Need: The app must be easy to use and adaptable to individual needs.

Need: The app should offer additional functions beyond matching mobility offers such as home and garden care, ways to increase pocket money for young people, scheduling and booking club activities etc. A kind of community platform is desired so that everyone can contribute according to their possibilities and needs.

The results of the empirical research address different responsibilities and issues: On the one hand, the results highlight and reinforce the current challenges in rural areas. Public transport is not available or difficult to access in many places, so citizens have to resort to their own cars. If elderly do not wish to drive longer distances any more, self-determined living in their habitual environment is at risk, because the citizens concerned face the severe challenge of reaching individual places. Therefore, public transportation should be available with regular connections in all villages. However, service providers argue that such services cause high costs and deficit.

The insights from the results show that mobility barriers can be overcome by the use of private cars and by voluntary driver services that are organized through a mobile app as a MaaS. A precondition for mobile digital services to work is sufficient broadband coverage in rural areas. Without stable internet connections, seniors cannot and do not want to use digital devices and apps. Most of the respondents still have doubts or substantive reservations about the content of digital functions and applications. The loss of data autonomy is one of the most common reasons for elderly not to use digital services. Training should be provided so that elderly learn and understand how digital services work and how they can use digital devices and apps properly. In this way, shyness about the technology should be overcome and user acceptance of both the app and e-government services should increase in the long term. Because most digital public transport services are not designed to be user-friendly, elderly refrain from using such solutions. The ease of use and simplicity of the SWiA app functions are particularly important to senior citizens and can be achieved by using a large font and symbols. Data scarcity and simplicity are further requirements, i.e. only the most relevant information should be displayed on the user interface (which corresponds to the aim of the project scope). Co-creation is a crucial approach to co-design the interaction, the functionality and the user navigation with the citizens. Therefore, the design of the SWiA app will be done in close collaboration with the senior citizens living in the region of Cochem-Zell.

Another important user need is the implementation of voluntary carpooling. Some users already offer carpooling among their friends, but there is no central platform available to manage such requests. By developing a central digital platform to bundle ride offers and communicate needs, mobility offers can be displayed in a user-friendly way and booked much faster by the MaaS users. A further aspect to be considered is that, while one might expect that elderly are more hesitant to use services of people they do not know in person, this aspect is less crucial in rural communities, where people know each other such as for SWiA. This aspect may need further investigation when expanding the MaaS to a wider geographical area beyond local communities.

7   Conclusion

To understand how a mobility app can be used in rural areas, this paper investigated key barriers, challenges and needs for such an app by applying qualitative content analysis. First, a literature review was conducted and coded along a category system to derive relevant findings. Subsequently, 60 citizens in rural areas were interviewed to gather empirical insights. Regarding RQ1, we found that user needs vary from user-oriented platforms to training in digital devices, services and apps to regional specifications, which need to be addressed by the responsible regional or local authorities. The results of RQ2 showed that citizens welcome the participation and collaboration in the development of a mobility app.

While not all user needs are directly related to the design and development of a mobility app, these are necessary to ensure the successful use and user's satisfaction of the overall MaaS solution. To ensure this, a crucial strategy in the project is to enable elderly to participate in the digital transformation process. Through the co-creation approach, users will be directly involved in the development of the app from the very beginning. In addition, the SWiA app should be promoted through various channels to draw attention to the new digital offer and to encourage its use.

Based on the insights from the qualitative content analysis of user needs for a MaaS in rural areas, the mobile app is currently developed by applying the co-creation approach through involving the citizens along the design and testing of the app. Along this step, interactive workshop sessions are used to discuss design options with the citizens. Due to the COVID-19 pandemic, however, these sessions take place online. We will report the findings of these interactive online co-creation sessions as well as on the technical concept of the SWiA app in future publications.

Acknowledgements. This research was supported by the Federal Office for Agriculture and Food, Germany, Ref. 2818LD026. For further info see swia-cochem-zell.de.

References

1. Bundesministerium für Ernährung und Landwirtschaft: Bericht der Bundesregierung zur Entwicklung der ländlichen Räume 2016, Berlin (2016)
2. Gans, P.: Urban population development in Germany (2000–2014): the contribution of migration by age and citizenship to reurbanisation. Comp. Popul. Stud. **42**, 319–352 (2018). https://doi.org/10.12765/CPoS-2018-01
3. Meyn, M.: Digitalization and its impact on life in rural areas: exploring the two sides of the Atlantic: USA and Germany. In: Patnaik, S., Sen, S., Mahmoud, M.S. (eds.) Smart Village Technology. MOST, vol. 17, pp. 99–116. Springer, Cham (2020). https://doi.org/10.1007/978-3-030-37794-6_5
4. Haefker, M., Tielking, K.: Alter, Gesundheit, Partizipation: Alternative Wohn- und Versorgungsformen im Zeichen des demografischen Wandels. Springer, Wiesbaden (2017). https://doi.org/10.1007/978-3-658-16801-8
5. Goltz, E., Treller, U.: Wohnsituation und Wohnzufriedenheit älterer Menschen in Mietwohnungen im Amt Gerswalde - Perspektiven zum Altersgerechten Wohnen. In: Ländliche Räume im demografischen Wandel, pp. 61–72. Bundesministerium für Verkehr, Bau und Stadtentwicklung (BMVBS) und Bundesinstitut für Bau-, Stadt- und Raumforschung im Bundesamt für Bauwesen und Raumordnung (2009)
6. Dauderstädt, K.: Der demografische Wandel als Herausforderung für den öffentlichen Dienst (2017)
7. Wimmer, M.A., Scherer, S.: Supporting communities through social government in co-creation and co-production of public services. Int. J. Publ. Adm. Digit. Age. **5**, 18–35 (2018)

8. Mayring, P.: Qualitative Content Analysis - Theoretical Foundation, Basic Procedures and Software Solution. Beltz, Klagenfurth (2014)

9. Litman, T.: Public transportation's impact on rural and small towns: a vital mobility link (2017)

10. Barreto, L., Amaral, A., Baltazar, S.: Mobility as as Service (MaaS) in rural regions: an overview. In: International Conference on Intelligent Systems (IS), pp. 856–860. IEEE (2018)

11. Plazinic, B., Jovic, J.: Mobility and transport potential of elderly in differently accessible rural areas. J. Transp. Geogr. **68**, 169–180 (2018)

12. Soder, M., Peer, S.: The potential role of employers in promoting sustainable mobility in rural areas: evidence from Eastern Austria. Int. J. Sustain. Transp. **12**, 541–551 (2018)

13. Hanson, T.R., Kroes, E., Van Ooststroom, H.: Can rural older drivers meet their needs without a car? Stated adaptation responses from a GPS travel diary survey. Transp. (AMST) **38**, 975–992 (2011)

14. Faria, R., Brito, L., Baras, K., Silva, J.: Smart mobility: a survey. In: International Conference on Internet of Things for the Global Community (IoTGC), pp. 1–8. IEEE (2017)

15. Porru, S., Misso, F.E., Pani, F.E., Repetto, C.: Smart mobility and public transport: opportunities and challenges in rural and urban areas. J. traffic Transp. Eng. (Engl. Ed.) **7**, 88–97 (2020)

16. Buehler, R., Pucher, J.: Demand for public transport in Germany and the USA: an analysis of rider characteristics. Transp. Rev. **32**, 541–567 (2012)

17. Apaoja, A., Eckhardt, J., Nykänen, L.: Business models for MaaS. In: ICoMaaS 2017 Proceedings, Tampere, pp. 8–20 (2017)

18. Finger, M., Bert, N., Kupfer, D.: Mobility-as-a-services: from the Helsinki experience to a European model? Eur. Transp. Regul. Obs. (2015)

19. Smith, G., Hensher, D.: Towards a framework for mobility-as-a-service policies. Transp. Policy **89**, 54–65 (2020)

20. Headicar, P.: Transport Policy and Planning in Great Britain. Routledge, London (2009)

21. Chun, S.A., Shulman, S., Sandoval, R., Hovy, E.: Government 2.0: making connections between citizens, data and government. Inf. Polity (2010). https://doi.org/10.3233/IP-2010-0205

22. Loebbecke, C., Picot, A.: Reflections on societal and business model transformation arising from digitization and big data analytics: a research agenda. J. Strateg. Inf. Syst. **24**, 149–157 (2015). https://doi.org/10.1016/j.jsis.2015.08.002

23. Williams, M.D.: E-government adoption in Europe at regional level. Transform. Gov. People, Process Policy **2**, 47–59 (2008)

24. Field, T., Muller, E., Edwin, L., Hélène, G.-R., Christian, V.: The case for e-government: excerpts from the OECD report: the e-government imperative. OECD J. Budg. **3** (2003)

25. Axelsson, K., Melin, U., Lindgren, I.: Public e-services for agency efficiency and citizen benefit - findings from a stakeholder centered analysis. Gov. Inf. Q. **30**, 10–22 (2013)

26. Charalabidis, Y., Loukis, E., Alexopoulos, C., Lachana, Z.: The three generations of electronic government: from service provision to open data and to policy analytics. In: Lindgren, I., et al. (eds.) EGOV 2019. LNCS, vol. 11685, pp. 3–17. Springer, Cham (2019). https://doi.org/10.1007/978-3-030-27325-5_1

27. Geiger, C.P., von Lucke, J.: Open government and (linked) (open) (government) (data). JeDEM-eJournal eDemocracy Open Gov. **4**, 265–278 (2012)

28. Nam, T.: Suggesting frameworks of citizen-sourcing via Government 2.0. Suggest. Fram. Citizen-Sourcing via Gov. 2.0 **29**, 12–20 (2011)

29. Wimmer, M.A., Pereira, G.V., Ronzhyn, A., Spitzer, V.: Transforming government by leveraging disruptive technologies: identification of research and training needs. eJournal eDemocracy Open Gov. **12** (2020). https://doi.org/10.29379/jedem.v12i1.594

30. Ronzhyn, A., Wimmer, M.A.: Literature review of ethical concerns in the use of disruptive technologies in Government 3.0. In: Berntzen, L. (ed.) ICDS 2019: The Thirteenth International Conference on Digital Society and eGovernments, pp. 85–93. IARIA, Athens (2019)

31. Wimmer, M.A.: Beiträge der Wissenschaft zur erfolgreichen e-government-Umsetzung. In: Zechner, A. (ed.) Handbuch E-Government: Strategien, Lösungen und Wirtschaftlichekeit, pp. 79–87. Fraunhofer IRB Verlag, Stuttgart (2007)

32. Ndou, V.D.: E-government for developing countries: opportunities and challenges. Electron. J. Inf. Syst. Dev. Ctries. **18**, 1–24 (2004)

33. Carter, L., Bélanger, F.: The utilization of e-government services: citizen trust, innovation and acceptance factors. Inf. Syst. J. **15**, 5–25 (2005)

34. Coursey, D., Norris, D.F.: Models of e-government: are they correct? Publ. Adm. Rev. **68**, 523–536 (2008)

35. Pestoff, V.: Co-production and third sector social services in Europe: some concepts and evidence. Voluntas. **23**, 1102–1118 (2012)

36. Bovaird, T.: Beyond engagement and participation: user and community co-production of public services. Publ. Adm. Rev. **67**, 846–860 (2007)

37. European Commission: A Vision for Public Services - Draft Version Dated (2013)

38. Karlsson, F., Holgersson, J., Söderström, E., Hedström, K.: Exploring user participation approaches in public eservice development. Gov. Inf. Q. **29**, 158–168 (2012)

39. Simonofski, A., Snoeck, M., Vanderose, B.: Co-creating e-government services: an empirical analysis of participation methods in Belgium. In: Rodriguez Bolivar, M.P. (ed.) Setting Foundations for the Creation of Public Value in Smart Cities. PAIT, vol. 35, pp. 225–245. Springer, Cham (2019). https://doi.org/10.1007/978-3-319-98953-2_9

40. Anthopoulos, L., Janssen, M., Weerakkody, V.: A unified smart city model (USCM) for smart city conceptualization and benchmarking. In: Smart Cities and Smart Spaces: Concepts, Methodologies, Tools, and Applications, pp. 247–264 (2019)

41. Mayring, P.: Qualitative content analysis. Forum Qual. Soc. Res. **1**, 10 (2000)

42. Krippendorf, K.: Models of messages: three prototypes (1967)

43. Huber, G.L.: Qualitative Analyse. Computereinsatz in der Sozialforschung. Oldenbourg Verlag, München (1992)

Adoption of E-Government Requirements to Higher Education Institutions Regarding the Digital Transformation

Christina Deutsch$^{(\boxtimes)}$ ⓘ, Matthias Gottlieb ⓘ, and Hans Pongratz ⓘ

Technical University of Munich (TUM), Munich, Germany
{christina.deutsch,matthias.gottlieb,pongratz}@tum.de

Abstract. Higher education institutions' (HEI) administrations in Europe are facing difficulties regarding their digitalization. However, to succeed in digital transformation, digital services' introduction, and optimization, the HEI needs to understand its digitalization requirements. As HEI administration reaches its highest digitalization level when it is in the development stage of e-government, the e-government's needs and requirements can be applied in the context of HEI administration. Therefore, we conducted a four-step approach: (1) a systematic literature review, (2) qualitative longitudinal and latitudinal coding, (3) creation of a concept matrix of the e-government's requirements analysis, and (4) its evaluation on an example of a German HEI. We extend the knowledge base with a requirements matrix for HEI administration to be obeyed. We conclude that e-government's requirements are comparable to HEI's administrative requirements with process-oriented digitalization as the basis. Given the requirements, HEIs digitalize their administrative processes more efficiently.

Keywords: E-government · Requirement · Higher education institution · Administration · Digitalization

1 Introduction

Higher education institutions' (HEI) administration is currently the HEI area with the lowest digitalization level in Germany [1]. However, the contradiction is that although HEI administration lacks the most on digitalization, its staff is at least ready (47.8%) to cope with the digital transformation compared to students (81.7%) and academic staff (68.5%) [1]. To make progress concerning the HEI administration's digitalization, the administration needs to understand its digital transformation requirements. Similar to HEIs, e-government relies on information and communication technologies (ICTs) in the public sector to transform the relations between public institutions and citizens [2]. Thus, we assume the e-government requirements to be comparable to those of HEI administration. A good understanding of the requirements supports the development and usage of new technologies, such as artificial intelligence and blockchain, and the digital transformation and optimization of existing services. Therefore, European HEI administrations can apply this understanding to resolve the transformation issues. We

N. Edelmann et al. (Eds.): ePart 2021, LNCS 12849, pp. 90–104, 2021.
https://doi.org/10.1007/978-3-030-82824-0_8

answer the research question: *What are the e-government's digitalization requirements evaluated in the context of HEI administration?* We extend the knowledge base by creating an e-government matrix for the HEI administration. Our results yield that HEI requirements are comparable to those of e-government and can improve the efficiency of HEI administrative processes' digitalization.

The remainder of this article is structured as follows. In the section Related Work and Definitions, we dig into the claim of e-government requirements' relevance for the HEI administration to get a common understanding and explain relevant terms. We illustrate our approach in the section Methodology and Framework. In section Results, we describe the e-government's requirements. Afterward, we discuss our findings in the context of HEI administration and shed light on requirements' applicability in HEI administration. We close with the Conclusion and Future Work.

2 Related Work and Definitions

Scientific contributions dealing with e-government's requirements focus on the process. To obtain requirements from citizens [3, 4], they define a model that guides the developer through the e-government's software creation process and evaluates the quality of the requirements [5]. In addition, there are governmental documents, such as the European Union (EU) e-government action plan of 2016–2020 [6], describing the European Commission's plans to improve e-government. The action plan aims for full digitalization but describes goals to be achieved rather than the requirements.

Referring to the applicability of the e-government's requirements in the HEI context, multiple researchers state the HEI administration's digitalization processes to follow e-governments' requirements, such as regulation approaches [1, 7–9]. E-government's requirements are contained in the German governmental regulations, such as the Bavarian E-Government Regulations (Bayerisches E-Government-Gesetz - BayEGovG) and E-Government Regulations of North Rhine-Westphalia (E-Government-Gesetz Nordrhein-Westfalen - EGovG NRW), which mention the applicability of these approaches to juristic persons under pub-lic law, including HEIs [10, 11]. We aim to evaluate e-government's requirements in the context of HEI administration. The relevant key terms are *digitalization*, *requirements*, *e-government*, and *HEI administration*.

2.1 Digitalization

The digitalization process transforms society, relying on ICTs [11]. It refers to technological changes and encompasses organizational and management innovations. Digitalization is the key driver of modifications in the e-government processes. Currently, digitalization supports the achievement of the HEI's strategic goals, which is an emerging trend regarding ICT adoption in HEIs [2].

2.2 Requirements

The requirement is a "[...] quality or qualification that you must have in order to be allowed to do something or to be suitable for something" [12]. Applied to e-government, a requirement is a quality or qualification that this institution needs for its successful digitalization and digital services provision. We assume this interpretation also to be valid for the HEI administration.

2.3 E-Government

The e-government (also electronic government, digital government) relies on ICTs for relations' transformation in the public sector [3]. This paper focuses on e-administration, referring to the administration's management processes and interactions between citizens and businesses with the administration [3, 13]. E-administration is responsible for implementing the policy framework and its maintenance, service management, such as providing subventions, facility management, financial, economic, and social issues. The other is e-democracy, including e-participation and corruption prevention, which supports citizens' opinions and decision-making processes regarding political problems with the help of electronic media [3, 13].

The e-government's communication matrix consists of: (1) Government to Government (G2G), (2) Government to Business (G2B), and (3) Government to Citizen (G2C) (see Fig. 1) [13]. G2G refers to the horizontal integration of three state powers and vertical integration of the state levels [1]. G2B deals with integrating state and private business actors who demand and provide services [1]. G2C is the integration of the state and citizens requesting public services [1]. Opposite directions also exist.

Although the term's core understanding is similar across different countries, the development states of e-government variate [12, 13]. European countries, such as Denmark and Finland, and the USA, show similarities regarding their basic e-government principles, such as one-stop services, service access, and data sharing [12].

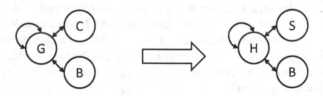

Fig. 1. E-Government matrix (left) vs. HEI matrix (right), based on [13].

2.4 Higher Education Institution

Multiple factors led to the HEIs' evolution: The Bologna Process initiated the structural transformation of HEIs in Europe, with numerous actors coordinating the transfer from HEIs to increase competence and scarce financial resources [14, 15]. Optimization and modernization became essential for administrations to improve the HEIs' services efficiency and quality [16]. HEIs now transform into process-oriented institutions where a process and its continuous adaptation to the organization's requirements are considered central aspects of the HEI implementation [14, 17].

E-government is process-oriented, and process optimization belongs to its prioritized targets [18]. Moreover, the HEI administration reaches the highest level of digitalization when it is in the development stage of the e-government [2]. Therefore, we can think of the HEI administration's matrix similar to the e-government's (see Fig. 1). (1) HEI to HEI (H2H) may refer to ICT usage within the HEI or interactions between different HEIs on the national or international levels. (2) HEI to Business (H2B) refers to the connections between a HEI and its external partners, including the student union, sponsors, and start-ups. (3) HEI to Student (H2S) is about services and applications offered to students, such as Student Information Systems (SISs) and Learning Management Systems (LMSs). Reverse directions, B2H and S2H, are also possible.

The Technical University of Munich (TUM) can be considered as representative German HEI (~600 professors, ~45,000 students, budget ~1.6 billion in 2019 (including the university hospital)) [19]. The HEI is highly process-oriented, referring to business processes, such as validating and submitting documents [20]. Due to its high overall digitalization level, established partners from the industry, and information systems targeted at the students' support, TUM has a matrix similar to the e-government's.

3   Methodology and Framework

In this paper, we carried out a literature review according to the four-step approach of Brocke et al. [21]. We addressed the first two steps in previous sections. We conducted the *AIS eLibrary* and followed Webster and Watson [22] by looking for contributions in leading journals and conference proceedings for literature search. We looked at eight journals from the Association for Information Systems (AIS) Senior Scholars' basket and the five recommended by the AIS Special Interest Group (SIG) Electronic Government. We also included four leading Information Systems (IS) conferences. To keep track of current developments, we considered only literature published in the last five years (2015–2020) and used the keywords *digital government*, *e-government*, and spelling variations. The literature search resulted in 433 hits. We read the titles and abstracts of the papers to identify relevant literature. Papers without any reference to e-government and those only focusing on its e-democracy component as well as articles discussing concrete technologies' applications in the e-government context, such as gamification, were excluded. We kept articles with a general focus and those discussing and (or) testing their findings' validity in European and American contexts. We found 16 relevant articles after screening the full texts.

4   Results

We found the top discussed concepts to be *stakeholder collaboration* (13 articles), *cost reduction* (nine articles), *interest diversity* (eight articles), and *legal regulations* (eight articles). Our findings revealed *complexity decomposition* and *reliability* as the concepts with a little discussion. We derived four requirement categories: three (G2G, G2B, G2C) from the communication matrix and one (Services) from the literature. Table 1 shows the inductively created concept matrix based on our findings.

1. **G2G** stands for the requirements of a single e-government and its interaction with other e-governments.
2. **G2B** consists of concepts describing stakeholder collaboration and their interest diversity.
3. **G2C** represents governmental needs when interacting with the citizens.
4. **Services** refer to the enabling services representing qualities of ICTs.

Table 1. E-government concept matrix (N.a. = not applicable).

Requirement	Description	Source/discussed	Application to HEI administration
G2G			
Ambidextrous organization	The e-government adopts conflicting values: efficiencies and innovations. Efficiencies are service improvements, whereas innovations stand for new technologies	[23, 24]	Yes
Adaptability	The e-government adapts to innovations and technological changes	[23–29]	Yes
Stability	The e-government maintains its fixed organizational structure. It is risk-averse to prevent the *failure trap*, i.e., taking too many risk-intensive actions	[23, 24, 30, 31]	Yes
Balanced power	The e-government aims for balanced power distribution within the organization	[23–25, 29, 30]	Yes

(continued)

Table 1. (*continued*)

Requirement	Description	Source/discussed	Application to HEI administration
Complexity decomposition	The e-government decomposes complex problems, such as software projects, into smaller parts	[23, 26]	Yes
Flexibility	The e-government has a flexible infrastructure. The decision-making life cycle times are short and final decisions are done as late as possible	[23, 31, 32]	Yes
Accountability	The e-government keeps its staff accountable with rules and regulations	[23, 24, 27, 30, 31, 33, 34]	Partially
Staff education	The e-government is responsible for educating its staff by providing it with the necessary ICT competencies to increase its openness to change	[23, 25, 26, 29, 32]	Yes
Cost reduction	Technologies applied in social services decrease expenses. However, governments only focusing on cost savings are at risk of failure	[25–27, 29, 31–35]	Yes

(*continued*)

Table 1. (*continued*)

Requirement	Description	Source/discussed	Application to HEI administration
Legal regulations	Regulations for digitizing have to be adapted. E-legislation's identification should happen as early as possible in a project	[23, 25, 27, 29–31, 33, 35]	Partially
G2B			
Interest diversity	The e-government has central role in digital projects and manages other parties. It should know its internal and external stakeholders, their capabilities, and interests	[23, 25–27, 30, 34, 36, 37]	Yes
Stakeholder collaboration	The e-government collaboration with its internal and external stakeholders allows the parties to create joint value propositions	[23, 25, 26, 29, 30, 32–39]	Yes
G2C			
Citizen centricity	The e-government focuses on its citizens and aims to satisfy their needs	[27, 29, 31, 34, 39]	Yes
Digital identity	The e-government allows its citizens to identify themselves with a digital ID or other means	[29, 38]	Yes

(*continued*)

Table 1. (*continued*)

Requirement	Description	Source/discussed	Application to HEI administration
Privacy	The e-government guarantees citizens' privacy	[27, 29, 33]	Yes
"No-stop shop"	The e-government proactively provides services to the citizens, i.e., when a life event occurs	[29, 38]	Unclear
Trust	The e-government builds and maintains a high level of trust of the citizens	[29, 31, 33–35, 39]	Yes
Engagement	The e-government motivates the citizens to engage with digital services, e.g., by informing them about the existing services	[25, 27, 31–33, 37, 38]	Yes
Services			
Quality	The service data is of high quality. The digital services are of high quality	[25–27, 29, 30, 32–34]	N.a.
Efficiency	The service is efficient	[23, 24, 34, 37, 38]	N.a.
Innovation	The e-government develops and introduces new technologies. It avoids the *failure trap*	[23, 24, 26, 27, 34]	Yes

(*continued*)

Table 1. (*continued*)

Requirement	Description	Source/discussed	Application to HEI administration
Transparency	The service is transparent, e.g., the citizen is able to track his service requests	[27, 29, 31, 33, 34]	N.a.
Accessibility	The service is accessible via various channels. The data is accessible across organizations	[29, 32–34, 38]	N.a.
Usability	The service is easy to use	[32, 34]	N.a.
Reliability	The service is reliable. It uses reliable data	[23, 25, 29, 30]	N.a.
Data management	The data necessary for the service is maintained, reused, and cleared up regularly	[25, 27, 29, 33]	N.a.
Interoperability/integration	The services are interoperable within the organization and between the internal and external services	[27, 29, 32–34]	N.a.
Standardization	The e-government establishes data and technical standards	[25, 27, 29]	Partially
Security	The e-government is security conscious. The services are secure	[23, 25, 27, 29, 30, 33]	Yes/N.a.

5 Discussion and Implications

In the following, we outline the applicability of the e-governments' requirements in the HEI administration context on the example of European HEIs, such as TUM.

5.1 H2H

The H2H category is related to the G2G category of e-government. The first requirement is the government's need to be *ambidextrous*. Ambidexterity stands for the digital government that continuously innovates and improves existing services. We discuss this concept using the organization of teaching processes in HEIs as an example. 95% of German representatives of higher education administrations think that online media support traditional face-to-face teaching, and 40% assume that completely online teaching is possible [40]. Therefore, most of the representatives are convinced of the proficiency of conflicting values simultaneously existing in the HEI context. However, HEI administrators should not be considered fully ambidextrous, as they tend to be digital-averse and in favor of *stability* [1]. Nevertheless, we see the degree of digitalization in student lifecycle actions at TUM as extraordinarily high compared to other HEIs.

Since the introduction of the Chief Information Officer (CIO) position in HEIs, universities actively participate in digital transformation and tailor to their needs digital systems, such as SISs [16], which demonstrates *adaptability*. Setting up innovation labs to work on innovative projects without disrupting existing processes can support ambidexterity [40]. At TUM, the *Big Data Innovation Lab* allows for developing and evaluating innovations on a research platform in different industry sectors. Such innovations often allow for cost reduction due to process automation.

Balanced power relations in e-government enable a clear assignment of roles and responsibilities of the parties involved. At TUM, the Extended Board of Management is responsible for the university's development plan, structural reorganization, and budget [41]. The roles are assigned, e.g., the President represents the university internally and externally, the Board of Management makes decisions on the university's key attributes: scientific, international, and entrepreneurial [41].

Complexity decomposition and *flexibility* are the next requirements to be discussed. An agile HEI can address both aspects [45]. An exemplary agile method is Design Thinking [43]. Given the customers' needs, this method allows the HEI to create a Minimum Viable Product (MVP) satisfying minimal users' requests. After being approved by the users, the product's adjustments are possible [43]. Thus, agile administration enables flexible solutions and product development in smaller pieces. The concept of smaller academic qualification units can become part of future academic study programs [44]. In general, the transformation of a HEI is complicated, as a bureaucratized rigid structure characterizes it, and public financing may envelope its digitalization. Therefore, its flexibility is not mainly determined by the market developments but by the legal regulations and academic culture [45]. The Bologna Process enhances, inter alia, the introduction of a system of comparable Bachelor and Master degrees, and promotes mobility of students and academic staff [46]. The Standing Conference of the Ministers of Education and Cultural Affairs responsible for coordinating and developing education in Germany is another example.

Art. 2 para. 1 sentence 7 of the Bavarian Higher Education Act (BayHSchG) obliges HEIs to promote the continuing *education* of their employees [47]. The employees can gain ICT capabilities, e.g., at the *TUM Institute for LifeLong Learning* that focuses on providing knowledge in the area of digitalization. The need for staff training is essential, as a lack of motivation is currently one of the main obstacles to digitizing HEIs.

Moreover, the e-government and, thus, the HEI should keep its employees *accountable*. Although the HEI administration can add internal control mechanisms, it cannot influence the Law on Academic Staff in Higher Education Institutions (Bayerisches Hochschulpersonalgesetz - BayHSchPG). As *legal regulations*, such as the BayEGovG, cannot be adjusted by the HEI administration directly according to its digitalization needs, their unchangeable nature may restrict the digital strategy. However, the Online Access Act (Onlinezugangsgesetz - OZG) may be the key digitalization enabler. There are already positive examples in higher education, and the Online Access Act will push even more activities in the context of online access via university web portals, authentication, and authorization, e.g., via Shibboleth, and data exchange via systems, such as LMS [48].

5.2 H2B

The H2B category is comparable to G2B and refers to various internal stakeholders being active in a HEI: students, teaching and scientific staff, personnel involved in the management and support processes. Libraries, data centers, and student unions can be considered external actors [14]. Therefore, the HEI's stakeholders' landscape is heterogeneous. This heterogeneity and the HEIs' process-oriented nature imply the need to consider *diverse interests* and collaborate with other stakeholders. In this collaboration, the HEI administration acts as an intermediary between the parties, including students, researchers, and business actors. Referring to the second requirement, *stakeholder collaboration*, only an intense interconnection and constant collaboration via online platforms can address the high digital transformation speed needed to maintain high teaching, research, and overall HEI's levels [45].

5.3 H2S

The H2S is similar to the G2C category regarding *citizen centricity* comparable to the HEIs' student centricity and student life cycle [14]. Moreover, a HEI student usually has a *digital identity*, and the EU General Data Protection Regulation guarantees student's *privacy*. However, this set of regulations may restrict the administration's actions regarding digitalization. New solutions, such as the self-sovereign identity (SSI) allowing students to control their private data, already exist [49]. With SSI, HEIs benefit from verifying, validating, and authenticating student data.

Currently, most HEI processes are realized as a one-stop-shop. However, *no-stop-shop* services arise at highly digitalized process-oriented HEIs, e.g., at TUM, the study progress monitoring is fully automated. The students' *trust* is necessary to prevent their resistance to using digital services. However, student concerns as digital natives are less complex than citizen clients of e-government, so encouraging their *engagement* and providing them with necessary information is easier to handle.

5.4 Services

We focus on the commonly discussed aspects of innovation, standardization, and security and refrain from discussing technology-specific requirements. HEIs already recognized the importance of *innovation* implementation [50]. The university is unlikely to experience the *failure trap* with the administrative staff being rather digital-averse.

Like the e-government, the HEIs collaboratively define standards and create interfaces, e.g., for the students' data transfer among institutions. *Standardization* is one of the operational challenges when introducing an IS at a HEI [16].

The *security* requirement encompasses cybersecurity and the HEI being aware of it. Events on security help to increase the awareness of the HEI's staff and students of this topic. At TUM, the *IT Security and Data Protection Days* take place regularly. Moreover, security control and innovations are part of the CIO's responsibilities.

6 Conclusion and Future Work

In this paper, we obtained the requirements of the e-government regarding its digitalization. Then, we evaluated these needs in the context of European HEIs, such as TUM, to assess their applicability to the HEI administration. We found most e-government's needs contained in Table 1 to apply to the administration fully. A HEI can only partially address some requirements which may represent boundary conditions, e.g., legal regulations may restrict its digitalization. Some H2H requirements are adaptability, flexibility, cost reduction, stakeholders' needs, collaboration, and interest diversity; H2C – privacy and student centricity; and service-specific – security, and standardization. During digital transformation, the administration can refer to the requirements matrix to obtain which of its needs may be covered or supported by an innovation and determine the technology's potentials.

Future research can determine additional requirements, including interdisciplinary contributions from research areas outside the IS leading journals and conferences. We considered papers dealing with the e-governments in Europe and the USA, whereby the contributions discussed institutions situated in different countries. These cross-country settings represent a limitation and may make the findings' comparability and transferability problematic [51]. Moreover, future research can focus on measurements and the coding of concepts that we did not address in our contribution. Therefore, researchers can extend the paper on generalizability to improve the external validity. In addition, future research can assess the requirements matrix with more HEIs and technological innovations.

Acknowledgment. The intention on which this report is based was funded by the German Federal Ministry of Education and Research under the funding code 534800. The responsibility for the content of this publication lies with the authors.

References

1. Gilch H., et al.: Digitalisierung der Hochschulen: Ergebnisse einer Schwerpunktstudie für die Expertenkommission Forschung und Innovation. Expertenkommission für Forschung und

Innovation (EFI), February 2019. https://his-he.de/publikationen/detail/digitalisierung-der-hochschulen. Accessed 18 Mar 2021

2. Veit, D.: Definition of E-Government. https://www.enzyklopaedie-der-wirtschaftsinformatik.de/wi-enzyklopaedie. Accessed 18 Mar 2021

3. Van Velsen, L., Van Der Geest, T., Hedde, T., Wijnand, D.: Requirements engineering for e-government services: a citizen-centric approach and case study. Gov. Inf. Q. **26**(3), 477–486 (2009)

4. Polak, P., Jurczyk-Bunkowska, M.: A framework for defining user requirement for e-government systems. In: Proceedings of the 18th European Conference on e-Government (ECEG), Santiago, Spain (2018)

5. Audytra, H., Hendradjaya, B., Sunindyo, W.D.: A proposal for quality assessment model for software requirements specification in Indonesian language for e-government. In Proceedings of the International Conference on Data and Software Engineering (ICoDSE) (2016)

6. Europäische Kommission: EU-eGovernment-Aktionsplan 2016–2020. Beschleunigung der Digitalisierung der öffentlichen Verwaltung. https://eur-lex.europa.eu/legal-content/DE/TXT/?uri=CELEX%3A52016DC0179. Accessed 18 Mar 2021

7. Öktem, M.K., Demirhan K., Demirhan H.: The usage of e-governance applications by higher education students. Educ. Sci. Theory Pract. **14**(5), 1925–1943 (2014)

8. Shrivastava, D.R.K., Raizada, D.A.K., Saxena, M.N.: Role of e-governance to strengthen higher education system in India. IOSR J. Res. Method Educ. (IOSRJRME) **4**(2), 57–62 (2014)

9. von der Heyde, M., Auth, G., Hartmann, A., Erfurth, C.: Hochschulentwicklung im Kontext der Digitalisierung - Bestandsaufnahme, Perspektiven, Thesen. In: Eibl, M., Gaedke, M. (eds.) Informatik Gesellschaft für Informatik (GI), pp. 1757–1772. International Federation for Information Processing, Bonn (2017)

10. Bayerisches E-Government-Gesetz (BayEGovG) (2016)

11. E-Government-Gesetz Nordrhein-Westfalen (EGovG NRW) (2020)

12. Fang, Z.: E-government in digital era: concept, practice, and development. Int. J. Comput. Internet Manag. **10**(2), 1–22 (2002)

13. Kim, C.-K.: A cross-national analysis of global e-government. Publ. Org. Rev. **7**(4), 317–329 (2007)

14. Altvater, P., Hamschmidt, M., Sehl, I.: Prozessorientierte Hochschule: Neue Perspektiven für die Organisationsentwicklung. Wissenschaftsmanagement, April 2010

15. Nickel, S.: Engere Kopplung von Wissenschaft und Verwaltung und ihre Folgen für die Ausübung professioneller Rollen in Hochschulen. In: Wilkesmann, U., Schmid, C.J. (eds.) Hochschule als Organisation, Wiesbaden, Germany, pp. 279–292 (2012)

16. Pongratz, J.C.A.: IT-Architektur für die Digitale Hochschule. TUM, Munich (2017)

17. Becker, J.: Was Ist Geschäftsprozessmanagement und Was Bedeutet Prozessorientierte Hochschule. Prozessorientierte Verwaltungsmodernisierung an Hochschulen, in Prozessorientierte Hochschule. Allgemeine Aspekte und Praxisbeispiele, pp. 8–22. BOCK + Herchen Verlag, Bielefeld, Germany (2011)

18. Scheer, A.-W., Kruppke, H., Heib, R.: E-Government Prozessoptimierung in der Öffentlichen Verwaltung. Springer, Heidelberg (2003). https://doi.org/10.1007/978-3-642-55456-8

19. TUM Facts & Figures. https://www.tum.de/en/about-tum/our-university/facts-and-figures/. Accessed 10 Mar 2021

20. Huppertz, C., Gottlieb, M., Pongratz, J.C.A.: Analysis of a digital business processes transformation: a case study on digitizing absence management. In: Proceedings der Community Tracks zur WI, Potsdam, Germany (2020)

21. Brocke, J., Simons, A., Niehaves, B., Riemer, K., Plattfaut, R., Cleven, A.: Reconstructing the giant: on the importance of rigour in documenting the literature search process. In: 17th European Conference On Information Systems, Verona, Italy (2009)

22. Webster, J., Watson R.T.: Analyzing the past to prepare for the future: writing a literature review. MIS Q. **26**(2), xiii–xxiii (2002)
23. Janssen, M., Van Der Voort, H.: Adaptive governance: towards a stable, accountable and responsive government. Gov. Inf. Q. **33**(1), 1–5 (2016)
24. Magnusson, J., Koutsikouri, D., Päivärinta, T.: Efficiency creep and shadow innovation: enacting ambidextrous IT governance in the public sector. Eur. J. Inf. Syst. **29**(3), 1–21 (2020)
25. Busch, P.A.: Conceptualizing digital discretion acceptance in public service provision: a policy maker perspective. In: 22nd Pacific Asia Conference on Information Systems (PACIS), Yokohama, Japan (2018)
26. Choi, T., Chandler, S.M.: Knowledge vacuum: an organizational learning dynamic of how e-government innovations fail. Gov. Inf. Q. **37**(1), 101416 (2020)
27. Goh, J.M., Arenas, A.E.: IT value creation in public sector: how IT-enabled capabilities mitigate tradeoffs in public organisations. Eur. J. Inf. Syst. **29**(1), 25–43 (2020)
28. Baird, A., Davidson, E., Mathiassen, L.: Reflective technology assimilation: facilitating electronic health record assimilation in small physician practices. J. Manag. Inf. Syst. **34**(3), 664–694 (2017)
29. Scholta, H., Mertens, W., Kowalkiewicz, M., Becker, J.: From one-stop shop to no-stop shop: an e-government stage model. Gov. Inf. Q. **36**(1), 11–26 (2019)
30. Li, Z., Liao, Q.: Economic solutions to improve cybersecurity of governments and smart cities via vulnerability markets. Gov. Inf. Q. **35**(1), 151–160 (2018)
31. Ranerup, A., Henriksen, H.Z.: Value positions viewed through the lens of automated decision-making: the case of social services. Gov. Inf. Q. **36**(4), 101377 (2019)
32. Berger, J.B., Hertzum, M., Schreiber, T.: Does local government staff perceive digital communication with citizens as improved service? Gov. Inf. Q. **33**(2), 258–269 (2016)
33. Sivarajah, U., Irani, Z., Weerakkody, V.: Evaluating the use and impact of web 2.0 technologies in local government. Gov. Inf. Q. **32**(4), 473–487 (2015)
34. Weerakkody, V., El-Haddadeh, R., Sivarajah, U., Omar, A., Molnar, A.: A case analysis of e-government service delivery through a service chain dimension. Int. J. Inf. Manag. **47**, 233–238 (2019)
35. Gil-Garcia, J.R., Sayogo, D.S.: Government inter-organizational information sharing initiatives: understanding the main determinants of success. Gov. Inf. Q. **33**(3), 572–582 (2016)
36. Gil-Garcia, J.R., Guler, A., Pardo, T.A., Burke, G.B.: Characterizing the importance of clarity of roles and responsibilities in government inter-organizational collaboration and information sharing initiatives. Gov. Inf. Q. **36**(4), 101393 (2019)
37. Rose, J., Flak, L.S., Sæbø, Ø.: Stakeholder theory for the e-government context: framing a value-oriented normative core. Gov. Inf. Q. **35**(3), 362–374 (2018)
38. Lindgren, I., Madsen, C.Ø., Hofmann, S., Melin, U.: Close encounters of the digital kind: a research agenda for the digitalization of public services. Gov. Inf. Q. **36**(3), 427–436 (2019)
39. Tummers, L., Rocco, P.: Serving clients when the server crashes: how frontline workers cope with e-government challenges. Publ. Adm. Rev. **75**(6), 817–827 (2015)
40. Schmid, U., Goertz, L., Radomski, S., Thom, S., Behrens, J.: Monitor digitale Bildung. Die Hochschulen im digitalen Zeitalter. Bertelsmann Stiftung (2017)
41. TUM Extended Board of Management. https://www.tum.de/en/about-tum/our-university/extended-board-of-management/. Accessed 18 Mar 2021
42. TUM Board of Management. https://www.tum.de/en/about-tum/our-university/tum-board-of-management/. Accessed 18 Mar 2021
43. Ehrhardt, A., Esche, T.: Agile Konzepte als Komplexitätslöser für die Hochschulen? Wissenschaftsmanagement **5/6** (2017)

44. HRK-Mitgliederversammlung: Micro-Degrees und Badges als Formate digitaler Zusatzqual-
    ifikation. https://www.hrk.de/positionen/beschluss/detail/micro-degrees-und-badges-als-for
    mate-digitaler-zusatzqualifikation/. Accessed 18 Mar 2021

45. Baecker, D.: Agilität in der Hochschule. Die Hochschule: Journal für Wissenschaft und
    Bildung. **26**(1), 19–28 (2017)

46. The Bologna Process. https://www.bmbf.de/en/the-bologna-process-1421.html. Accessed 18
    Mar 2021

47. Bayerisches Hochschulgesetz (BayHSchG) (2006)

48. Auth, G.: Digitalisierungstreiber Onlinezugangsgesetz - auch für Hochschulen relevant?
    (2019)

49. Tobin, A., Smith., J.: Self-sovereign identity for higher education. https://www.evernym.com/
    blog/self-sovereign-identity-higher-education/. Accessed 18 Mar 2021

50. Barton, T., Mueller, C., Seel, C.: Hochschulen in Zeiten der Digitalisierung: Lehre, Forschung
    und Organisation. Springer, Wiesbaden (2019). https://doi.org/10.1007/978-3-658-26618-9

51. Bannister, F.: The curse of the benchmark: an assessment of the validity and value of e-
    government comparisons. Int. Rev. Adm. Sci. **73**(2), 171–188 (2007)

Digital Government

Developing Cross-border E-Governance: Exploring Interoperability and Cross-border Integration

Robert Krimmer[1,2] ⓘ, Stefan Dedovic[2] ⓘ, Carsten Schmidt[1,2(✉)] ⓘ,
and Andreea-Ancuta Corici[3] ⓘ

[1] Johan Skytte Institute for Political Studies, Center for IT Impact Studies, University of Tartu,
Lossi 36, 51003 Tartu, Estonia
{robert.krimmer,carsten.schmidt}@ut.ee

[2] Ragnar Nurkse Department of Innovation and Governance, Tallinn University of Technology
(TalTech), Akadeemia tee 3, 12618 Tallinn, Estonia
{robert.krimmer,stefan.dedovic,carsten.schmidt}@taltech.ee

[3] Fraunhofer FOKUS, Berlin, Germany
andreea.ancuta.corici@fokus.fraunhofer.de

Abstract. The recent policy and regulatory initiatives of the EU, such as Digital Single Market Strategy, Single Digital Gateway, European Interoperability Framework and eIDAS, identify the need for digital cross-border integration in the EU. The achievement of the digital single market within the EU is challenging governments at all levels to transform or update their governance systems in order to establish the cross-border e-governance. The existing stage models in the e-Government literature, do not address the cross-border integration in the evolution phase of the e-Government. The heterogeneity and the legacy systems of the cross-border data exchange infrastructures hinders the process of seamless cross-border data exchange. This heterogeneity of cross-border data exchange infrastructures and complexity of the cross-border integration in the EU requires high level of interoperability in the legal, organisational, technical and semantic environment. Therefore, we explore the cross-border data infrastructures and its state of play in the EU by following the predominant framework that ensures the interoperability of the digital public services, EIF. We found that the most successful approach for cross-border e-governance and the cross-border integration might be the federated approach.

Keywords: Cross-border integration · Data-exchange solutions · EIF · Single Digital Gateway · eIDAS · OOP

1 Introduction

One of the main initiatives of the EU in the field of digital transformation is the achievement of the Digital Single Market. In the Digital Single Market, individuals and businesses are able to seamlessly exercise and access online activities across borders without

N. Edelmann et al. (Eds.): ePart 2021, LNCS 12849, pp. 107–124, 2021.
https://doi.org/10.1007/978-3-030-82824-0_9

any discrimination and under a high level of personal data protection. The Digital Single Market was already part of the strategy of the European Commission 2014–2019 and the work is continued as part of the EC priorities for 2019–2024. One of these priorities is to make Europe fit for the digital age and one of the pillars of the Digital Single Market strategy is to create a better access for consumers and businesses to digital goods and services across Europe. e-Government, smart government and smart governance, as corner stones of the activities in Europe can provide a wide variety of benefits including more efficiency and savings for governments and businesses, increased transparency, and greater participation of citizens, e.g. in political life and cross border services. Therefore, we have analysed "what are the different approaches for cross-border e-governance and the cross-border integration in the wider arear of e-Government?" We have recognised that an overview in this field is missing. The goal of this paper is to report and summarize the state of play and highlight weaknesses and good practices along the line of the European Interoperability Framework (EIF).

1.1 Methodological Approach

In order to identify drivers, barriers and opportunities for cross-border e-Government we made a literature review, analysed several e-Government initiatives and examined the related legal- and organisational framework.

In e-Government literature, so called stage or maturity models have played an important role to describe current ongoing and planned or expected future development in the digital transformation of public administration. Stage models take either an evaluatory, normative, or positive approach, which were identified in the seminal study by Meyerhoff Nielsen [1] where he reviewed 42 different stage models. In this study, one of the identified foci is dedicated to integration and transformation dimension. Here the most widely cited paper by Layne and Lee stands out, which is identifying a vertical and horizontal integration within a given context [2]. Andersen and Henriksen included Layne and Lee model and additionally identified full transformation by emphasising the user-centricity [3]. However, none of the identified models, look at the cross-border integration, however the recent developments by the European Commission and the Member States clearly identified this policy goal.

Consequently, we are exploring the topic of cross-border data exchange infrastructure and its state of the play in the EU. First, we conduct a preliminary literature analysis on the drivers, barriers and benefits to cross-border data exchange. Second, we follow the predominant framework that ensures the interoperability with other digital public services, the EIF and its layers: 1) Legal, 2) Organisational and 3) Technical and Semantic Interoperability. The EIF is developed by the EC to give specific guidance on how to set up interoperable digital public service and to improve the quality of European public services [5]. The EIF criteria and a mapping against them, allows us to explore the topic comprehensively. Last, we compare existing approaches to cross-border data exchange and provide a first evaluation for this break-through development finally enabling the Digital Single Market (DSM). At the end we provide an overview of the findings and recommendations based on the descriptions, analysis and evaluation in the respective parts of this paper.

2 Background

Achieving the Once-only principle (OOP) is one of the priorities of the EU. Understanding of the OOP varies, in some countries it means store data only once and link to this single source, while in others, it means that citizens and business need to provide personal data only once, thus copies can exist [4].

In this section we describe the relevant policy initiatives and legislation's background addressing the interoperability policy and cross-border data exchange on the EU level. Since interoperability is a necessary condition for reliable and trustworthy cross-border access to procedures and cross-border data exchange, this section is inspired by the European Interoperability Framework interoperability model; more specifically, it includes interoperability governance and integrated public service governance layers.

2.1 Interoperability Governance

As defined in the EIF, interoperability governance, among other things, can be understood as all decisions on interoperability, policies and institutional agreements that enable interoperability at the national and EU level [5]. In this subsection we describe the policies and initiatives on the EU level in ensuring the digital government transformation.

European Commission (EC) adopted the Digital Single Market Strategy communication (2015) to harmonise the initiatives and incentivise the development of digital transformation in the EU. A Digital Single Market can be understood as an ecosystem in which the citizens and businesses can assess the online services under fair competition conditions and personal data protection, irrespective of their nationality or place of residence. One of the barriers that are hindering the development of the Digital Single Market is the lack of open and interoperable systems and services, and the lack of common data portability infrastructures [6]. To overcome these barriers for cross-border data exchange, suggested solution is to reuse the existing building blocks of the Connecting Europe Facility programme, with further integrating the existing platforms, portals, networks and systems into the one Single Digital Gateway [6].

The EU has adopted the e-Government Action plan 2016–2020 to set up conditions and define actions to achieve the Digital Single Market's strategic objectives, such as modernising public administrations, achieving cross-border interoperability and enabling easy interactions with the citizens. Main objective of this plan is to enable citizens and businesses to fully benefit from the interoperable digital public services and enable access to cross-border digital public services. To achieve these objectives public administrations should enable the access to digital public services for cross-border users and to prevent further fragmentation in the digital environment [7].

The latest policy initiative by the EU is the Digital Europe Programme (DEP) for 2021–2026. The DEP aims to reinforce the impact of the Digital Single Market's policy achievements. The DEP's primary objective is to create investment opportunities within the EU, national, regional and local level in the critical technological industries [8]. This investment programme is the key programme in the next following years to achieve seamless cross-border public services and citizen-centric public service in the EU. To achieve these objectives EC agreed on three key actions; first is the creation of the digital transformation platform, second the rollout of the OOP, and third the implementation of the interoperability incubator. The EC committed to support the full integration of the CEF Telecom building blocks, ISA^2 actions and the European Data portal into one ecosystem Digital Transformation Portal [8]. This will provide the basis especially for the implementation of the OOP in the cross-border settings under the Single Digital Gateway. Proposed actions in the DEP could further enable interoperability among the public administrations at all administration levels and achieve seamless cross-border digital public services.

To achieve the Digital Single Market, ministers of the EU Member States signed the Tallinn Declaration on e-Government, adopted in 2017. In this declaration, ministers of the EU Member States agreed on the shared vision and actions to enable and provide borderless and interoperable digital public services to all citizens and business [9]. Among the common principles for digital public services, Tallin Declaration also addressed specific actions that the Member States will work on to achieve the objectives. In particular, they agreed to collaborate to implement the OOP for the key public services and also to adhere to EIF for the cross-border digital public services to achieve the principle of interoperability-by-default [9].

Recognizing the importance of the united support and political commitment towards the digital transformation of the public services and the importance of the goals addressed in the Tallinn Declaration, ministers of the Member States agreed to continue and further support the development of the digital public services ecosystem in the EU. The Berlin Declaration [10] has been adopted with the objective to achieve value-based digital transformation by supporting and strengthening digital participation and inclusion in the EU. They agreed to continue coordination to achieve cross-border interoperability and also to strengthen the EIF. In particular, one of the priorities is to strengthen Europe's digital sovereignty and interoperability. To achieve this priority, Member States will collaborate to reduce the administrative burdens on European citizens and businesses and promote the cross-border implementation of the OOP by supporting interoperability by design policies and solutions [10].

2.2 Integrated Public Service Governance at the EU Level

In this subsection we describe relevant policies and initiatives that ensure integrated public service governance at the EU level. Digital public services in the EU are achieved by many interconnections and collaboration of multiple organisations to provide digital public services, which requires coordination and governance on the EU level. Thus, in the cross-border data exchange, the EU programmes that enable the coordination and governance of the EU, digital public services are described.

EC created "Interoperability solutions for public administrations, businesses and citizens – ISA^2" and the "Connecting Europe Facility – CEF" funding programmes to support and enable the governance of the interoperable cross-border digital public services. These programmes aim to facilitate and enable the cross-border digital public services between the public administrations at the cross-border, national, regional and local level [11, p. 5].

The ISA^2 programme was running from 2016 until 2020, aiming to support the development of cross-border digital interoperable solutions. The interim evaluation of the ISA^2 shows that in the absence of ISA^2, the overall objectives for cross-border inter-operable public services would not be achieved by only national or subnational interventions [12]. Also, the ISA^2 has contributed to improving the cross-border interoperability in the EU, by raising awareness on the topic of interoperability and by facilitating the exchanges between Member States [12].

Similarly, the CEF is a funding programme that supports the development of the infrastructure and technical solutions for digital public services, facilitating cross-border interactions between public administrations, citizens and businesses [13]. CEF supports cross-border interactions by deploying key building blocks, Digital Service Infrastructures (DSIs), to create an interoperable European digital ecosystem for public administrations [14]. The value of these building blocks is the reusability and extensibility. They can also be integrated into other IT projects and combined with each other [14]. Building blocks that CEF has been developed, inter alia, are eID, eSignature, eInvoicing, eDelivery, Automated Translation and EBSI.

Alongside the EC funding programmes, EC has also addressed the interoperability of public services in the EU level by adopting the revised EIF in 2017. The EIF provides guidance and recommendations to public administrations on developing and achieving interoperable digital public services. In the EIF, interoperability is defined as "the ability of organisations to interact towards mutually beneficial goals, involving the sharing of information and knowledge between these organisations, through the business processes they support, by means of the exchange of data between their ICT systems" [5, pp. 4–5]. The purpose of this framework is to inspire public administrations to develop and deliver interoperable digital public services to other public administrations, business and citizens; to provide guidance to public administrations on how to design their own national interoperability framework; and lastly but not least, to contribute to the establishment of the Digital Single Market by creating and supporting cross-border interoperable European public services [5]. Three main elements of the EIF, are the core interoperability principles, interoperability layers (Legal, Organisational, Semantic and Technical) and integrated public services model. Legal interoperability layer as described in the EIF, ensures that the public administrations are able to interconnect and work together under different legal frameworks, policies and strategies [5]. Organisational interoperability is described as "documenting and integrating or aligning business processes, and relevant information exchanged" [5, p. 24]. Semantic interoperability is more focused on the data and therefore "ensures that the precise format and meaning of exchanged data and information is preserved and understood throughout exchanges between parties" [5], p. 25]. Technical interoperability ensures the communication between different technical infrastructures linking systems and services [5].

One of the recommendations, inter alia, within the EIF is addressing the functioning of the Digital Single Market and the data exchange systems, in which is recommended that the designers of public services should address the data portability infrastructures in order to avoid lock-in and to support the free movement of data [5].

As previously mentioned, the structure of this article is inspired by the EIF interoperability layers, in order to present the state of play of the cross-border data exchange systems in the EU.

3 Drivers and Barriers to Cross-border Data Exchange

This section describes the drivers, barriers and benefits to cross-border exchange.

The reason why the OOP is accepted as a priority in the EU policies on digital government transformation lies in the promise that it will reduce the burden on citizens, businesses, and public administrations when it comes to provision and collection of data [15–18]. Mainly, several authors are agreeing on that implementing OOP will bring various benefits for public administrations, business and citizens [4, 15, 18–20]. The benefits for public administration can be time savings, costs savings, higher administrative gains, increased efficiency and effectiveness, proactive public services, and the creation of better public services [15, 21]. Also, the OOP might lead to the process optimisation and no duplication of tasks [21]. Similarly, implementation of OOP in the government brings positive outcomes also to the citizens and business, mainly in time savings, reduced administrative burden, less cumbersome and more convenient procedures, increased transparency of the use of resources by the state [18, p. 3]. Finally, it is estimated that the implementation of the OOP in cross-border settings can increase cost savings up to 5 million euros [17]. However, although OOP brings various benefits to stakeholders in the public services creation, it is still poorly understood, as Krimmer *et al.* [19] state, most likely due to the novelty of the concept and lack of cross border OOP initiatives (p. 7).

The drivers for the implementation of OOP are mostly generated by the external triggers, such as in the demand of the citizens and business for reduced administrative burden, in the legal obligation (e.g. SDGR), or in improved service quality and better governance [16, 19, 22]. Moreover, Krimmer *et al.* [19] note that the participation in cross-organisational and cross-border knowledge transfer with strong leadership by the managers can be seen as a driver at the organisational level for the implementation of the OOP. Also, it is found that the maturity of the technical infrastructure and the existence of the OOP in the country can be seen as a driver for the implementation at the cross-border level [16]. This shows that the difference in the maturity levels of the e-Government and heterogeneity of data exchange infrastructures within the Member States might have hindering effects on the adoption of the Single Digital Gateway.

Besides these drivers, there are several factors hindering the process of OOP implementation on cross-border level. Mainly, research has shown that the Member States are mostly concerned about the privacy and data protection issues, the legality of the data sharing across-borders, procedural differences, lack of political and managerial support and lack of financial support [19, pp. 4–5]. Furthermore, the existing governmental silos and lack of organisational interoperability, hinders the process of the OOP implementation in the cross-border setting [19, p. 3].

Technological heterogeneity and maturity of the e-Government systems are perceived by many authors and Member States as the main barrier for the cross-border implementation of the OOP [16–19, 21]. Moreover, Mamrot and Rzyszczak [23] state that the fragmentation of the data exchange infrastructures in the Member States has a negative impact on extending EU-wide OOP. Similarly, Cave *et al.* [17] stated that the local solutions that are implemented in national borders are not designed for the cross-border data exchange while at the same time they so embedded, and the changes will be resisted. This has been proven by the research of Krimmer *et al.* [19], in which is found that the Member States are not willing to undertake major changes to their legacy systems for cross-border reasons. The lack of technical interoperability can be seen in, inter alia, in the heterogeneity of the data exchange infrastructure systems, different approaches to handling data, access to distributed data sources. More specifically, due to the heterogeneity of the data-exchange infrastructures in the EU, it is difficult to achieve cross-border interconnection between local databases, and the solution needs to ensure a high degree of compatibility with the existing technological systems [21]. In addition, one of the major challenges in the implementation of the OOP at the cross-border level is the mutual trust between the public administration on the cross-border level [24]. Similarly, citizens in the DACH region are also concerned about the seamless data exchange across borders, where two-thirds of respondents are having a negative impression of the cross-border OOP implementation [25].

4 Legal Interoperability

Following the overarching political initiatives in the field of e-Government and also the funding programmes and frameworks in the field of interoperability, in this section, the main focus will be on the legal interoperability and the regulations adopted by the EU that addresses the cross-border data exchange ecosystem. The following regulations enable mainly the legal and technical interoperability among the Member States by requiring them to collaborate and enable interoperability at all levels.

One of the milestones for achieving interoperable cross-border digital public services is the adoption of the eIDAS Regulation in 2014 [26]. In cross-border data exchange systems, one of the key building blocks is electronic identification and authentication. One of the main objectives of the eIDAS is to improve trust among the stakeholders and remove barriers in the cross-border use of national electronic identification by providing a framework for interoperable recognition of the national identifications in cross-border settings [26]. eIDAS also sets up the framework for electronic registered delivery service (ERDS), which is essentially the data exchange IT system that enables the transfer of data and provides proof of evidence that data is transmitted [26]. Recognition of the legal validity for the data sent through ERDS is also provided in eIDAS. However, there is no implementing act for ERDS adopted yet, which means that standards for ERDS are still unclear [27]. The recognition of eID and electronic delivery services are one of the reasons why the eIDAS Regulation is of huge importance for successful cross-border data exchange among public administrations in the EU.

Following the achievements of eIDAS regulation, the EU has adopted the resolution on Single Digital Gateway in 2018 [28]. The SDG regulation aims to create one single gateway in which the citizens and business would be able to get information, give feedback and to access online public procedures. The Single Digital Gateway will be implemented into the EU portal Your Europe which will act as a single access point to existing national portals [25]. The SDG regulation requires all Member States to enable access to 21 digital public procedures[1] also for the cross-border users. One of the important goals of SDG regulation, inter alia, is to enable the access to these online procedures by implementing the OOP through safe and secure technical system [28].

5 Organisational Interoperability

The main focus in this section is on organisational interoperability through which will be explained the data exchange ecosystem in the EU.

As already explained, the lack of organisational interoperability and the heterogeneity of the data-exchange infrastructure are considered a major barrier to the development of the Single Digital Gateway. In this section we explore the national solutions that Member States are using for the data exchange purposes. The focus in this section is on the Member States that mostly participated in the large-scale projects in the EU such as STORK[2], TOOP[3], DE4A[4].

One of the pioneers in the digital transformation in government is Estonia, also considered as the leading country in the digitalisation of public services. This high development in digital transformation can be prescribed to their data exchange system X-Road. This secure exchange internet-based communication protocol is considered as a backbone of the OOP in Estonia because it enables the connection between multiple databases and enables data sharing among them [23]. During the phase of the creation of the system, the aim of this data-exchange system was not to replicate existing data in database systems but rather to re-use and connect different database systems to communicate and to enable the secure sharing of data [22]. The main characteristics of the X-Road, inter alia, are that it is open-source, autonomous, confidential, interoperable and secure [20]. Next to the X-Road system, it is important mentioning that Estonia has a mature and high degree of uses of its eID solution, which enables the implementation of the OOP. Also, other countries are using the X-Road solution, such as Finland, which uses the X-Road solution for their data-exchange purposes. Consequently, Estonia and Finland are also the pioneers in the cross-border implementation of OOP. With the bilateral agreement and connection of the Finland databases in the central server of X-Road, data stored in databases in both countries are shared by utilising the X-Road system [25]. It is very important to mention that X-Road is centrally governed and that it is used by all public administrations for all kinds of data exchanges, while it also allows uses by private parties [29].

The Netherlands, however, is using multiple data exchange systems to enable the implementation of the OOP. This is the reason because the institutional structure requires a demarcation between private and public infrastructures [29, p. 41]. These systems are Digikoppeling, Digilevering, Digimelding, and Stelselcatalogus, and they are employed

---

[1] These procedures are related to seven life events: "Birth"; "Residence"; "Working"; "Studying"; "Moving"; "Retiring"; "Starting, running and closing the business".

[2] Secure Identity Across Borders Linked (STORK); https://ec.europa.eu/digital-single-market/en/content/stork-take-your-e-identity-you-everywhere-eu.

[3] The Once-Only Principle Project (TOOP); https://www.toop.eu/.

[4] Digital Europe for All (DE4A); https://www.de4a.eu/.

in order to enable seamless data exchange between public administrations. The Netherlands also has a system of agreements for data exchange systems, Diginetwerk, which includes multiple networks and databases by employing the above-mentioned systems.

In Austria, the implementation of the OOP is enabled by its data exchange system Register and System Network (RSV) [24]. This data exchange system interconnects 130 databases of the various public administrations, and it acts as an interconnector between the databases and front-end solutions [24]. RSV is considered a prerequisite for OOP implementation by the Austrian authorities because it facilitates the exchange of data in a transparent and secure environment [24].

Slovenia, instead, similarly to the Netherlands, use different systems to implement OOP. Three main building blocks for data-exchange are Tray, IO module and Asynchronous Module. These building blocks were developed primarily for the e-social security data exchange, but it is also used for other purposes [30]. Slovenia has developed a central system for electronic delivery, SI-CeV, which enables the secure exchange of documents between public administrations, citizens and businesses [31]. This system can also be used for cross-border connection and implementation of the cross-border OOP [31].

Belgium, as a federal state, uses different exchange systems at the federal and state level. For instance, the Flemish government uses the MAGDA (Maximum Data Sharing between Administration and Agencies) platform to enable data exchange between 190 agencies and 13 departments of the Flemish government and 308 local governments [21]. On the federal level, Belgium utilises Federal Service Bus to enable data exchange between different public administrations and multiple ministries [24]. Federal Service Bus is also used for cross-border purposes and acts as a cross-border connector that allows access to the national registries while taking into consideration security and data protection principles [24].

Finally, these different national solutions for data exchange purposes shows that the development of the solutions was undertaken mostly for national purposes. Further to the technical differences, the additional divergence among these solutions is also based on the governance and control of these solutions. For instance, some countries have centralised data exchange solutions (such as Estonia and Slovenia), while in some countries, there are multiple solutions for the data exchange (such as the Netherlands).

6 Semantic and Technical Interoperability

In this section, we describe the semantic and technical specifications of the cross-border data exchange infrastructure by using the TOOP architecture as an example.

Regarding Data Quality and more specifically the data accuracy, the semantic modules play an important role in the data exchange. The semantic interoperability view specifies only one process, the semantic mediation and the TOOP project attempted/proposed a loosely coupled semantic architecture, as the monolithic approach is hindering the once-only principle.

The semantic mediation service is necessary on the Data Consumer (DC) side for evidence identification, as well as evidence interpretation and on the Data Provider (DP) for evidence extraction.

As founding aspects of the semantic view, the ontology handling components can be defined as:

- an OOP Semantic Model that describes entities relevant when the Once-Only Principle is applied and are generic. This comprises the reused ISA^2 core vocabularies concepts, e.g. Natural Person.
- a methodology for modelling Domain Semantic Models based on the methodology proposed by ISA^2 "e-Government Core Vocabularies handbook".

For this, the domain specific information has to undergo several stages of modelling having transformed into a computable semantic model and representational format (RDF, OWL).

For the generic concepts, the DG GROW eCERTIS component is available for multiple Member States and languages.

A special case comes from the eHealth domain. One of the communication standards, HL7, has been upgraded in the last years with a data model that allows REST operations and semantic interoperability of patient health record by introducing the HL7 Fast Healthcare Interoperable Resources (FHIR) framework. The initiatives and projects where it is employed range from International Patient Summary (IPS), clinical studies data storage and processing to bioresearch apps [32].

Regarding the semantics of the exchanged data, a set of Service-oriented Architecture (SOA) based Common Terminology Services were defined by the HL7 standardization organization [33]. Thus, services like retrieving the appropriate value from the ConceptMap for encoding purposes, validation of used value and display in different languages is possible. The maturity of the FHIR standard has invited the EU eHealth Digital Service Infrastructure (eHDSI or eHealth DSI) to use it when defining the semantic service specification.

In the TOOP project, the extended set of Core Vocabularies are implemented in the semantic data models of the central components like the Data Services Directory (DSD), the Criterion & Evidence Type Rule Base (CERB) (making use of the DG GROW eCERTIS) and the TOOP Exchange Data Model (EDM), with the goal to achieve horizontal, cross-service and cross-actor semantic interoperability. Regarding technical interoperability, both authentication and data exchange levels have evolved in the recent years. The eIDAS network can be employed for user identification.

At the base of the technical interoperability for data exchange lays the CEF eDelivery solution based on a distributed model called the "4-corner model". In this model, the back-end systems of the users don't exchange data directly with each other but do this through Access Points. The data or documents pass through four layers - the backend of the sender (C1), the senders' Access Point (C2), the receiver Access Point (C3) and the backend of the receiver (C4). The communication between these layers is enabled by the AS4 messaging protocol. These Access Points are the nodes that enable the technical interoperability between the heterogeneous IT systems in the EU (Fig. 1).

The Service Metadata Publishing (SMP) standard can be used for discovery of communication endpoint (DP or DC) and of the access point for evidence exchange. The list of qualified trust service providers and the provided services are administered by the Member States on trust list servers. Thus, a discoverable service has to perform a

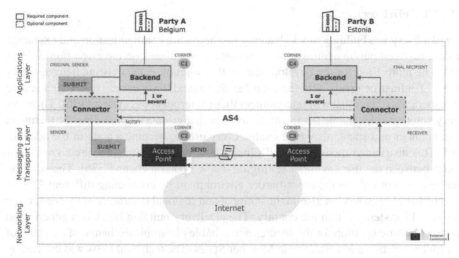

Fig. 1. eDelivery 4-corner model [34].

SMP endpoint registration to the Service Metadata Locator (SML) server. As a remark, OASIS renamed the SML component to Business Document Metadata Service Location (BDXL).

The mGov4EU project is focusing its activity on online services that citizens need to access from a mobile device in a cross-border context due to moving to another Member State or having multiple citizenships (thus having multiple eIDs and residencies).

Single Digital Gateway Regulation (SDGR) (EU) 2018/1724 of the European Parliament and of the Council, introducing a single digital gateway aiming at specifying the requirements for evidence exchange for online services in the light of the European Single Digital Market and Services. The "4-corner model" eDelivery can be only regarded as a starting point for the specification and implementation for this regulation, as key components related to the interplay of the eID and the required user explicit request together with the eDelivery concepts and components are still to be designed and validated. Taking into account the implementing act of the SDGR including the refined guidelines, available in a draft format and to be published end of June 2021, well established technologies like Security Assertion Markup Language (SAML), together with the eIDAS Technical Specifications and the OAuth2.0 constitute the anchor points for the design inside the mGov4EU project.

7 Cross-border Solutions

Currently, there are several solutions offering options for data exchange on the cross-border level. These solutions are mostly initiated by the European Commission as the leading organisation in enabling cross border interoperability.

7.1 CEF eDelivery

The eDelivery is a building block that enables the secure communication and exchange of data between public administration, business and citizens on the cross-border level [35]. The motivation for the development of this solution is the existing heterogeneity of the IT infrastructures within the Member States and the necessity to create a secure interoperability layer that will interconnect these heterogeneous systems [36]. The eDelivery solution helps public administrations to exchange data by providing the technical specifications and standards which enable every user to become a node in the network [36]. This distributed model of the eDelivery building block enables direct communication between the users without setting up a new bilateral channel [36]. The solution can be used not only in the cross-border environment by connecting different IT systems of Member States but also in the national and regional environment by connecting different IT systems within the country. The eDelivery building block is a generic and content agnostic solution for the secures and reliable electronic exchange of any kind of information within and between the Member States. The technical basis was created by different large scale EU projects, mainly the e-SENS[5] project. The results are taken up by the CEF as part of the long-term sustainability strategy for eDelivery. The eDelivery solution is technically based on the 4-corner model.

7.2 Business Registers Interconnection System

Another relevant EU initiative that enables cross-border data exchange between the Member States is the Business Registers Interconnection System (BRIS). The BRIS infrastructure provides a cooperation platform for all Business Registers in the EEA countries. It provides to the citizens, business and public administrations a single point of access on the European eJustice portal[6], on which they can search and find the relevant information on companies and their branches [21]. The purpose of the BRIS infrastructure is improved cross-border access to business information and is achieved by enabling communication between business registries. BRIS is using a public network in order to enable access to citizens business and public administrations to find a piece of information. The system is distributed with a central component of storing and indexing the published information [37, 38]. To enable secure and reliable data exchange, BRIS uses the CEF eDelivery solution. Finally, the benefits of BRIS are that it reduces administrative burden, increases consumer confidence, increases legal certainty and efficiency of procedures [21, 38].

7.3 EESSI

The Electronic Exchange of Social Security Information System (EESSI) is the IT platform that enables data exchange by social security institutions across borders. Most exchanges between public administrations related, inter alia, to sickness, occupational disease and accidents at work, pension, unemployment, were paper-based which was

---

[5] Electronic Simplified European Networked Services (e-SENS); www.esens.eu.

[6] www.e-justice.eu.

being replaced by the electronic data exchanges by the rollout of EESSI [39]. The first data exchange related to the social security of EU citizen took place in 2019, and since 2019 all EEA countries are required to connect to the system [39]. To exchange the information, EESSI uses a private network, and it has a routing component that enables the secure and reliable exchange of information [39]. Use of EESSI benefits public administrations but also to citizens by enabling: Faster and more efficient information exchange, more accurate data exchange, safe IT environment for data exchange, secure handling of personal data and verification of social security rights [40].

7.4 EUCARIS

The European Car and Driving Licence Information System (EUCARIS) is a decentralised IT system that connects the Member States, which enables the sharing of information related to vehicle and driving licence and other transport-related data [41]. EUCARIS is an exchange mechanism and not a database nor a central repository, and it is developed in order to reduce car theft and registration fraud within the EU [42]. The value of EUCARIS is that it enables the cross-border data exchange within the transport and mobility sector by enabling a peer-to-peer connection between the Member States. Also, the goal of EUCARIS is to avoid the creation of the new system for data exchange every time when a new agreement, treaty or directive comes into force [43]. By having one exchange information system, it achieves costs and time savings and higher interoperability [43].

7.5 OpenPEPPOL

OpenPEPPOL provides a set PEPPOL-based ICT products and services that enables the cross-border interconnection of eProcurement systems through loosely coupled building blocks. The PEPPOL eDelivery network uses Access Points and gateways to enable the interconnection between multiple parties in the EU. This solution provides technical specification and open-source software for data exchange related to public eProcurement processes by enabling the communication between heterogeneous data exchange infrastructures. Exchange of information, similarly to the eDelivery building block, is enabled through the 4-corner model and access Points acting as interoperable nodes. This enables a many-to-many interoperability environment, and it reduces costs and burden on creating bilateral agreements and the creation of new systems [44].

7.6 TOOP

The OOP solution created by the TOOP project was discussed and analysed in the previous section on technical and semantic interoperability. TOOP architecture proved the feasibility of achieving a OOP in a cross-border setting, and therefore having SDGR as a basis of the creation is the best example to explain the technical and semantic interoperability of federated data-exchange architecture.

7.7 Evaluation

Evaluation Matrix presents the collection of the cross-border solutions and the specifications criteria on the features of the cross-border solutions. The selection of criteria is done on the basis of the public access, Public Network (the general public can access the solution and search for information) or Private Network (only public administrations have access to the solution); the system distribution, Purely Distributed System (the system is purely distributed when it enables peer-to-peer communication without a central platform or routing component) or Central Platform/Routing Component (the system is connected to the routing component and/or central platform); organisation level, Centralised organisation (the solution is maintained and administrated by one authority) or Decentralised organisation (the solution is maintained and administrated by the users). The results of this evaluation matrix can be seen in Table 1.

Table 1. Evaluation matrix

Evaluation matrix	Public access		System distribution		Governance level	
	Public network	Private network	Purely distributed system	Central Platform/routing component	Centralized organisation	Decentralized organisation
BRIS	x			x	x	
EUCARIS		x	x			x
EESSI		x		x	x	
TOOP		x		x	x	
OpenPeppol		x		x		x

This number of existing and ongoing projects in development provide a heterogenous landscape, when looking at the national and European level. At the national level, we can differentiate between two different cross-border service participation types – either as 1) data provider or 2) as data consumer. In the former case, the public authority is providing data for a cross-border use case, while in the latter, the public authority is requesting data and thus consuming it. Usually, such data providers and data consumers are organised in the form of base registries, in particular when public IT systems are organised following the OOP model. In rare cases, such base registries interact with other, foreign, base registries directly. This forms the first type of connection to national data, 1) the direct access. More commonly, the access is provided through some form of mediator, either 2) data aggregators which pool data of a sector, or 3) national/context-dependant data exchange layers.

Next to these organisation and access types on MS-level, the cross-border integration can also take place on a 1) vertical level in a domain-specific way, e.g. within sector specific private networks (EESSI, EUCARIS). Alternatively, and this is what is proposed within the TOOP project, a horizontal, content- and sector-agnostic, integration, in the format of a federation of federations. Within TOOP, this hierarchy has also been put together in a graphical format, see the figure below (Fig. 2).

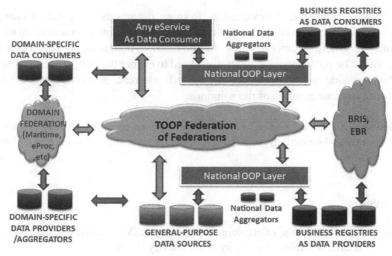

Fig. 2. The TOOP cross-border framework [45]

8 Conclusions

To summarise, the different approaches for cross-border e-governance and the cross-border integration were analysed based on the different layers of the EIF to identify the **drivers**, **barriers** and **opportunities** in the wider context of e-Government. The main **barriers** for the EU-wide cross-border implementation, inter alia, are the heterogeneity of the data exchange infrastructures, existing legacy systems, and lack of willingness to undertake significant technological changes for the sake of enabling it on the cross-border level. Several authors address these barriers by stating that Member States should re-use already developed cross-border solutions such as CEF eDelivery [21, 46]. Furthermore, the lack of interoperability can be solved by following and adopting the solutions created by the CEF, ISA^2, and by designing interoperable public services following recommendations, principles, and interoperability model suggested by the EIF. Legislation is perceived to be the most significant **barrier** and **driver** (once it exists) at the same time for European data integration [16].

Finally, as already mentioned, the Single Digital Gateway regulation must be seen as an **opportunity**; it requires that all Member States offer access to fully online procedures by also cross-border users through the Your Europe portal. Having multiple agreements between the Member States and also bilateral agreements might create many interconnection points and networks, which might further deepen the heterogeneity of IT systems within the EU.

As recommendations, based on the analysis of the projects, the following can be concluded; the possibly best option to overcome this hurdle and to enable cross-border data-exchange could be through a data-exchange connector which will enable the interconnection of different IT infrastructures of public administrations. Therefore, the technically most successful solution for cross-border integration probably would be a federated approach as proposed in the Single Digital Gateway Regulation.

Besides that, related to the evaluation, from an organisational point of view, it is important to establish a governance structure that ensures the involvement of all relevant stakeholders (e.g. EC, Member States, standardisation bodies etc.). This governance structure should be on the one side institutionalised to ensure the long-term sustainability and on the other side provide the necessary flexibility to react as fast as necessary to any kind of needs for amendments of the solutions.

Acknowledgement. The work for this paper has received funding from European Union's Horizon 2020 research and innovation programme under grant agreement Nos. 857622, 737460 and 959072.

References

1. Nielsen, M.M.: The demise of eGovernment maturity models: framework and case studies. Doctoral dissertation, Tallinn University of Technology (2020)
2. Layne, K., Lee, J.: Developing fully functional e-government: a four stage model. Gov. Inf. Q. **18**(2), 122–136 (2001). https://doi.org/10.1016/S0740-624X(01)00066-1
3. Andersen, K.V., Henriksen, H.Z.: E-government maturity models: extension of the Layne and Lee model. Gov. Inf. Q. **23**(2), 236–248 (2006). https://doi.org/10.1016/j.giq.2005.11.008
4. Krimmer, R., Kalvet, T., Toots, M., Cepilovs, A., Tambouris, E.: Exploring and demonstrating the once-only principle. In: 18th Annual International Conference on Digital Government, pp. 546–551 (2017). https://doi.org/10.1145/3085228.3085235
5. European Commission: Final European Interoperability Framework - Implementation Strategy: COM(2017) 134 final (2017)
6. European Commission: A Digital Single Market Strategy for Europe
7. European Commission: EU eGovernment Action Plan 2016–2020: Accelerating the Digital Transformation of Government
8. Digital Europe Programme: Draft Orientations of the Programme 2021–2022
9. Tallinn Declaration on eGovernment: at the Ministerial Meeting During Estonian Presidency of the Council of the EU on 6 October 2017
10. Berlin Declaration: on Digital Society and Value-Based Digital Government at the Ministerial Meeting on 8 December 2020
11. Wimmer, M.A., Boneva, R., Di Giacomo, D.: Interoperability governance: a definition and insights from case studies in Europe. In: Proceedings of the 19th Annual International Conference on Digital Government Research: Governance in the Data Age, May 2018, pp. 1–11 (2018). https://dl.acm.org/doi/10.1145/3209281.3209306
12. Iacob, N., Renda, A., Simonelli, F., Campas, A.: Evaluation study supporting the interim evaluation of the programme on interoperability solutions for European public administrations, businesses and citizens (ISA2): final report (2019)
13. CEF Digital: Connecting Europe Facility - Innovation and Networks Executive Agency - European Commission. https://ec.europa.eu/inea/en/connecting-europe-facility. Accessed 22 Feb 2021
14. CEF Digital: Connecting Europe Facility in Telecom - Shaping Europe's Digital Future - European Commission. https://ec.europa.eu/digital-single-market/en/connecting-europe-facility-telecom. Accessed 22 Feb 2021
15. Halmos, A.: Cross-border digital public services. CESCI, Budapest (2018)
16. Krimmer, R., Kalvet, T., Toots, M.: The once-only principle project drivers and barriers for OOP. In: TOOP (2017). https://www.toop.eu/sites/default/files/D27_Drivers_and_Barriers.pdf

17. Cave, J., Botterman, M., Cavalini, S., Volpe, M.: EU-wide digital once-only principle for citizens and businesses: policy options and their impacts (2017)
18. Wimmer, M.A., Marinov, B.: Scoop4c: reducing administrative burden for citizens through once-only - vision and challenges (2018)
19. Krimmer, R., Kalvet, T., Toots, M.: Contributing to a digital single market for Europe barriers and drivers of an EU-wide once-only principle. In: dg.o 2018: Proceedings of the 19th Annual International Conference on Digital Government Research, 30 May–1 June 2018, pp. 1–8 (2018). https://doi.org/10.1145/3209281.3209344
20. Rashid, N.: Deploying the Once-Only Policy: A Privacy-Enhancing Guide for Policymakers and Civil Society Actors. Harvard Kennedy School (2020)
21. Kalvet, T., Toots, M., Krimmer, R., Cepilovs, A.: Position Paper on Definition of OOP and Situation in Europe (Updated Version) (2017)
22. LOBO Georges (CNECT): 2017 ISA2 Work Programme Detailed Action Descriptions (2020)
23. Mamrot, S., Rzyszczak, K.: Implementation of the 'once-only' principle in Europe. In: Krimmer, R., Prentza, A., Mamrot, S. (eds.) The Once-Only Principle. LNCS, vol. 12621, pp. 9–37. Springer, Cham (2021). https://doi.org/10.1007/978-3-030-79851-2_2
24. Fedko, E.: Ekaterina Fedko once only principle: implementation of the once-only principle in the cross-border context: analysis of good practices. Master thesis, Chair for Information Systems and Information Management, Westfälische Wilhelms-Universität, Münster, Germany (2020)
25. Akkaya, C., Krcmar, H.: Towards the implementation of the EU-wide "once-only principle": perceptions of citizens in the DACH-region. In: Parycek, P., et al. (eds.) EGOV 2018. LNCS, vol. 11020, pp. 155–166. Springer, Cham (2018). https://doi.org/10.1007/978-3-319-98690-6_14
26. P. Office, Regulation (EU) No 910/2014 of the European Parliament and of the Council of 23 July 2014 on Electronic Identification and Trust Services for Electronic Transactions in the Internal Market and Repealing Directive 1999/93/EC: Regulation (EU) No 910/2014 (2014)
27. Stasis, A., Demiri, L.: Secure document exchange in the Greek public sector via eDelivery. In: Katsikas, S.K., Zorkadis, V. (eds.) e-Democracy 2017. CCIS, vol. 792, pp. 213–227. Springer, Cham (2017). https://doi.org/10.1007/978-3-319-71117-1_15
28. P. Office, Single Digital Gateway Regulation (EU) 2018/1724 of the European Parliament and of the Council of 2 October 2018 Establishing a Single Digital Gateway to Provide Access to Information, to Procedures and to Assistance and Problem-Solving Services and Amending Regulation (EU) No 1024/2012: Single Digital Gateway Regulation (2018)
29. Bharosa, N., Lips, S., Draheim, D.: Making e-government work: learning from the Netherlands and Estonia. In: Hofmann, S., et al. (eds.) ePart 2020. LNCS, vol. 12220, pp. 41–53. Springer, Cham (2020). https://doi.org/10.1007/978-3-030-58141-1_4
30. SCOOP4C: Slovenian building blocks for secure and reliable data exchange between institutions _ SCOOP4C. https://scoop4c.eu/cases/slowenian-building-blocks-secure-and-reliable-data-exchange-between-institutions. Accessed 26 Feb 2021
31. NIO: Centralni sistem za e-vročanje SI-CeV—Izdelki—Portal NIO. https://nio.gov.si/nio/asset/centralni+sistem+za+evrocanje+sicev-813?lang=sl. Accessed 26 Feb 2021
32. Leroux, H., Metke-Jimenez, A., Lawley, M.: Towards achieving semantic interoperability of clinical study data with FHIR. J. Biomed. Semant. (2017). https://jbiomedsem.biomedcentral.com/articles/10.1186/s13326-017-0148-7
33. HL7: HL7 Version 3 Standard: Common Terminology Services (2009). http://www.hl7.org/documentcenter/public/standards/dstu/2009may/V3_CTS_R2_DSTU_2009OCT.pdf. Accessed 20 Feb 2021
34. Frade, J.R.: Electronic Registered Delivery Service (ERDS) and the eIDAS Regulation (2016)
35. Joinup: About CEF eDelivery. https://joinup.ec.europa.eu/collection/connecting-europe-facility-cef/solution/cef-edelivery/about. Accessed 18 Feb 2021

36. CEF eDelivery: Introduction to the Connecting Europe Facility eDelivery Building Block (2015)
37. European Commission: Report on the interconnection of national centralised automated mechanisms (central registries or central electronic data retrieval systems) of the member
38. Ajpes: Business Registers Interconnection System. https://www.ajpes.si/Registers/Sloven ian_Business_Register/BRIS. Accessed 22 Feb 2021
39. European Commission: Digitalisation in social security coordination - employment, social affairs & inclusion - European Commission. https://ec.europa.eu/social/main.jsp?catId= 869&langId=en#:~:text=EESSI%20is%20an%20IT%20system,rules%20on%20social%20s ecurity%20coordination. Accessed 22 Feb 2021
40. European Commission: Social security goes digital: quicker and easier exchange of social security information throughout the EU and beyond - employment, social affairs & inclusion - European Commission. https://ec.europa.eu/social/main.jsp?langId=en&catId=869&furthe rNews=yes&newsId=2836. Accessed 1 Mar 2021
41. SCOOP4C: European Car and Driving Licence Information System (EUCARIS). https:// scoop4c.eu/cases/european-car-and-driving-licence-information-system-eucaris. Accessed 1 Mar 2021
42. EUCARIS: European Car and Driving Licence Information System. https://www.eucaris.net/. Accessed 17 Feb 2021
43. EUCARIS Secretariat: EUCARIS Brochure (2020)
44. PEPPOL eDelivery Network - An Overview - Peppol. https://peppol.eu/what-is-peppol/pep pol-transport-infrastructure/. Accessed 1 Mar 2021
45. Tepandi: D2.2 Generic Federated OOP Architecture, 2nd version
46. Wimmer, M.A., Neuroni, A.C., Frecè, J.T.: Approaches to good data governance in support of public sector transformation through once-only. In: Viale Pereira, G., et al. (eds.) EGOV 2020. LNCS, vol. 12219, pp. 210–222. Springer, Cham (2020). https://doi.org/10.1007/978-3-030-57599-1_16

Accountable Federated Machine Learning in Government: Engineering and Management Insights

Dian Balta[1]([✉]), Mahdi Sellami[1], Peter Kuhn[1] [iD], Ulrich Schöpp[1],
Matthias Buchinger[1], Nathalie Baracaldo[2], Ali Anwar[2], Heiko Ludwig[2],
Mathieu Sinn[2], Mark Purcell[2], and Bashar Altakrouri[3]

[1] fortiss GmbH, Munich, Germany
balta@fortiss.org
[2] IBM Research, San Jose, USA
[3] IBM Cloud and Cognitive Software, Armonk, USA

Abstract. Machine learning offers promising capabilities to improve administrative procedures. At the same time, adequate training of models using traditional learning techniques requires the collection and storage of enough training data in a central place. Unfortunately, due to legislative and jurisdictional constraints, data in a central place is scarce and training a model becomes unfeasible. Against this backdrop, federated machine learning, a technique to collaboratively train models without transferring data to a centralized location, has been recently proposed. With each government entity keeping their data private, new applications that previously were impossible now can be a reality. In this paper, we demonstrate that accountability for the federated machine learning process becomes paramount to fully overcoming legislative and jurisdictional constraints. In particular, it ensures that all government entities' data are adequately included in the model and that evidence on fairness and reproducibility is curated towards trustworthiness. We also present an analysis framework suitable for governmental scenarios and illustrate its exemplary application for online citizen participation scenarios. We discuss our findings in terms of engineering and management implications: feasibility evaluation, general architecture, involved actors as well as verifiable claims for trustworthy machine learning.

Keywords: Accountability · Federated learning · Framework · Verifiable claims

1 Introduction

Machine learning (ML)–a concept that incorporates various characteristics of intelligent systems that follow particular goals, have a formal representation of knowledge and an automated logical interference [1]–is expected to represent a huge leap from data analysis to high quality and efficiency predictions, and increases the value of informed judgements [2].

© IFIP International Federation for Information Processing 2021
Published by Springer Nature Switzerland AG 2021
N. Edelmann et al. (Eds.): ePart 2021, LNCS 12849, pp. 125–138, 2021.
https://doi.org/10.1007/978-3-030-82824-0_10

At the same time, ML has to address general issues such as fairness, ethics, robustness and explainability of trained models (cf. e.g. [3, 4]), in order to address legal, economic and political uncertainty. The existing uncertainty regarding machine learning exposes government practice to **engineering and management challenges** (cf. e.g. [5]) and applications have yet to deliver sustainable and reproducible results in the government domain.

Three noteworthy challenges are **accountability** [6], **data sharing** (cf. e.g. [7, 8]) and **privacy preservation** (c.f. e.g. [9]). Accountability represents a relation, where a government is accountable for ML to the users of its ML-based services by providing transparency means as well as mechanisms that allow them to enforce control. For instance, users should be able to resolve responsibilities in case of data and model bias (cf. e.g. [10]), to request changes to existing policies (cf. e.g. [11]) as well as to install third-party audits (cf. e.g. [12]).

The second challenge, data sharing in government, emerges out of technical issues such as interoperability and heterogeneity of data infrastructure, but also legal constraints and organization resistance. For instance, in governments where jurisdiction is split along federal levels as well as department competencies, the lack of data sharing is motivated by a missing legal basis and corresponding administrative procedures. Moreover, a common information model is often needed (cf. e.g. [13, 14]). The third challenge, preserving privacy, is a cornerstone of digitization and machine learning, and is of crucial importance for governments. For instance, GDPR in the EU and CCPA as well as HIPAA in the USA are legal frameworks that introduce extensive requirement for government information systems.

The objective of this paper is to provide an *analysis framework* for addressing the described engineering and management challenges in government based on an approach named *Accountable Federated Machine Learning (AFML)*. In this context, accountability is focused on creating verifiable claims [15] towards trustworthy engineering of machine learning [12]. Federated Machine Learning (FML) is a novel approach to apply machine learning to generated knowledge based on shared models, but keep the data private at each participating party's side during the training process (cf. e.g. [16]). FML allows parties to collaborate on one of the main challenges of machine learning: quality and quantity of the training data.

With the analysis framework based on AFML, we address the question: *What engineering and managerial aspects should be considered along the process of introducing novel ML approaches in the government domain?* We discuss an argument that standardization artefacts (e.g. business processes, models, shared terminologies, software tools etc.) are required in the course of analysis. To support this argument, we present findings from a prototype setup of AFML within a use case of citizen participation in Germany and discuss their implications. We believe that our research should be of value to both researchers and practitioners, given the current progress in similar domains.

2 Theoretical Background

2.1 Federated Machine Learning

The term federated learning was recently introduced by McMahan et al. [16]: *"We term our approach Federated Learning, since the learning task is solved by a loose federation of participating devices (which we refer to as clients) which are coordinated by a central server."*. The real-world challenge addressed was primarily to learn from millions of devices (e.g. smart phones) by federating models [17]. Since then, interest in the research community evolved and included data-silos across organizations rather across single end-users. With respect to this development, a broader definition was introduced:

> *"Federated learning is a machine learning setting where multiple entities (clients) collaborate in solving a machine learning problem, under the coordination of a central server or service provider. Each client's raw data is stored locally and not exchanged or transferred; instead, focused updates intended for immediate aggregation are used to achieve the learning objective."* [17].

In this paper, we chose to use the term federated machine learning (FML) instead of federated learning in order to avoid confusion among researchers outside the machine learning community. Thereby, we refer to the clients as FML **parties** and to the services provider as FML **aggregator**.

2.2 Accountability

Accountability can be generally defined as a *"a relationship between an actor and a forum, in which the actor has an obligation to explain and to justify his or her conduct, the forum can pose questions and pass judgment, and the actor may face consequences"* [18]. Accountability has been considered as a guiding principle for system design back in the 1960s (cf. e.g. [19]). In this paper, accountability is focused on creating verifiable claims [15] towards trustworthy FML [12]. In accordance with [20], trustworthiness from an engineering perspective can be represented as argument that aims at explaining the design of a system. Moreover, the argument should explain checks and tests performed during its development to ensure particular system properties. The argument should be organized around particular claims (or goals) and supporting evidence about the system. One can visualize it as a tree, broken down into claims and subclaims (the interior is the reasoning) with evidence at the leaves. To make the claims verifiable, they should be formalized and their evolvement (as well as of the supporting evidence) should allow for an audit trace (cf. e.g. [12, 21–23]).

From a management perspective, trustworthiness concerns assignable responsibilities, distributed obligations and corresponding rules and agreements (cf. e.g. [24]). Consequently, accountability can be presented in terms of: (i) compliance concerned with ensuring that activities are in accordance with prescribed and/or agreed norms (cf. e.g. [25–27]), (ii) control among the parties involved in a process that influence the conditions of the process (cf. e.g. [24]) and (iii) a regulatory framework that defines the requirements, goals, and completion criteria of a process in a satisfactory manner to the parties, who can build a consensus regarding their judgement on the completion of the process in a verifiable way (cf. e.g. [24, 25]).

2.3 Standardization

Standardization artefacts, representing among others a uniform set of agreements or specifications between the actors who develop and apply them, are a suitable approach to study the applicability of a technology in government [28]. In order to analyze IT standardization artefacts in government, the following framework that consist of two dimension can be applied [29, 30]. The first dimension includes three levels of interoperability and the second dimension includes five functional views. The interoperability dimension is structured along three layers. First, business processes applied in delivering public service are found on the organizational layer. Second, exchange of information and data as well as to their meaning between parties involved is found on the semantic layer. Third, data structure and format, sending and receiving data based on communication protocols, electronic mechanisms to store data as well as software and hardware are situated on the technical/syntactic layer.

The second dimension includes five functional views. The administration view includes predominantly non-technical standards. They affect personnel and process aspects as well as communication within or between public administrations. Second, the modeling view includes reference models and architectures, as well as modelling languages for each corresponding interoperability level. Third, standards that focus on the computation of data are included in the processing view. Fourth, corresponding standards for data and information exchange between different public administrations is handled in the communication and interaction view. Fifth, the security and privacy view contains standards that aim at addressing issues such as definition of access management policies, cryptography methods or requesting a required minimum of personal data.

3   Research Approach

We follow a qualitative analysis approach to explorative research. We aim at developing a descriptive artefact (analysis framework) that can be categorized as a theory for analyzing [31]. Our research approach is rooted in the paradigm of pragmatism [32]. We studied the findings through an argumentative-deductive analysis [33], which comprised theoretically-founded concept development and prototype development. We conducted a hermeneutic literature review [30] to study the theoretical foundations. Thereby, we started to develop our understanding of the concepts of accountability [19, 34, 35] and FML [16, 17, 36, 37] and derived implications from a standardization perspective [28, 29].

For our prototype, we used data and a list of challenges from a research project on online citizen participation [28], where missing data showed the potential of data sharing while at the same time data privacy concerns hampered any progress on sharing. Online citizen participation can be described as a form of participation that is based on the usage of information and communication technology in societal democratic and consultative processes focused on citizens [38].

The envisioned application of machine learning with a particular relevance for online citizen participation is a methodology named natural language processing (NLP). NLP has been already applied in government practice (e.g. [39]) as well as in online citizen participation (e.g. [40]). With respect to methodological development and practical tool availability of NLP, we decided to create a prototype architecture that involves *classification of ideas sampled during online citizen participation* and focuses on the following challenge: *How to apply FML for NLP classification tasks that are traditionally performed in a centralized manner?*

The data used for NLP in the prototype were collected during several citizen participation sessions in a German city. The dataset is a collection of citizen ideas –describing their problems, concerns and suggestions in German text form– including other information like title and category. Since the data originated from heterogeneous sources, several preprocessing steps were conducted to obtain a consolidated dataset: a collection of 3903 ideas with 8 categories, with stratified sampling into a training (90% - 3,512 ideas) and a test (10% - 391 ideas) set, and ultimately the training set was randomly split into 3 slices à ~1170 ideas each, simulating the three participating cities.

The prototype implements the use case as follows. Each city is represented by a party in the FML. The parties agree that an aggregator (as an independent actor responsible for the provision of the required technology) will manage the FML process and generate a global model based on local model updates from each party. Moreover, they agree on the set of test data that will be used to benchmark each updated version of the model. Each party can train locally the models in numerous rounds and store the required data locally. Technical components such as messaging and routing of the FML communication, storage of encrypted models as well as accountability-related rules and log data (verifiable claims and evidence about training data set, number of rounds, model updates, reached model quality, configuration of each party etc.) are stored on a cloud infrastructure. For running and orchestrating the FML process, we used the IBM FL framework [36]. The component for accountability rules and data (cf. for details https://git.fortiss.org/evidentia) is built atop a logic database named Datalog [41] and Hyperledger Fabric [42].

4 AFML Engineering

4.1 Feasibility Evaluation for FML

In order to structure FML approaches in a comprehensive manner, we provide the following overview (cf. Table 1) based on substantial extant research [37, 43, 44]. The overview has nine dimensions with corresponding characteristics. It is rather selective and does not claim to be fully exhaustive, since its sole purpose is to provide a starting point for evaluation the feasibility of engineering FML in the government context (for additional details cf. e.g. [45]).

The dimension *data partitioning* is characterized by the type of learning implied in terms of samples (data to learn from) and feature space (individual measurable property or characteristic of the data) to consider when labeling data. *Horizontal* implies that the data samples differ between the FML parties, but the feature space is the same. For example, departments with the same jurisdiction at different federal levels or at different cities share knowledge about user preferences about consumption of a public service.

Vertical implies that the features differ between the FML parties, but the data space is the same. For example, departments with different jurisdictions share knowledge about relevant user attributes to create a more detailed user profile. *Hybrid* approaches concerns difference in both samples and features and are rather interesting in academic research, but have limited practical implications.

Table 1. Feasibility evaluation of FML.

Dimension	Characteristics		
Data partitioning	Horizontal	Vertical	Hybrid
ML model	Linear model	Decision tree	Neural network
Training data input	Featured	Raw	
Training data output	Structured	Unstructured	
Data federation	Cross-silo	Cross-device	
Privacy preservation	Differential privacy	Cryptographic techniques	
Network topology	Centralized	Decentralized	
Federation need	Economic incentive	Regulation	
Technology grade	Research	Industry	

The *machine learning model* dimension describes different types of approaches that can be applied in FML. It is important the profound understanding of the mechanics of these approaches is present at each party's side, since the parties should agree on one approach and be able to justify potential attacks and malfunctions (cf. e.g. [17]).

The dimensions *training data input* and *output* as well as *data federation* are of particular relevance for FML in a government setup, when parties are organizations. This is the case, since *cross-device federation* typically addresses the challenge of applying FML to a large number of end devices (smart phones, IoT devices etc.), where challenges emerge out of scalability issues but the variety of data types is rather limited. In *cross-silo federation*, different organizations participate with different data. For instance, different public administrations have to agree on which data to use for building models and for which purpose. In this case, the involved parties should agree on the characteristics of data input and output and in case of heterogeneity, additional data pre- and post-processing should be introduced (cf. e.g. [44]).

Privacy preservation is typically addressed by either *differential privacy* or through *cryptographic methods* [12]. Basically, differential privacy aims at handling data in way that does not allow to reverse engineer any privacy-relevant information from the model or from queries based on the model. In practice this task is often challenging, due to the tension between robustness, fairness and privacy (cf. e.g. [17]). Cryptographic methods focus on securing that data stays private throughout the FML process, i.e. that computation is performed without revealing privacy related information. Practical and theoretical challenges include analyzing potential attacks as well as reaching the desired level of performance, since communication and processing effort is high.

The *network topology* could be centralized (e.g. aggregator) or decentralized (e.g. the model is aggregated among the parties in a peer-to-peer like setup). Practical implementations vary based on the type of data partitioning involved. A rather common topology is the centralized one combined with suitable privacy preservation.

Federation need represents a generic engineering dimension that addresses alignment with business and management. Economic incentives imply a clear efficiency or effectiveness need from the parties to collaboratively develop a model with corresponding privacy requirements. Needs that results from regulation are often derived from the legal framework and limitations regarding data sharing. Federation can be required from a mixture of needs, e.g. initial economic drivers and consideration of GDPR and jurisdiction legal norms among public administrations.

Technology grade implies the practical need to analyze and select a suitable technology stack. While research is active and ongoing, there are industry frameworks and service offerings available that take care of non-FML specific tasks such as authentication and identity management (cf. e.g. [17, 46]).

4.2 Architecture of AFML

Based on our prototype, we generalize the following architecture (cf. Fig. 1) for AFML and extend the feasibility evaluation for FML with focus on practical implications. First, parties in the government domain should be capable of applying machine learning. AFML does not provide a remedy for missing machine learning pipelines and, in fact, only adjusts the way machine learning is applied. Moreover, data preprocessing is still a traditional challenge to be mastered, and in the context of AFML this might lead to additional effort when defending against attacks and malfunctions (cf. e.g. [17]).

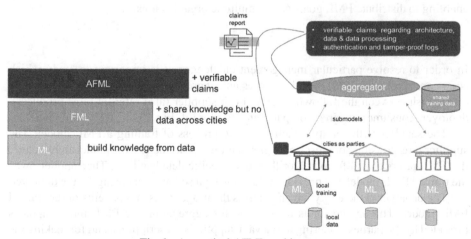

Fig. 1. A practical AFML architecture.

Second, in the context of government practice particular FML setups seem more feasible. We argue that *data partitioning would be rather horizontal, data federation would be cross-silo, network typology would be rather centralized and considered technologies should be industry or near-industry grade.* In the prototype developed, we gathered initial insights in support of our argument, since cities were willing to experiment but pointed out that a service provider should take over the FML setup and cross-device federation is currently lacking corresponding infrastructure and applications.

Based on our prototype and concept development, we also found that accountability of FML represents a potential enabler for accepting a novel technology. This is the case, since fairness, ethics and privacy are intensively discussed in the context of machine learning (cf. e.g. [3]) and, ultimately, trustworthiness of machine learning (cf. e.g. [12]), which is sometimes hampering public administrations to act.

From an engineering point of view, this challenge could be addressed with **verifiable claims**. Such claims should be defined regarding the architecture, data and data processing of FML. Examples include the framework configuration, data samples and features, model configuration and lineage along the training rounds, and, of course, continuous integration of changes (cf. e.g. [47]). Moreover, verifiable claims should be built upon corresponding authentication and ID management, as well as tamper-proof logs (cf. e.g. [21–23, 48]). Consequently, the additional feasibility requirement would be to introduce accountability and to make it accessible to a broad number of stakeholders through **claims report**.

5 AFML Management

Managing accountability for FML comprises transparent assignment and ownership of responsibilities based on rules and agreements about the expected results and obligations, facilitating to judge whether all parties have fulfilled their responsibilities. Moreover, it might comprise mechanisms to impose sanctions if obligations are not fulfilled, thereby enabling to distribute FML goals across multiple organizations.

5.1 Actors in AFML

In order to resolve particular management challenges, it is important to study which actors are involved in FML besides parties and aggregators. Based on our analysis, we distinguish between the following actors [47]: supplier (also referred to as producer), deployer (consumer), aggregator, party and auditor (cf. Fig. 2).

The supplier is the entity which owns the process of training a FML model. The supplier is responsible for prescribing global training parameters, the model architecture, the FML protocol and fusion algorithm, and specific data handlers. The supplier owns the trained FML model and provides it (e.g. through software licensing) to the deployer.

The deployer is the entity which controls the usage, risks and benefits of the trained FML model. The aggregator is responsible for aggregating the FML model updates provided by the parties, adhering to relevant supplier's prescriptions, and for making the trained FML model accessible to the supplier. The parties are responsible for providing the aggregator with FML model updates, adhering to relevant supplier's prescriptions. The auditor is an independent (potentially accredited) body which verifies and/or certifies that the deployment of the FML model (and/or the FML model itself) adheres to technical standards and/or applicable governance, risk & compliance (GRC) obligations.

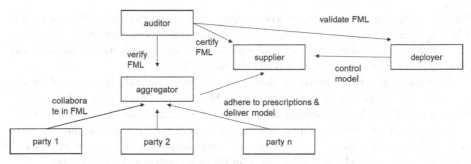

Fig. 2. Overview of actors in AFML.

5.2 Trust Between Parties

Another aspect of addressing management challenges of AFML is the mapping of rules and agreements between the parties according to their responsibilities and obligations. Since the parties are different organization, from a management perspective FML activities takes place in setup where different organizations carry out activities jointly to achieve a common business objective. In particular, compliance challenges of linking regulation with governance, business processes and their execution across organizations pose threats to coping with responsibilities and obligations [27]. In order to cope with the latter, a corresponding level of trust is required. Achieving trust is challenging in the case of FML due to potentially unequal power relations (e.g. who provides the data, who is interested in the model) and the possibility of protecting the interests of individual organizations (e.g. what is a "good model") by manipulating and controlling collaborative learning processes (e.g. attacks and/ or malfunction).

As a remedy, accountability in management of FML would include introducing **verifiable claims** that link (i) compliance with prescribed and/or agreed norms (cf. e.g. [25–27]), control mechanism for the parties involved in a process (cf. e.g. [24, 49]) as well as (iii) a regulatory framework. Such claims should represent the basis for operationalizing trust among the actors in a satisfactory manner. In particular, this would result in a non-repudiable consensus regarding the actors' judgement on the completion of the process in a verifiable way (cf. e.g. [24, 25]).

Claim reports could represent a feasible artefact that operationalizes accountability. The purpose of such reports (sometimes referred to as factsheets [47, 50]) is to provide transparency and instill trust into ML services. They are to be "completed by AI service providers for examination by consumers" and shall contain "sections on all relevant attributes of an AI service", in particular "how the service was created, trained, and deployed" [47]. Yet, it is still an open issue what level of detail and which claims are most suitable for a report to adhere to a required level of trust.

6 Discussion and Conclusion

In this paper, we formulated the need to face challenges of accountability, data sharing and privacy preservation along the course of machine learning in a government context.

We address this need by introducing a novel approach named federated machine learning, which relaxes limitations of data sharing and privacy constraints. Moreover, we address the formulated need by introducing accountability from an engineering and management perspective towards generating verifiable claims for FML.

Through an argumentative-deductive analysis of literature and a prototype of AFML for online citizen participation, we explored AFML from an engineering and a management perspective. The engineering perspective includes feasibility evaluation of FML and adds an accountability perspective based on a corresponding architecture for practical applications in government. The management perspective includes an analysis of actors involved in AFML and means to establish trustworthiness between them.

Based on this analysis framework, we approach the question of introducing AFML in the government domain based on the following overview of standardization artefacts (cf. Table 2, [7, 28]). Exemplary artefacts in bold show that substantial progress has already been made or industry-ready solutions already exist, which is promising for exploring improvements of existing approaches (cf. e.g. [39]). Regarding the other exemplary artefacts, the status is either an open research problem or the current solutions are for application in a research setup.

Our research has a number of limitations. First, the engineering analysis is rather general and omits details that might be of relevance for a thorough feasibility evaluation in practice, especially from a methodological perspective given the fact that we developed the prototype and used it as a basis for interpretation. Second, the presented architecture is focused on a cross-silo data federation. Emerging developments (e.g. smart city, edge computing) might pose the need for a cross-device FML in government, which is out of our research scope. Third, the management analysis was solely based on argumentation and deduction from relevant literature as well as prototype development, due to the novelty of FML and the limited access to suitable interviewees in the government domain for sampling of primary empirical data. Fourth, a limitation for ML in general is a possible security and privacy breach by reverse engineering a model, which might leak the data.

We believe that future research should build on our findings and address the describing limitations of our research. We strongly encourage researchers to explore potential use cases and to derive engineering and management requirements for AFML. We also believe that practitioners can directly benefit from the presented findings and apply them as a basis for exploring novel FML techniques to overcome traditional challenges.

Table 2. Implications for streamlining AFML in government.

	Administration	Modeling	Processing	Communication & interaction	Security & privacy
Organizational/managerial	Governance of incentives vs. regulations	**Lifecycle blueprint**	**FML training integration**	**Enterprise infrastructure integration**	Compliance
Semantic	Claim report semantics	Trust semantics	Explain-ability	Data & model metadata	**Guarantees for attacks and threats**
Technical/syntactic	**Evidence granularity & tamper-proof guarantees**	Common accountability criteria	**Toolchain**	Tool & model interoperability	**Cryptography & differential privacy, ID mgmt**

Acknowledgements. This research was partially funded by the Bavarian Ministry of Ministry of Economic Affairs, Regional Development and Energy in the context of the project BayernCloud (funding code 'AZ: 20-13-3410.1-01A-2017').

We thank our reviewers for their careful reading and their constructive remarks.

References

1. Russell, S.J., Norvig, P.: Artificial Intelligence: A Modern Approach. Pearson Education Limited, Kuala Lumpur (2016)
2. Agrawal, A., Gans, J., Goldfarb, A.: Prediction Machines: The Simple Economics of Artificial Intelligence. Harvard Business Press, Boston (2018)
3. Winfield, A.F., Michael, K., Pitt, J., Evers, V.: Machine ethics: the design and governance of ethical AI and autonomous systems [scanning the issue]. Proc. IEEE **107**, 509–517 (2019)
4. Dwivedi, Y.K., et al.: Artificial intelligence (AI): multidisciplinary perspectives on emerging challenges, opportunities, and agenda for research, practice and policy. Int. J. Inf. Manag. 101994 (2019)
5. Sun, T.Q., Medaglia, R.: Mapping the challenges of artificial intelligence in the public sector: evidence from public healthcare. Gov. Inf. Q. (2018)
6. AUPP Council: Statement on algorithmic transparency and accountability. Commun. ACM (2017)
7. Scholl, H.J., Klischewski, R.: E-government integration and interoperability: framing the research agenda. Int. J. Publ. Adm. **30**, 889–920 (2007)
8. Wang, F.: Understanding the dynamic mechanism of interagency government data sharing. Gov. Inf. Q. **35**, 536–546 (2018)
9. Janssen, M., van den Hoven, J.: Big and open linked data (BOLD) in government: a challenge to transparency and privacy? Gov. Inf. Q. **32**, 363–368 (2015). https://doi.org/10.1016/j.giq. 2015.11.007
10. Howard, A., Borenstein, J.: The ugly truth about ourselves and our robot creations: the problem of bias and social inequity. Sci. Eng. Ethics **24**, 1521–1536 (2018)
11. Cath, C., Wachter, S., Mittelstadt, B., Taddeo, M., Floridi, L.: Artificial intelligence and the 'good society': the US, EU, and UK approach. Sci. Eng. Ethics **24**, 505–528 (2018)
12. Brundage, M., et al.: Toward trustworthy AI development: mechanisms for supporting verifiable claims. arXiv preprint arXiv:2004.07213 (2020)
13. Scholta, H., Niemann, M., Halsbenning, S., Räckers, M., Becker, J.: Fast and Federal— Policies for Next-Generation Federalism in Germany (2019)
14. Scholta, H., Balta, D., Räckers, M., Becker, J., Krcmar, H.: Standardization of forms in governments. Bus. Inf. Syst. Eng. **62**, 535–560 (2020)
15. Küsters, R., Truderung, T., Vogt, A.: Accountability: definition and relationship to verifiability. In: Proceedings of the 17th ACM Conference on Computer and Communications Security, pp. 526–535. ACM (2010)
16. McMahan, B., Moore, E., Ramage, D., Hampson, S., Arcas, B.A.: Communication-efficient learning of deep networks from decentralized data. In: Artificial Intelligence and Statistics, pp. 1273–1282. PMLR (2017)
17. Kairouz, P., et al.: Advances and open problems in federated learning. arXiv preprint arXiv: 1912.04977 (2019)
18. Bovens, M.: Analysing and assessing accountability: a conceptual framework 1. Eur. Law J. **13**, 447–468 (2007)
19. Eriksén, S.: Designing for accountability. In: Proceedings of the Second Nordic Conference on Human-Computer Interaction, pp. 177–186. ACM (2002)

20. Bloomfield, R., Rushby, J.: Assurance 2.0: a manifesto. arXiv preprint arXiv:2004.10474 (2020)
21. Cleland-Huang, J., Gotel, O., Zisman, A.: Software and Systems Traceability. Springer, London (2012). https://doi.org/10.1007/978-1-4471-2239-5
22. Cleland-Huang, J., Gotel, O.C., Huffman Hayes, J., Mäder, P., Zisman, A.: Software traceability: trends and future directions. In: Future of Software Engineering Proceedings, pp. 55–69 (2014)
23. Gotel, O., et al.: Traceability fundamentals. In: Cleland-Huang, J., Gotel, O., Zisman, A. (eds.) Software and Systems Traceability, pp. 3–22. Springer, London (2012). https://doi.org/10.1007/978-1-4471-2239-5_1
24. Baldoni, M., Baroglio, C., Micalizio, R., Tedeschi, S.: Accountability and responsibility in business processes via agent technology. In: Workshop on Experimental Evaluation of Algorithms for Solving Problems with Combinatorial Explosion (RCRA 2018), pp. 1–18. CEUR-WS (2018)
25. Yao, J., Chen, S., Levy, D.: Accountability-based compliance control of collaborative business processes in cloud systems. In: Nepal, S., Pathan, M. (eds.) Security, Privacy and Trust in Cloud Systems, pp. 345–374. Springer, Heidelberg (2014). https://doi.org/10.1007/978-3-642-38586-5_12
26. Sadiq, S., Governatori, G., Namiri, K.: Modeling control objectives for business process compliance. In: Alonso, G., Dadam, P., Rosemann, M. (eds.) BPM 2007. LNCS, vol. 4714, pp. 149–164. Springer, Heidelberg (2007). https://doi.org/10.1007/978-3-540-75183-0_12
27. Hashmi, M., Governatori, G., Lam, H.-P., Wynn, M.T.: Are we done with business process compliance: state of the art and challenges ahead. Knowl. Inf. Syst. 57(1), 79–133 (2018). https://doi.org/10.1007/s10115-017-1142-1
28. Balta, D., Kuhn, P., Sellami, M., Kulus, D., Lieven, C., Krcmar, H.: How to streamline AI application in government? A case study on citizen participation in Germany. In: Lindgren, I., et al. (eds.) EGOV 2019. LNCS, vol. 11685, pp. 233–247. Springer, Cham (2019). https://doi.org/10.1007/978-3-030-27325-5_18
29. Balta, D.: Effective Management of Standardizing in E-Government, pp. 149–175. Corporate Standardization Management and Innovation (2019). https://doi.org/10.4018/978-1-5225-9008-8.ch008
30. Balta, D., Krcmar, H.: Managing standardization in eGovernment: a coordination theory based analysis framework. In: Parycek, P., et al. (eds.) EGOV 2018. LNCS, vol. 11020, pp. 60–72. Springer, Cham (2018). https://doi.org/10.1007/978-3-319-98690-6_6
31. Gregor, S.: The nature of theory in information systems. MIS Q. 611–642 (2006)
32. Goldkuhl, G.: Pragmatism vs interpretivism in qualitative information systems research. Eur. J. Inf. Syst. 21, 135–146 (2012)
33. Wilde, T., Hess, T.: Forschungsmethoden der Wirtschaftsinformatik. Wirtschaftsinformatik 49(4), 280–287 (2007). https://doi.org/10.1007/s11576-007-0064-z
34. Nissenbaum, H.: Computing and accountability, https://link.galegroup.com/apps/doc/A15020194/AONE?sid=lms. Accessed 06 Oct 2019
35. Beckers, K., Landthaler, J., Matthes, F., Pretschner, A., Waltl, B.: Data accountability in socio-technical systems. In: Schmidt, R., Guédria, W., Bider, I., Guerreiro, S. (eds.) BPMDS/EMMSAD -2016. LNBIP, vol. 248, pp. 335–348. Springer, Cham (2016). https://doi.org/10.1007/978-3-319-39429-9_21
36. Ludwig, H., et al.: IBM Federated Learning: An Enterprise Framework White paper V0.1. arXiv:2007.10987 [cs] (2020)
37. Li, Q., Wen, Z., Wu, Z., Hu, S., Wang, N., He, B.: A survey on federated learning systems: vision, hype and reality for data privacy and protection. arXiv preprint arXiv:1907.09693 (2019)

38. Susha, I.: Grönlund, \AAke: eParticipation research: systematizing the field. Gov. Inf. Q. **29**, 373–382 (2012)

39. Androutsopoulou, A., Karacapilidis, N., Loukis, E., Charalabidis, Y.: Transforming the communication between citizens and government through AI-guided chatbots. Gov. Inf. Q. (2018)

40. Maragoudakis, M., Loukis, E., Charalabidis, Y.: A review of opinion mining methods for analyzing citizens' contributions in public policy debate. In: Tambouris, E., Macintosh, A., de Bruijn, H. (eds.) ePart 2011. LNCS, vol. 6847, pp. 298–313. Springer, Heidelberg (2011). https://doi.org/10.1007/978-3-642-23333-3_26

41. Greco, S., Molinaro, C.: Datalog and logic databases. Synth. Lect. Data Manag. **7**, 1–169 (2015)

42. Androulaki, E., et al.: Hyperledger fabric: a distributed operating system for permissioned blockchains. In: Proceedings of the Thirteenth EuroSys Conference, pp. 1–15 (2018)

43. Mothukuri, V., Parizi, R.M., Pouriyeh, S., Huang, Y., Dehghantanha, A., Srivastava, G.: A survey on security and privacy of federated learning. Futur. Gener. Comput. Syst. **115**, 619–640 (2021)

44. Verma, D., White, G., de Mel, G.: Federated AI for the enterprise: a web services based implementation. In: 2019 IEEE International Conference on Web Services (ICWS), pp. 20–27. IEEE (2019)

45. Song, L., Wu, H., Ruan, W., Han, W.: SoK: training machine learning models over multiple sources with privacy preservation. arXiv preprint arXiv:2012.03386 (2020)

46. Torkzadehmahani, R., et al.: Privacy-preserving artificial intelligence techniques in biomedicine. arXiv preprint arXiv:2007.11621 (2020)

47. Arnold, M., et al.: FactSheets: increasing trust in AI services through supplier's declarations of conformity. IBM J. Res. Dev. **63**, 6–1 (2019)

48. Spanoudakis, G., Zisman, A.: Software traceability: a roadmap. In: Handbook of Software Engineering and Knowledge Engineering: Recent Advances, vol. 3, pp. 395–428. World Scientific (2005)

49. Baldoni, M., Baroglio, C., May, K.M., Micalizio, R., Tedeschi, S.: Computational accountability. In: Deep Understanding and Reasoning: A Challenge for Next-generation Intelligent Agents, URANIA 2016, pp. 56–62. CEUR Workshop Proceedings (2016)

50. Piorkowski, D., González, D., Richards, J., Houde, S.: Towards evaluating and eliciting high-quality documentation for intelligent systems. arXiv:2011.08774 [cs] (2020)

Agile Development for Digital Government Services: Challenges and Success Factors

Maximilian Kupi[✉][ID] and Keegan McBride[ID]

Hertie School, Centre for Digital Governance, Berlin, Germany
{kupi,mcbride}@hertie-school.org

Abstract. Many governments have problems with developing digital government services in an effective and efficient manner. One proposed solution to improve governmental digital service development is for governments to utilize agile development methods. However, there is currently a lack of understanding on two important and related topics. First, whether or not agile development might help to overcome common failure reasons of digital government projects. Second, what the challenges and success factors of agile digital government service development are. This paper addresses both of these gaps. By gathering insights from six cases where agile methods were used in the development of new digital services, it identifies five core categories of challenges and success factors encountered when utilizing agile development methods for governmental digital service development: organizational, methodological, end-user-related, technological, and regulatory. Furthermore, based on these findings, it makes initial recommendations on when and how to best use agile methods for digital government service development.

Keywords: Agile development · Digital government · Public administration · e-government · Failure · Public services

1 Introduction

As governments begin to become more "digital", one important aspect is the digitalization of services. While governments are more than just service providers, this is a core part of a digital government. Yet, many digital government services are developed slowly and do not materialize as initially planned [16]. One potential reason for this is due to a disconnect between historically grown governmental approaches, processes, and regulations for non-digital services, and the more agile nature of new software development projects.

The private sector has innovated on their service development processes and many software companies now rely on some form of agile development methods for rapidly implementing services that are in line with user needs and expectations [4,11]. Such methods have the potential to bring out gains in effectiveness,

© IFIP International Federation for Information Processing 2021
Published by Springer Nature Switzerland AG 2021
N. Edelmann et al. (Eds.): ePart 2021, LNCS 12849, pp. 139–150, 2021.
https://doi.org/10.1007/978-3-030-82824-0_11

efficiency, and user satisfaction. For this reason, governmental organizations are now beginning to experiment with integrating agile development methods into their own digital public service development toolkits [1,16,30].

However, governments are not businesses, governmental services are not private sector services, and citizens are not customers [15]. For these reasons, undifferentiated claims that agile methods or agile development will, normatively, improve governmental digital service development are flawed. There are substantial differences between the private sector and government. Governments face a unique set of challenges such as those related to risk aversion in the governmental mindset, resistance to change, and user (aka. citizen) demand for stability [15].

Thus, in order to investigate the role agile development may or may not play in the development of governmental digital services, there are at least two concrete areas that must be explored. First, what are common causes of digital government project failure and could these potentially be overcome by applying agile methods? Second, what challenges and success factors emerge when agile development methods are utilized for digital government service development?

In regard to the first question, a large amount of research has been done to identify common sources of digital government project failures [6,9,10,14,25]. Additionally, there is a large strand of literature on similar topics from other domains such as organizational management, management information systems, and computer science literature [8,13,26]. With regard to agile methods, there are some first studies that examine the use of agile methods in government organizations more broadly [18,32]. However, in regard to the second question, when it comes to exploring and conceptualizing which new challenges and success factors may arise when applying these methods in digital government service development, the literature is scant. Thus, it is against this background that the following research question emerged to guide this paper:

RQ: *What are the commonly occurring challenges and success factors during the agile development of digital government services?*

In order to answer this research question, a systematic review of six case studies selected via a theoretical sampling approach from the OECD's Observatory of Public Sector Innovation (OPSI) database was conducted. Each case represents a self-reported successfully developed digital government service where agile development was utilized in some aspect. By exploring these cases it is possible to begin to provide new insight into how agile development methods are applied inside digital government service development projects, and what challenges and success factors may emerge as a result. In answering this question, using such a method, the core contribution of this paper is related to its elucidation of the relationship between, and the empirical exploration of, the effects of agile methods during digital government service development.

2   Background

Inside the domain of digital government, sources of digital government project failure is a widely discussed topic (e.g., [6,10,14]). Although not all failure sources of digital government projects are necessarily transferable to service development, such research provides a strong foundation for initial exploration and shows clear relationships to problems identified in traditional software development projects. On the topic of digital government project failure, researchers often distinguish between failure reasons and failure factors [2]. Failure reasons are related to particularities that lie within a project's life-cycle, like a missing focus or execution issues, and hence might be tackled by applying new development methods. Failure factors, which exist in a project's ecosystem—also beyond the project period—are unlikely to be effected by new development methods, and are therefore not relevant for the analysis within this paper. One of the clearest literature-based classifications of digital government project failure reasons comes from Anthopoulos et al. [2]. This classification consists of eight primary failure reasons: design-reality gaps, missing focus, content issues, skill issues, execution issues, regulatory issues, external factors, and missing user satisfaction.

In order to explore how agile development could, in theory, help to overcome the aforementioned challenges, it is valuable to start with a brief description and overview of agile development. Agile development methods involve creating, testing, and improving technology products incrementally [16]. Largely, all agile methods adhere to the tenets of the Agile Manifesto [3]. The Agile Manifesto was formulated by 17 thought leaders of agile software development in 2001 to lay down the four values and twelve guiding principles of agile methods [27].[1] Agile development is an umbrella term, with a number of different methodological approaches lying within it, such as Scrum, eXtreme Programming, Lean Software Development, and Feature-Driven Development [7,27]. Each method has its own strengths and weaknesses, yet most are similar in the importance they place on constant and continuous integration of users and their feedback, as well as small and iterative design delivery cycles.

Looking at the categorization of common reasons for digital government project failure by Anthopoulos et al. [2], it appears to be the case that many of these are challenges and inefficiencies similar to those within software development projects that were identified, and therefore targeted by, the pioneers of agile development. With this in mind, it is possible to map the values and principles associated with agile development against the respective failure reasons that they may help to overcome. This mapping is shown below in Table 1.

Table 1. Potential counteractive agile development values and principles mapped on common reasons for digital government project failure.

Failure Reasons	Design-reality gaps	Missing focus	Content issues	Skill issues	Execution issues	Regulatory issues	External factors	Missing user satisfaction
Counteractive Values & Principles	V3, V4, P1, P2, P7, P9	V2, V3, P1, P3, P7, P9, P10	V3, V4, P2, P4, P10, P12	V1, P4, P5, P6, P11, P12	V2, V4, P2, P4, P8, P12	V4, P2, P4	V4, P2, P12	V2, V3, P1, P2, P3, P7, P9, P12

Authors' mapping based on [2,3].

---

[1] These principles and values can be found at: https://agilemanifesto.org.

3   Research Method

While, theoretically, agile development may help overcome common failure sources due to its respective values and principles, it is important to explore empirically the actual implementation of agile methods in digital government service development. In order to conduct such exploration, this paper utilizes a case-based methodological approach, where relevant cases were identified from the OPSI innovation database via a theoretical sampling approach [5,31]. The OPSI innovation database collects and maintains self-selected and self-submitted descriptions and reflections of innovation projects; these are the basis for the analysis in this paper. However, for this reason, there is a high amount of selectivity and survivorship bias in the data used. Nevertheless, due to the nature of this research, the cases are likely still of interest. One of the clearest reasons is that, though increasing, there is still a limited number of agile methods-based digital government service development projects. Thus, the OPSI database provides a critical resource for identifying developments of this nature. Furthermore, if this paper was studying how agile development helps to overcome governmental digital service development failure specifically, then this data would not be appropriate as it does not include failures. Yet, this is not the purpose of this paper. It only wishes to understand how, in successfully delivered digital government service development projects, agile methods did or did not aid in their success, and how agile influenced—and was influenced by—the context factors of these projects.

In this research, cases were selected using a six-step sampling process. For a case to be included, it needed to specifically mention "agile" within the case description, be at the highest governmental level (e.g., federal or national), and be related to a specific development of a digital government service. Based on these criteria it was possible to select 6 cases from the entirety of the database (421 cases at the time of writing). An overview of this process is shown below in Fig. 1.

421	cases in *OECD Observatory of Public Sector Innovation* data base
75	cases mentioning keyword "agile"
57	cases on *National / Federal Government Level*
28	cases with focus on *Public Administration Modernization and Reform*
15	cases with tag *Digital and Technology Transformation* and/or tag *Public Service Delivery*
6	cases after final eligibility assessment

Fig. 1. Case selection process (authors' visualization).

With the cases selected, the next step was to analyze each case description directly from the OPSI database. For this task, a qualitative methodological approach based on content analysis was selected [12,28]. Each description was read, and recurring themes and concepts were identified using an inductive coding strategy [29]. The coding was done independently by each of the authors of this paper. After this was done, final codes were discussed and agreed upon via a collaborative process involving all authors.

4   Case Descriptions

(1) **SmartStart.** The SmartStart service is a life-event-based service aiming to improve access to information on services that are available for new parents dealing with the birth of a child in New Zealand. The service integrates information from a number of different agencies, and has increased the efficiency and effectiveness of government service provision within this domain. The challenges faced fell under the organizational, regulatory, methodological, and technological categories. For example, during the development of the service it was clear that there was different level of maturity, both technical and organizational, among the collaborative partners [22]. There were also issues related to procurement, technology interoperability, as well as misunderstandings about the agile method itself [22]. Success factors were related to the availability of funding for the development, cross-agency collaboration, a lean and agile-based approach, offering a minimum viable product (MVP), and engaging heavily with the end-user for continuous feedback [22].

(2) **Blockchain of Frequencies.** The blockchain of frequencies service was built in France and utilizes blockchain technology to ensure "the integrity, the immutability, the transparency, the traceability, the audibility of the reservations of frequencies" [23]. The developmnent utilized agile software development methods, following a sprint-based approach for the creation of the service. In regard to core challenges, categorically these were mostly technological and methodological. The technology (blockchain) was complicated for the developers and the agile method required the organization to redesign and rethink certain organizational processes [23]. Similar to the first case, end-user feedback and interactions, as well as the continuous development and testing of an MVP were viewed as critical for the success of the developmnent [23].

(3) **Digital Mobile Key.** The digital mobile key facilitates the identification and authentication of citizens for online service use in Portugal. This solution was also built using agile development, and, notably, relied heavily on a modular architecture, reusing components and standards, thus improving the overall agility and adaptivity of the service [19]. The challenges faced can be categorized into groups of end-user-related, technological, and organizational. For example, the service was organizationally and legislatively complex due to a large number of involved actors and influencing regulation, was subject to initially poor user uptake, and was technically dependent on a number of different components that required integration [19]. The relevant identified success factors were the importance of top-level managerial support, citizen interaction and end-user feedback, as well as the use of open standards [19].

(4) MyService. MyService was built by the Australian Government and aimed to provide an easier way for veterans to access services. The project brought together a number of different services, enabled data sharing among said services, and improved the speed and ease at which a user could navigate through the services. In regard to agile development, the project was end-user-oriented, utilized human-centered design, and employed multidisciplinary and cross-organizational development teams [21]. The service faced challenges primarily related to organizational issues—such as low support and commitment of the implementation team and low levels of internal organizational capacity for digital service development—as well as regulatory issues, e.g., redefining and improving the service business processes [21]. Identified success factors were related to the importance of human-centred design, the use of multi-discplinary teams, and focusing on development of internal agency capacities [21].

(5) GOV.UK step-by-step navigation. The step-by-step navigation service was built for the British government domain GOV.UK and aimed to improve the understandability of digital service journeys for citizens. The project was reliant on agile development methods, carried out by a multi-disciplinary and cross-governmental team, utilized human-centered design, and took end-user feedback into account throughout the entire duration of the development [24]. Challenges encountered were primarily technical, related to the actual usability of the service at its initial development stages [24]. Success factors identified during the development were having top-level managerial support and possessing the internal capacity to engage in cross-agency collaboration [24].

(6) GOV.UK Verify. GOV.UK Verify is a service that was created to provide a digital identity to British citizens allowing them to authenticate themselves on both public and private digital services. The service was delivered via a public private partnership managed by the Government Digital Service applying an agile and iterative process which built on multiple user research activities [20]. The challenges faced during the development can be categorized as end-user-related, organizational, and technological [20]. There were issues related to obtaining user adoption, changing organizational processes and business cases, complying with relevant legislative requirements and regulations, as well as service scalability [20]. Clearly identified success factors were related to multi-disciplinary teams and inter-agency cooperation, end-user engagement, and ensuring a transparent engagement approach across public and private sector stakeholders throughout the development process [20].

5   Results and Discussion

As a result of the analysis, it was possible to identify five categories that encompass the relevant challenges and success factors with regard to the use of agile methods in digital government service development, as well as the ways in which agile development seems to have helped foster perceived digital government service 'successes'. These categories are: organizational, methodological, end-user-related, technological, and regulatory. The following subsections explore the identified challenges and success factors within these categories.

5.1   Identified Challenges

Organizational. The first group of challenges identified are organizational barriers. Primarily, these occurred due to missing or low levels of capacity within the specific organization. For example, in case 4, MyService, it was noted that "too often we look to outsource technological risks instead of owning them. We try to solve the easy problems, instead of taking on the difficult ones" [21]. Other organizational challenges were those related to structures within the organization as implementing agile development methods required structural changes, especially with respect to work and team processes. This can be seen clearly in case 1, where it was noted that when adopting an agile approach, "you'll need to change how you're organized for and lead work. Accept that there will be new roles and teams created within your organization and across the agencies involved" [17]. Further organizational issues were primarily related to project management and project complexity. Though agile development should focus on the use of small and multi-disciplinary teams, sometimes this still requires cross-agency collaboration, and such collaboration can be difficult if the appropriate experience is lacking, as was the case in cases 1, 2, and 4.

Methodological. The second group of challenges were those related to the actual methodology of agile development. These challenges occurred in cases 1, 2, and 4 the clearest, and were primarily related to organizations attempting to do agile development for the first time, thus having an incomplete or inaccurate understanding about the method. These misunderstandings were most often associated with when and how to integrate or gather user feedback (case 1 and 2), the actual agile development process (case 1), or how to build and make available an MVP (case 1 and 4).

End-user-related. The third categorization of identified challenges were those related to the end-user. These challenges were specific to the uptake and adoption of a created service. Interestingly, even though the studied cases used agile development methods, which, in theory, emphasize customer orientation and end-user involvement in order to counteract these sort of failures, some still suffered difficulties with respect to the adoption of the service. For example, in case 6, it was noted that one of the biggest challenges was being able to "engage with government departments and to convince them to adopt the service" and that it was "challenging to think of a customer-centric solution, rather than a department-centric solution" [20]. The fact that the studied services were built involving customer feedback throughout and still had issues with adoption raises interesting questions to be investigated in future research.

Technological. The fourth grouping of challenges were those related to technological challenges. In some of the cases, the solution being developed was fairly new, disruptive, or innovative, thus, there was missing knowledge about how to best build or implement certain technologies. This was identified in both cases 2 and 3 as a challenge. In case 2, it was noted that there was a need to "study it [the technology] well in order to grab all the implications, make sure that it was fitting our requirements" [23]. One of the most common issues with technology was related to interoperability. Many of the services were pointed for citizen use, but were built with multi-disciplinary teams across different agencies. In order for such services to be delivered correctly, the technical systems of these agencies needed to be interoperable and integrated. As these systems had different technical specifications—also influenced by the regulatory challenges discussed in the next paragraph—such interoperability took time and effort, thus slowing down service development.

Regulatory. The final categorization of challenges identified in the cases were those related to regulations. Oftentimes, regulations are not in favor or amenable to agile development methods. In many cases, an unsupportive legislative environment was listed as a challenge that needed to be overcome. This obstructive environment could be, for example, issues with procurement (case 6). Agile development implies that projects are changeable and flexible, as the end result is not necessarily known. Yet, governmental processes, especially those related to procurement, rather require clear deliverables and goals as well as a clearly defined end-product; thus, there is a need for regulatory innovation or a change of procurement practices. Other regulatory challenges that needed to be overcome involved cross-agency collaboration and data sharing, or were specific to the domain of the service itself, for example related to GDPR or KYC regulations (see cases 3 and 6 respectively).

5.2 Identified Success Factors

Organizational. Starting with the organizational factors, for example, while lack of organizational capacity or inexperience with cross-agency collaboration was perceived as a challenge in some digital government service development, in the cases where this experience did exist, cross-agency collaboration was highlighted as a success factor. Additionally identified important success factors were the presence of funding, as well as strong organizational and managerial support for the service development. For example, in case 6, it was noted that "the key to this [the service] is getting the upfront investment right, both in terms of strong senior support and enough money to allow the idea and team to move quickly" [20].

Methodological. In regard to methodological success factors, a majority of the cases highlighted that the use of lean and agile development played a strong role in ensuring the success of their service development. One of the clearest examples of this comes from case 1, where a waterfall method was trialed, but failed, and an agile and lean approach was adopted instead [17]. Other success factors highlighted, and directly related to agile development methodologies, were the use of multi-disciplinary teams, focusing on human-centric design, the use of MVPs, and striving for transparency through the entire process. The analyzed cases, as a majority, found that services delivered using such methods were cheaper, more efficient, and more in line with user needs.

End-user-related. For the end-user category, the primary identified success factor was end-user engagement. In every case analyzed this was listed as a key and crucial part of ensuring the service was delivered properly. While some services still faced issues with regard to end-user adoption, by involving end-users throughout the process of the design and development of the service, services were generally believed to better match citizens' needs, and thus lead to higher levels of satisfaction with the service.

Technological. Among the technological success factors, two in particular were identified: open standards and modular development. In case 3, for instance, it was highlighted that "the use of open standards also brings benefits, such as interoperability and data exchange, minimizes the risk of an application to become obsolete, and enables the solution's reuse" [19]. In other words, integrating already existing standards and modules into new technological solutions not only speeds up the development, but also helps to potentially avoid legacy software issues, and further contributes to the development of technological and software ecosystems.

Regulatory. For the final group of success factors, regulatory, there were no clearly identified success factors mentioned in the cases. Regulation was only viewed as a challenge that needed to be overcome when delivering services in an agile manner. This raises the question of why this is the case, and should encourage research into how regulation and legislation must change so as to not hinder innovation or agile development of services, but instead encourage or foster such approaches.

5.3   Discussion

It turns out that there are a number of interesting challenges and success factors that one may encounter when applying agile methods to the development of digital government services. While there is an increasing amount of literature that puts agile development forward as a panacea for governmental digital service development issues, this study clearly shows that the use and implementation of agile development methods brings along its own set of issues and challenges that must be overcome and weighed against its potential benefits. In particular, it became apparent that while agile methods, by virtue of their values and principles, are a promising approach to counteracting failures related to design-reality gaps or missing user satisfaction and focus, challenges related to technological complexity or regulatory and skill issues remain, albeit with a different twist. Based on these results and the identified success factors that appeared to be associated with the use of agile development methods within the specific digital government services studied, it is possible to highlight some initial recommendations:

- If you are building a new digital government service that needs to be delivered quickly, and if it is unclear how it should best look or operate to meet citizen needs, it may be possible to experiment with or use an agile development approach.

- If an agile approach is to be used, it is important that there is strong managerial support, appropriate funding, and motivated team members with the proper experience supporting the service development.
- When working with multidisciplinary and cross-agency teams, it is important to ensure already at the beginning that there is a clear and shared understanding about the development strategy, service goals, and operating procedures.
- If the service is being built in-house, it is of the utmost importance that there is the necessary technological and administrative capacity for service development. If this does not exist, it should be brought in either via hiring staff or drawing on experienced employees from other agencies.
- Expect challenges—agile does not always mean easier, but it certainly does mean different. While providing the opportunity to overcome some common failure sources, in some respects, it may even be harder than traditionally developed services and create new and unfamiliar challenges.
- Talk with the legal team. While lawyers are often thought of being the antithesis of agility, agilely developed services may face regulatory resistance and uncertainty; having legal support to overcome and manage such issues is thus necessary.
- Don't be afraid to be wrong. Agile methods and service development works best when initial MVPs are released and feedback is gathered repetitively over the development duration. The goal is not to end up with exactly what was planned at the beginning, but to deliver a functioning service in line with user expectations and needs.

6   Conclusion

This paper analyzed the potential of agile methods for digital government service development and compiled the respective challenges and success factors. It was possible to map potentially counteractive values and principles of agile development to commonly occurring digital government project failure reasons stated in the literature. As, following this analysis, agile development appeared to offer some opportunities for digital government service development, the next step of the research was to understand and untangle the potential challenges and success factors one may expect when implementing agile within digital government service development. In order to gain such knowledge, the paper utilized a theoretical sampling methodology to select six successful digital government service development projects where agile was utilized to elucidate five commonly occurring themes using a qualitative content analysis approach.

As a result of this research, there are three concrete contributions to the literature made in this paper. First, mapping the agile development principles and values to commonly occurring sources of digital government project failures and shortcomings. This mapping should set the stage for future research that explores empirically whether or not following such principles and values can—in practice—overcome, prevent, or preempt failure when developing governmental digital services. Second, the paper identified five categories of challenges and success factors that one may experience if utilizing agile methods for digital government service development. Therefore, this research is likely to be useful to any organization interested in understanding what to expect if it decides to adopt agile development approaches. Finally, based on the findings, the paper was able to make concrete recommendations for those who may wish to experiment with agile methods for their own digital government service development.

References

1. Alleman, G.B., Henderson, M., Seggelke, R.: Making agile development work in a government contracting environment-Measuring velocity with earned value. In: Proceedings of the Agile Development Conference, 2003. ADC 2003, pp. 114–119 (2003). https://doi.org/10.1109/ADC.2003.1231460
2. Anthopoulos, L., Reddick, C.G., Giannakidou, I., Mavridis, N.: Why e-government projects fail? An analysis of the Healthcare.gov website. Govern. Inf. Q. **33**(1), 161–173 (2016). https://doi.org/10.1016/j.giq.2015.07.003
3. Beck, K., et al.: Manifesto for Agile Software Development (2001). https://agilemanifesto.org. Accessed 19 Mar 2021
4. Cockburn, A., Highsmith, J.: Agile software development: the people factor. Computer **34**(11), 131–133 (2001). https://doi.org/10.1109/2.963450
5. Corbin, J., Strauss, A.: Chapter 7 — Theoretical Sampling. In: Basics of Qualitative Research: Techniques and Procedures for Developing Grounded Theory. SAGE Publications Inc. (2012). https://doi.org/10.4135/9781452230153
6. Dada, D.: The failure of e-government in developing countries: a literature review. Electron. J. Inf. Syst. Develop. Ctries. **26**(1), 1–10 (2006). https://doi.org/10.1002/j.1681-4835.2006.tb00176.x
7. Dingsøyr, T., Nerur, S., Balijepally, V., Moe, N.B.: A decade of agile methodologies: towards explaining agile software development. J. Syst. Softw. **85**(6), 1213–1221 (2012). https://doi.org/10.1016/j.jss.2012.02.033
8. Dwivedi, Y.K., et al.: IS/IT project failures: a review of the extant literature for deriving a taxonomy of failure factors. TDIT 2013. IFIP Advances in Information and Communication Technology, vol. 402, pp. 73–88. Springer, New York (2013). https://doi.org/10.1007/978-3-642-38862-0_5
9. Gichoya, D.: Factors affecting the successful implementation of ICT project in government. Electron. J. E-Govern. (2005). https://doi.org/10.1108/13552519910282601
10. Goldfinch, S.: Pessimism computer, failure, and information systems development in the public sector. Public Adm. Rev. **67**(5), 917–929 (2007). https://doi.org/10.1111/j.1540-6210.2007.00778.x
11. Highsmith, J.: What is agile software development? J. Defense Softw. Eng. **15**(10), 4–9 (2002). https://doi.org/10.1109/2.947100
12. Hsieh, H.F., Shannon, S.E.: Three approaches to qualitative content analysis. Qual. Health Res. **15**(9), 1277–1288 (2005). https://doi.org/10.1177/1049732305276687
13. Kappelman, L.A., McKeeman, R., Zhang, L.: Early warning signs of IT project failure: the dominant dozen. Inf. Syst. Manage. **23**(4), 31–36 (2006). https://doi.org/10.1201/1078.10580530/46352.23.4.20060901/95110.4
14. Loukis, E., Charalabidis, Y.: Why do e-government projects fail? risk factors of large information systems projects in the Greek public sector: an international comparison. Int. J. Electron. Govern. Res. **7**(2), 59–77 (2011)

15. McBride, K., Kupi, M., Bryson, J.: Untangling agile government: on the dual necessities of structure and agility. In: Stephens, M., Awamleh, R., Salem, F. (eds.) Agile Government: Concepts and Practice for Future-Proof Public Administration. World Scientific Publishing, Singapore (2021). https://doi.org/10.31235/osf.io/qwjcx

16. Mergel, I.: Agile innovation management in government: a research agenda. Govern. Inf. Q. **33**(3), 516–523 (2016). https://doi.org/10.1016/j.giq.2016.07.004

17. New Zealand Government: SmartStart Lessons learned from the first cross-agency life event project. Technical report, New Zealand Government (2017). https://www.publicservice.govt.nz/assets/Legacy/resources/smartstart-lessonslearned-v2.pdf. Accessed 19 Mar 2021

18. Nuottila, J., Aaltonen, K., Kujala, J.: Challenges of adopting agile methods in a public organization. Int. J. Inf. Syst. Project Manage. **4**(3), 65–85 (2016). https://doi.org/10.12821/ijispm040304

19. OPSI: Digital Mobile Key (2014). https://oecd-opsi.org/innovations/digital-mobile-key/. Accessed 19 Mar 2021

20. OPSI: GOV.UK Verify - the digital identity platform for the UK public sector (2016). https://oecd-opsi.org/innovations/gov-uk-verify-the-digital-identity-platform-for-the-uk-public-sector/. Accessed 19 Mar 2021

21. OPSI: MyService (2016). https://oecd-opsi.org/innovations/myservice/. Accessed 19 Mar 2021

22. OPSI: SmartStart (2016). https://oecd-opsi.org/innovations/smartstart/. Accessed 19 Mar 2021

23. OPSI: Blockchain of Frequencies (2018). https://oecd-opsi.org/innovations/blockchain-of-frequencies/. Accessed 19 Mar 2021

24. OPSI: GOV.UK step-by-step navigation (2018). https://oecd-opsi.org/innovations/gov-uk-step-by-step-navigation/. Accessed 19 Mar 2021

25. Paulin, A.: Twenty years after the hype: is e-Government doomed? Findings from Slovenia. Int. J. Publ. Adm. Digital Age **2**(2), 1–21 (2015). https://doi.org/10.4018/ijpada.2015040101

26. Pinto, J.K., Mantel, S.J.: The causes of project failure. IEEE Trans. Eng. Manage. **37**(4), 269–276 (1990). https://doi.org/10.1109/17.62322

27. Rigby, D., Sutherland, J., Takeuchi, H.: The secret history of agile innovation (2016). https://hbr.org/2016/04/the-secret-history-of-agile-innovation. Accessed 19 Mar 2021

28. Strauss, A., Corbin, J.M.: Basics of Qualitative Research: Grounded Theory Procedures and Techniques. SAGE Publications Inc., Thousand Oaks (1990)

29. Thomas, D.R.: A general inductive approach for analyzing qualitative evaluation data. Am. J. Eval. **27**(2), 237–246 (2006). https://doi.org/10.1177/1098214005283748

30. Upender, B.: Staying agile in government software projects. Proc. AGILE Conf. **2005**(2005), 153–159 (2005). https://doi.org/10.1109/ADC.2005.41

31. Urquhart, C., Lehmann, H., Myers, M.D.: Putting the 'theory' back into grounded theory: guidelines for grounded theory studies in information systems. Inf. Syst. J. **20**(4), 357–381 (2009). https://doi.org/10.1111/j.1365-2575.2009.00328.x

32. Vacari, I., Prikladnicki, R.: Adopting agile methods in the public sector: a systematic literature review. In: Proceedings of the International Conference on Software Engineering and Knowledge Engineering, SEKE 2015, pp. 709–714 (2015)

Data-Driven Personalized E-Government Services: Literature Review and Case Study

Mariia Maksimova$^{(\boxtimes)}$, Mihkel Solvak , and Robert Krimmer

Johan Skytte Institute of Political Studies, University of Tartu,
Ülikooli 18, 51003 Tartu, Estonia
{mariia.maksimova,mihkel.solvak,robert.krimmer}@ut.ee

Abstract. Better targeted and more personalized service offering to citizens has the potential to make state-citizen interactions more seamless, reduce inefficiencies in service provision, and lower barriers to service access for the less informed and disadvantaged social groups. What constitutes personalization and how the service offering can be customized to meet individual user demand is, however, much less clear and underdeveloped partially due to the technical and legal dependencies involved. The paper gives an overview of how personalization and customization of digital service offering have been discussed in the literature and systematizes the main strand emerging from this. It follows up with a case study of the Estonian X-road log data as one potential way to detect latent user demand emerging from an experienced life-event that could form a basis for letting users define their service needs as holistically as possible. The results show the existence of distinct service usage clusters, with specific user profiles behind them, a clear indication of latent demand that leads to a simultaneous consumption of otherwise independent digital services.

Keywords: Life event e-service · Personalized digital service · e-Service logs

1 Introduction

Improving the quality and accessibility of public services is a priority for governments regardless of their digital development level. The introduction of electronic government portals has become a widespread means of doing this. However, the interaction between the citizen and the state in such a digital gateway remains one-sided. The provision of services still has a one-fits-all approach and the state, as a service provider, does not analyze the individual needs of citizens. Personalization of service offering where user demand and supply matched by advanced

The work for this paper has received funding from European Union's Horizon 2020 research and innovation programme under grant agreement No.s 857622 and 959072.

© IFIP International Federation for Information Processing 2021
Published by Springer Nature Switzerland AG 2021
N. Edelmann et al. (Eds.): ePart 2021, LNCS 12849, pp. 151–165, 2021.
https://doi.org/10.1007/978-3-030-82824-0_12

data analytics and AI approaches have the potential to make state-citizen interactions seamless on an entirely new level [29]. At least, this is the hoped potential
of applications utilizing recent advantages in machine learning and AI. In most
cases, the reality is still a situation where the citizen needs to actively seek out
the service from the relevant authority instead of being offered proactively based
on individual needs. Often, a service needs to be pulled by the citizen instead of
being pushed by the state, and seamless interactions still a faraway dream.

The technological advances in machine learning and AI are, however, can
improve service delivery only when they are embedded in a service delivery design
that allows for personalization to happen in the first place, i.e., capture data that
is indicative of demand. It can be used to offer a tailor-made service response
that overcomes legal and organizational boundaries set by a state organization
that is hierarchical and horizontally organized in domains that don't cooperate
nor share data. Such a situation is still very much a rarity, but this is starting
to change slowly. The ongoing pandemic might paradoxically be a force that
expedites movement towards more personalized service delivery in Europe.

The European Recovery and Resilience Facility (RFF), established in 2021
to overcome the damage brought about by the coronavirus pandemic, prescribes
that the each recovery and resilience plan by member states has to spend a
minimal of 20% to "foster digital transformation"[1], these are substantial funds
that some digitally more advanced countries are planning to use to do exactly
that, develop new service delivery ways that are much closer to citizen demand
understood holistically, the Estonian government foresees that up to a total of
5–6% of the full RRF fund for Estonia to be spent on life-event and pro-active
service delivery development.

Focusing on citizen needs is increasingly supported both in the research literature and in government development strategies. It is believed to be an important element in the process of public administration transition towards a new
interaction model between the state and society. An individual approach to each
citizen, as a consumer, will allow analyzing the needs, interests, and rights of a
citizen to receive a particular service and create a more convenient and up-to-
date list of services. Thus, the state policy is formed from a more active position
as a supplier of services, moving towards the model of service state. The case of
Estonia supports this statement by introducing a way to see if and how latent
user demand could be detected based on the X-road log data. It opens up an
opportunity for more personalization and letting users define their service needs
as holistically as possible.

2   Methodology

For this paper, two methodological approaches were selected. First, to explore
the relevant approaches in personalized, data-driven, and life-event strategies
for electronic state portal design, a systematic literature review (SLR) was performed, which consists of consecutive steps, according to which all publications

---

[1] Recovery and Resilience Facility https://ec.europa.eu/info/business-economy-euro/
recovery-coronavirus/recovery-and-resilience-facility_en.

containing the results of the studies on the phenomenon in interest are collected, followed by an assessment of their quality and the synthesis of the results. The steps are as follows: (1) planning and formulating the research question; (2) localization and searching the literature; (3) data gathering and quality evaluation; (4) data extraction and data analysis; and (5) interpretation and presenting results [5,25]. This research method helps to analyze existing studies and creates a foundation to conclude what is already known and what is unknown [24]. Using it in this study helps to identify current trends in the research literature and highlight their shortcomings.

The selected sources for the search were Scopus, Web of Science, and Google Scholar databases. The relevant articles were searched using the combination of chosen terms as most commonly used in articles on the topic of more data-driven citizen-oriented design of electronic service provision: "data driven", "life-event", "proactive", "personalized", "public administration", "e-government", "electronic service", "e-service", and "portals" as titles and keywords. There were no limitations concerning the year of the publication. In total, 864 articles were identified; however, after duplicates were deleted and the second round of screening based on the title, 103 publications remained. The third round included the paper's abstract analysis, after which 33 papers were selected. Further examination of each article took place upon retrieving the full text, after which an additional ten articles were excluded, as they did not fit the inclusion criteria: 1) the subject of study – approaches for more personalized services provision via electronic state portals; 2) the language of the paper – English; 3) type of the paper - journals papers, international conferences and book chapters; 4) the paper is not a summarizing paper of the previous research by the same author. The final sample of articles consists of 23 studies. The studies' date of publication ranged from 2002 to 2020.

Second, the paper conducts a case study based on log file data from the Estonian x-road data exchange layer. The hierarchical cluster analysis using Ward's linkage for individual unique service usage was carried out on a random sample of 100 000 individuals. Estonia was chosen as a critical case [27], as it is one of the few countries (if not the only one) where such a large number of base registries is connected in one eco-system, whose logfiles and thus exchanges between databases can be analyzed. Limitations include, but are not limited to, the lack of comparative data and a possible bias due to researchers' location in Estonia. Due to the uniqueness of the case, these shortcomings need to be in future research.

3   Literature Review

3.1   Conceptual Foundations

Before turning to the literature analysis, it is necessary to dwell in more detail on the conceptual foundations of this study. There are quite a few theoretical approaches to personalization. In a broad sense, personalization is understood as the process of selecting suitable electronic services for a citizen on any criteria related to the citizen at a given time. It can affect different sets of the government web portal functionality e.g., prefiltered search results, tailored recommendations, banners to match a person's interests, or links to other related to the topic of interest sites [11]. It is one of the most promising solutions that can be implemented in state electronic portals due to its' ability to establish a dialogue between citizens and the state. Sometimes personalization and customization are used interchangeably [6] or customization considered to be a part of personalized electronic service [7].

One of the most common personalization methods is a recommendation system whose task is to provide recommendations by automatic filtering of unnecessary services. In most solutions, ontology-based semantic reasoning is used for the data organization and management of information. Accurate data description, qualitative classification, knowledge management, and defined relationships between data entities create a system where information is ontologically grouped, making it much easier to process, sort, and present it [3,6,12,16,21,26]. Personal recommendations are divided into 'auto' and 'on-demand'. On-demand recommendations are performed at the user's request, such as searching for a specific service on a website. Auto recommendations are carried out by processing personal information and preferences linked to the user's profile and presenting information or changing site interface based on it [3,28].

The user profile on the state portal can be used for personalization in several ways. From all the variety, the main ones can be distinguished: content-based, CF-based, knowledge-based, and a hybrid approach [3,6]. A content-based is using historical information about the user's interaction with the site. The profile is compared with the content of the services in which the user was previously interested. Within this framework, various weighted schemes compile indices based on different indicators that help rank services for a specific user. A CF-based compares an array of users to find similar profiles and recommends services based on the preferences of the user's group. In this way, the user submits their rating or uses the service. After that, the system algorithm compares users and groups them based on the similarity of patterns. Recommendations are provided based on which services were liked or used by the group to which the user belongs. A knowledge-based approach is using a knowledge base with predefined possible interests as a reference model for content filtering. It is based on a system that contains a knowledge base with a set of specific solutions and algorithms, on the basis of which recommendations are given. A hybrid is a mixture of the listed above approaches in different configurations.

Another way to provide citizens with more personalized services and simplify access to them is the life-event approach. The life-event based state portals use a model that groups services by the most critical events in a person's life. The assumption behind this is that most users don't know what kind of service they need but assume the end result [23]. This grouping often implies a hierarchical system of services [6] connected by the fact that they are used to solve any question that arises at a particular period of life. There are different ways to define the life-event, however, it is possible to trace their similarity to the life stages of a person. This division of a person's life into stages helps separate services using the same logic and sequence of events. Using life events to categorize services allows the user to navigate the electronic portal better, as this division is intuitive.

3.2 Literature Analysis

Studying a personalized approach to serving citizens in the public sector goes in different directions, both as a purely technical solution and as something that requires more conceptualization and understanding of this process. The analysis of selected studies allows us to identify four main directions in the study of the personalization of state portals: (1) developing of models and frameworks for electronic portals personalization; (2) implementation of different techniques for better personalization of government electronic portals; (3) modelling of web portal/model/framework from end-user perspective; (4) discussion about existing cases of government electronic portals personalization.

As part of the first research direction, the study of personalization in state electronic portals is carried out based on prototypes or reference models. This category includes attempts by several researchers to conceptualize the life event and propose how it can be integrated into government systems. The main focus is on the categorization of life-even services and producing working prototypes of active web portals [16,19,22,23] and the construction of multi-level systems that take the selected categories as a basis [13]. Researchers use different classification criteria but similarly note the diversity of personalization models and the prospects for implementing them in government electronic systems. Another characteristic of this category is that the concepts of "life-event" and "user-centric personalization" presented in these works do not have explanatory power but are more fragmented and descriptive.

The second group of researchers considers personalization in the context of its implementation in electronic portals. It suggests the possibility of a better application of it by complementing various technologies and data analysis methods. One of the proposed solutions is ontology-based semantic reasoning for the data organization and management of information. Accurate data description, qualitative classification, knowledge management, and defined relationships between data entities create a system where information is grouped ontologically, making it much easier to process, sort, and present it [3,6,12,26]. Another approach is focusing on the different data mining techniques like web mining [11], association rules mining [20], mining with the use of time-decayed Bayesian algorithm [10] and algorithm for computing an item-based CF similarity [26] used to improve recommendation accuracy and coverage. This also includes works that pay more attention to the use of various user data obtained from profiles on the service [2,4,28] or from social media [1] to understand the needs of users better.

The third direction of research on personalization focuses on modeling the architecture of proactive electronic portals, taking into account the process participants' point of view on what obtaining an electronic service should look like. For a better understanding of the processes, it is proposed to get insights from civil servants and experts [15] as well as end-user [8,14,21] to create a methodology for proactive service design. These studies are also based on the analysis of existing services, taking them into account to improve the proposed methodology. The fourth group also focuses on the analysis of implemented personalization cases. Thus, D. Linders et al. (2018) look at Taiwan's approach to proactive actions based on sending notifications to citizens based on data on the due dates for fines, fees, and taxes [9]. In turn, V. Homburg & A. Dijkshoorn (2013) consider the factors influencing the adoption and diffusion of personalized e-government services in Dutch municipalities and develop a set of recommendations for future adoption [7].

The proposed solutions are creating top-down approaches since pre-designed structural elements are used. This kind of design leads to limited personalization, as matches can mostly occur across large categories. In case if some service is not included in the logic of a predefined system, then it is likely that the search for this service will be difficult. In addition, existing research is primarily theoretical and does not use real data, which can significantly increase its applicability of proposed solutions. Thus, despite a significant amount of academic research, there is still no single approach to the personalization of government electronic portals, making it necessary to search for new frameworks and models that integrate real empirical data.

3.3   Dynamic Bundling of Services to Meet Demand

The discussion above shows that all possible approaches taken to align user needs better with the service offering and provide a seamless service consumption experience depend on distilling user needs in the first place and not simply concerning one service, but the total universe of possible services from the user perspective. In essence - the citizens need the service bundle that addresses the particular needs arising out of the experienced events. This leads to holistic service demand where the adequate supply depends on multiple organizational, legal, and technical dependencies. Overcoming these involves substantial legislative, administrative and organizational challenges. One needs to bear in mind that state portals tend to be service gateways and actual service owners are usually separate institutions. Though forming one single digital gateway, they do not include the whole digital service universe and hence also don't allow to take the personalization very far since they have limited user information, service selection, and in most cases, no access to secondary data sources to be able to complement the limited information to truly personalize user experience after authentication.

It is safe to say that proof-of-concept (POC) types of studies and trials are needed before any administrative or organizational changes to address user demand holistically are possible. But these studies are faced with difficulties, as such POCs depend on the availability of service consumption data on individuals that still spans domains, institutions, and time, i.e., combined datasets that capture the full service demand from the client point of view regardless of the service owner. As a rule such combined datasets do not exist or cannot even be created due to data privacy reasons. Next we explore one possible workaround for solving this problem by using service call logs from a data exchange layer to determine the latent service demand structures.

4   User Defined Service Demand

4.1   Client Data Source

Short of a single super database on everything citizens do, some state information system organizational methods might allow for a potential workaround for this problem, albeit limited in nature. The possible solution stems from the need to exchange data and the subsequent interoperability inherent in providing (most) digital services. In the Estonian case, such interoperability is ensured through a centrally managed distributed data exchange layer called X-road, which allows public and private institutions to exchange data for offering various public and private digital services. As of 2021, roughly 2900 different digital services are offered over the X-road (https://www.x-tee.ee/factsheets/EE/#eng), which generate approximately 100 million service request queries a month. The cumulative service call queries stand at 7.6 billion since the inception of X-road in 2002. Though a majority of these involve machine-machine interactions, close to 3%, i.e., 3 million are human-initiated service call queries which are logged centrally by X-road Center in the central log for compliance monitoring (see Fig. 1). The actual data exchange happens between the parties, and no one outside of this has access to the data, but the identities of the parties, which mostly make up base registries and service portals, are stored centrally. Therefore, the central log stores limited information on service consumption, such as who issued when a service request to what service producer and when was that answered for traffic monitoring and compliance purposes. The byproduct of this central log is a single, albeit limited dataset that includes all service call requests by citizens. This entails a substantial share of total citizen interactions with the state.

Estonia is offering most state services also or only digitally, but they are still owned by separate institutions resulting in a fractured service delivery landscape from the client point of view. Citizens still need to: a) have a clear understanding of which services are designed for their specific needs; b) whether they are eligible for these; c) seek the service out and; d) actively pull it by requesting the service through various service portals or the central digital gateway www.eesti.ee. This state of affairs is due to different state service providers not offering services in a conjoined way even though they might be sharing data with other service providers in the back-end over X-road. Such service offering design does not reflect how the citizens' needs arise.

In reality, a life event, for example having a child, leads to a bundle of service needs – child health care needs, parental benefits registration, tax exemptions on certain benefits, and other in kind and monetary benefits requests. The state observes these as single service consumption instances consumed by the individual – the latent demand for which is determined by some life event of the citizen. While we can reasonably deduct what basic needs arise from specific life events, everything outside of this theoretical cluster is by definition excluded

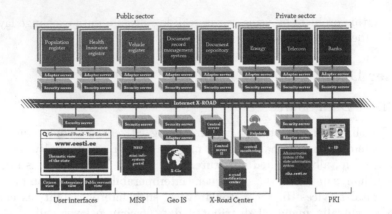

Fig. 1. Schematic picture of X-road (Reprinted from: [18])

even though additional services might be consumed in close temporal space or a particular order and be related through the latent unobserved demand triggered by the life-event. This leads to the unnecessary need to pull different services from different institutions while they could be proactively offered based on the currently unobserved latent event leading to service demand.

Rather than redesign the administrative structure of state service provision, we propose to study and pilot the applicability of service call query clustering to identify if certain service needs cluster together temporally or follow a specific temporal sequence. We also look for lead events that can seem to be triggering more service consumption events. By identifying actual service consumption bundles from the service consumption logs, we pinpoint single domains and domain crossing areas in which service consolidation could bring the most significant value for both the client and the service provider. Value for the citizen would be a reduced need to pull services, reducing informational inequalities on knowledge of and eligibility for services, and more seamless interactions with various service-providing state organizations. Value for the service provider would be to reduce customer support need and channel more clients directly to service provision gateways/portals.

4.2 Service Consumption Patterns

Logged Information. Table 1 shows how a service call query looks like by example of the query 5875968103, the data is available as open data at https:// logs.x-tee.ee/EE/gui/, this particular one is a service request made on the 16th January 2021 by the East Tallinn Central Hospital (client) for a digital health record made to the Health and Welfare Information Systems Center (service provider logged as a member in the log) which maintains this particular service under the auspice of the Ministry for Social Affairs. When an individual makes the service request, the client ID is anonymized in the open data, but a pseudonymized version of the logs has been made available to us for academic research. The individual only shows in the logs if he or she has accessed the service personally through authenticating before requesting the service, if a medical health record of a patient was accessed by a doctor in a hospital or private practice through a mini-information system portal (MISP) then this is recorded a service request by the owner of this particular MISP. As told above, the actual data exchange happens between the two parties to the exchange, and only the metadata of the request is logged by the X-road Center.

The fields of interest for us are marked in the table and are client ID, timestamp, and the service type based on which we can connect individual logs and see which services are consumed either temporally close together or in specific temporal sequences empirically without any theoretical priors to what should go together theoretically.

Table 1. Example of a X-road log from central log (not all fields shown)

```
{
    "id":                        5875968103,
    "clientMemberClass":         "COM",
    "clientMemberCode":          10822068,
    "clientSubsystemCode":       "ehealth",
    "clientXRoadInstance":       "EE",
    "messageProtocolVersion":    4,
    "requestAttachmentCount":    0,
    "requestInDate":             16.02.2021,
    "requestInTs":               1613509200000,
    "requestMimeSize":           "None",
    "requestSoapSize":           4348,
    "responseMimeSize":          "None",
    "responseSoapSize":          23578,
    "securityServerType":        "Client",
    "serviceCode":               "hl7",
    "serviceMemberClass":        "GOV",
    "serviceMemberCode":         70009770,
    "serviceSubsystemCode":      "digilugu",
    "serviceXRoadInstance":      "EE",
    "succeeded":                 "TRUE",
    "totalDuration":             1122
},
```

Service Usage Groups. A prior look at the service usage depth and duration showed two wider user groups emerging [17]. People who use a large number of services on a large number of days over the duration of a year and user with a small amount of service consumed over a few days a year. Solvak et al.

[17] speculate that the former group is mainly civil servants for whom some of the work is organized around digital services. However, the latter is most likely regular citizens who need to pull such services to interact with the state and solve everyday issues related to the service.

We examine the potential latent demand structure based on log data from 2003 to 2015, i.e., the first 13 years since the establishment of the X-road system. Figure 2 shows the average annual service call queries (on a logarithmic scale) and the average number of unique services consumed. The query heatmap (Fig. 2a) indicates that the most active user groups are 20–29 and 30–39 year olds[2].

The average number of unique services by age groups (Fig. 2b) shows a roughly similar picture indicating that not only is this group using services more intensely as indicated by the query number, but they also have a wider selection of services which they use. Therefore, there is variance in service usage depth and number. Moreover, it is non-randomly distributed across age groups, which already indicates that demand differs substantially and could be driven by life events.

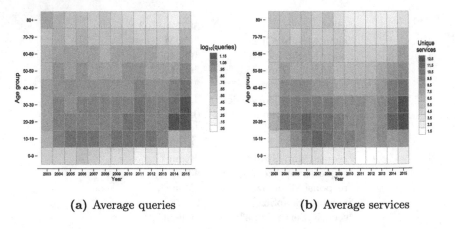

(a) Average queries   (b) Average services

Fig. 2. Annual averages of service call queries and unique services used by age group

Clusters of Service Usage Time-Series. We further selected a random sample of 100 000 individuals out of the total dataset and performed a hierarchical cluster analysis using Ward's linkage for individual unique service usage time-series' by the year the individuals first appeared in the logs. Figure 3 shows the four biggest and most distinct clusters that emerged out of this exercise for each year of first appearance in the logs. We computed four independent clusters for the usage time series that started in the given year.

---

[2] Minors show in the graph when parents are using some services - mainly health record-related - as legal custodians in their name.

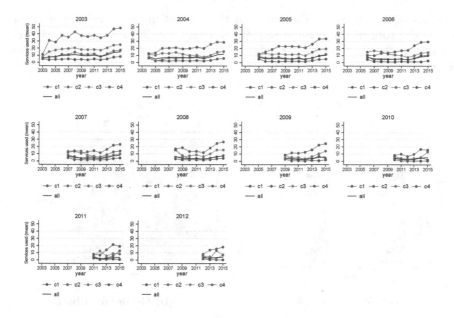

Fig. 3. Clusters in individual service usage time-series, calculated according to the time series that starts in the given year.

Particularly interesting are the third and fourth clusters, where the service usage rate is initially the same for both, but it starts to grow continually in the fourth, whereas it starts to fall or stagnates in the third cluster. Interestingly this pattern repeats itself across the years in varying degrees. While the time series clustering does not tell us anything about the real content of the latent service demand, it nevertheless indicates clear, structured differences in usage intensity and service numbers. Given the relatively large number of unique services consumed per year in the fourth cluster (between 20 to 50 depending on the starting year) there seems to be room for consolidating service offering if these numbers are driven by some shared life-event driven latent demand.

This potential is further strengthened when one peeks into what kind of individuals cluster in the given groups. This is done in Fig. 4, which shows substantial differences in the age and gender structure. The third and fourth clusters have an age distribution peak at 20–30 years and have a significantly higher share of women. While the first cluster is biggest in terms of individuals, it has a relatively flat age distribution, combining this with the low service usage number in the cluster, we can conclude that this includes widely different individual needs across age groups with most likely very heterogeneous service demand menu.

The preliminary empirical investigation therefore points already towards promising results as we have demonstrated that usage patterns take different paths over time, with some of them - characterized by heavy demand for a wide variety of services - being taken by a quite narrow age group with an above average share of female users. The fact that the highest intense service user groups include disproportionally more women in active childbearing age (20–30 year old) points clearly towards some latent demand structure, possibly life-event driven.

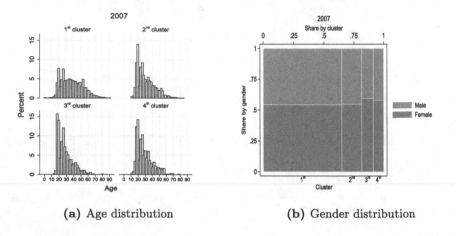

(a) Age distribution   (b) Gender distribution

Fig. 4. Age and gender distributions in four clusters of individuals who appeared in logs in 2007 for first time

5   Discussion and Conclusion

The literature review showed that the personalization of digital service offerings is not uniformly understood nor defined. There is a lack of understanding of how user demand can be correctly captured and integrated into the service delivery channel design and structure. Possible workarounds through getting additional data from outside the knowledge domain of the service owners - such as using social media data - are not viable strategies and place a heavy additional data collection and managing burden, let alone possibly infringing on user privacy. A content-based approach proposes to examine the user's prior interaction with a given site, focusing only on a small selection of services and will not be viable in a situation where the user demands are dynamic and time-dependent.

The alternative has been a knowledge-based approach where personalization patterns are fixed based on a theoretical understanding of what users want and what needs seem to go together. The live-event based approach is one of such approaches. However, here further limitations enter, as a life-event is by defini-tion a major structuring force in the individual's life which does trigger a large cluster of potential needs hard to comprehend from the service owners point of view or even impossible to detect due to the legal and organizational barriers stopping effective data merging that might show co-consumption of widely dif-ferent services by the same client. State portals tend not to include such wide selection, and hence the data captured through usage sessions on the portal is, as a rule, not sufficient to cover all the needs that arise, as these cross many domains and are very likely leading to a sophisticated drawn out need for state support.

We propose a fully bottom-up life event definition that is purely empirical and hence also user-defined - something that combines all aspects of the personalization strategies outline in the literature - user data, data from widely different domains, major structuring events, and a dynamic sequence of combinations of service being consumed. Taking a client-centric view of a life event - something that is big and triggers a myriad of service needs only the individual can comprehend - comes with the major challenge of properly identifying the latent needs arising from it. The latent needs are by definition not observable, but the latent demand leads to observable service consumption clusters if we find ways of joining data from different service owners as it is easier to move data than it is to move institutions or people. We use limited technical service call logs of a data exchange layer for a distributed state information system to switch the view from 2000 separate service owners to one individual that has a need that can be addressed with a specific collection of some of these 2000 services.

The results show that usage is clustered, and some clusters exemplify patterns that indicate a life-vent driven demand - high service usage intensity with multiple unique services being consumed by a narrow age group. Though potentially heterogeneous in content, the service consumption bundles are not overly large when one counts the consumption events and the usage intensity. A further examination of the actual service content of such clusters plus additional clustering definitions on updated data is ongoing. This will show what type of latent demand - defined by the combination of specific services in a service shopping basket - describes what groups.

We consider this latent demand detection one fundamental building block of fully personalized service menus that are dynamic over time and adjusted underlining population dynamics change. Though the full integration of the services in the identified bundles is still a major obstacle, we can demonstrate that the demand can be empirically detected and the content exposed, which paves the way for possible integration solutions.

References

1. Abdellatif, A., Ben Amor, N., Mellouli, S.: An intelligent framework for e-government personalized services. In: Proceedings of the 14th Annual International Conference on Digital Government Research, pp. 120–126 (2013)
2. Abdrabbah, S.B., Ayachi, R., Amor, N.B.: A dynamic community-based personalization for e-government services. In: Proceedings of the 9th International Conference on Theory and Practice of Electronic Governance, pp. 258–265 (2016)
3. Al-Hassan, M., Lu, H., Lu, J.: A framework for delivering personalized e-government services from a citizen-centric approach. In: Proceedings of the 11th International Conference on Information Integration and Web-based Applications & Services, pp. 436–440 (2009)

4. Alsoud, A., Nakata, K.: A conceptual life event framework for government-to-citizen electronic services provision (2011)
5. Cooper, H.M.: Synthesizing Research: A Guide For Literature Reviews, 2nd edn. Sage, Thousand oaks (1998)
6. Guo, X., Lu, J.: Intelligent e-government services with personalized recommendation techniques. Int. J. Intell. Syst. **22**(5), 401–417 (2007)
7. Homburg, V.M., Dijkshoorn, A.: Diffusion of personalized e-government services among Dutch municipalities: an empirical investigation and explanation. Int. J. Electron. Govern. Res. (IJEGR) **7**(3), 21–37 (2011)
8. Kõrge, H., Erlenheim, R., Draheim, D.: Designing proactive business event services. In: Panagiotopoulos, P., et al. (eds.) ePart 2019. LNCS, vol. 11686, pp. 73–84. Springer, Cham (2019). https://doi.org/10.1007/978-3-030-27397-2_7
9. Linders, D., Liao, C.Z.P., Wang, C.M.: Proactive e-governance: flipping the service delivery model from pull to push in Taiwan. Govern. Inf. Q. **35**(4), S68–S76 (2018)
10. Liu, B., Chen, T., Jia, P., Wang, L.: Effective public service delivery supported by time-decayed Bayesian personalized ranking. Knowl. Based Syst. **206**, 106376 (2020)
11. Markellos, K., Markellou, P., Panayiotaki, A., Tsakalidis, A.: Semantic web mining for personalized public services. In: Global E-Government: Theory, Applications and Benchmarking, pp. 1–20. IGI Global (2007)
12. Sanati, F., Lu, J.: Multilevel life-event abstraction framework for e-government service integration. In: Proceedings of the European Conference on e-Government, ECEG (2009)
13. Sanati, F., Lu, J.: Life-event modelling framework for e-government integration. Electron. Govern. Int. J. **7**(2), 183–202 (2010)
14. Sirendi, R.: Designing proactive public services as sociotechnical systems by using agent-oriented modelling. In: Decman, M., Jukic, T. (Eds.), Proceedings of the 16th European Conference on e-Government (ECEG), Ljubljana, Slovenia, 16–17 June, pp. 308–316 (2016)
15. Sirendi, R., Taveter, K.: Bringing service design thinking into the public sector to create proactive and user-friendly public services. In: Nah, F.H., Tan, C.H. (eds.) HCIBGO 2016. LNCS, vol. 9752, pp. 221–230. Springer, Cham (2016). https://doi.org/10.1007/978-3-319-39399-5_21
16. Skokan, M., Sabol, T., Mach, M., Furdik, K.: Integration of governmental services in semantically described processes in the access-eGov system. In: 2008 International Multiconference on Computer Science and Information Technology, pp. 415–419. IEEE (2008)
17. Solvak, M., Unt, T., Rozgonjuk, D., Võrk, A., Veskimäe, M., Vassil, K.: E-governance diffusion: population level e-service adoption rates and usage patterns. Telemat. Informat. **36**, 39–54 (2019)
18. Solvak, M., Vassil, K.: E-voting in estonia: Technological diffusion and other developments over ten years (2005–2015) (2016)
19. Tambouris, E., Tarabanis, K.: A dialogue-based, life-event oriented, active portal for online one-stop government: the onestopgov platform. In: Proceedings of the 2008 International Conference on Digital Government Research, pp. 405–406 (2008)
20. Tang, H., Zhang, P., Song, S., Yan, H.: Using association rules mining to provide personalized information in e-government. In: 2011 International Conference on E-Business and E-Government (ICEE), pp. 1–4. IEEE (2011)
21. Tawfik, H., Anya, O.: Towards lifestyle-oriented and personalised e-services for elderly care. In: 2013 Sixth International Conference on Developments in eSystems Engineering, pp. 357–360. IEEE (2013)

22. Todorovski, L., Kunstelj, M., Vintar, M.: Reference models for e-services integration based on life-events. In: Wimmer, M.A., Scholl, J., Grönlund, A. (eds.) EGOV 2007. LNCS, vol. 4656, pp. 92–103. Springer, Berlin, Heidelberg (2007). https://doi.org/10.1007/978-3-540-74444-3_9
23. Vintar, M., Leben, A.: The concepts of an active life-event public portal. In: Traunmüller, R., Lenk, K. (eds.) EGOV 2002. LNCS, pp. 383–390. Springer, Berlin, Heidelberg (2002). https://doi.org/10.1007/978-3-540-46138-8_62
24. Webster, J., Watson, R.T.: Analyzing the past to prepare for the future: writing a literature review. MIS Q. **26**, xiii–xxiii (2002)
25. Whittemore, R., Knafl, K.: The integrative review: updated methodology. J. Adv. Nursing **52**(5), 546–553 (2005)
26. Xu, C., Xu, L., Lu, Y., Xu, H., Zhu, Z.: E-government recommendation algorithm based on probabilistic semantic cluster analysis in combination of improved collaborative filtering in big-data environment of government affairs. Pers. Ubiquit. Comput. **23**, 475–485 (2019). https://doi.org/10.1007/s00779-019-01228-x
27. Yin, R.K.: Case Study Research and Applications: Design and Methods. Sage Publications, Thousand Oaks (2017)
28. Zaoui, I., Elmaghraoui, H., Chiadmi, D., Benhlima, L.: Towards a personalized e-government platform. Int. J. Comput. Sci. Theory App. **2**(2), 35–40 (2014)
29. Zuiderwijk, A., Chen, Y.C., Salem, F.: Implications of the use of artificial intelligence in public governance: a systematic literature review and a research agenda. Govern. Inf. Q. **38**, 101577 (2021)

Legal Issues

Application of Process Modelling and Simulation to Evaluate Administrative Burdens at the Law-Making Stage

Szymon Mamrot$^{(\boxtimes)}$ (iD)

Lukasiewicz Research Network - Institute of Logistics and Warehousing, ul. Estkowskiego 6, 61-755 Poznań, Poland
szymon.mamrot@ilim.lukasiewicz.gov.pl

Abstract. The number of the legal regulations is increasing, which implies additional administrative burdens for entrepreneurs. Evaluation of the legal acts efficiency in terms of administrative burdens, is usually conducted after the adoption of provisions. Improvement of existing legislation is a difficult and time-consuming task. Therefore, the aim of conducted research was to develop a method permitting the assessment of administrative burdens in the course of law-making. We propose to apply techniques of business process modelling and reengineering to improve quality of law during law-making. The main contribution of the article is a method based on application of Business Process Model and Notation (BPMN) to design processes introduced by the legal acts. The presented method, due to application of modeling and simulation analysis, permits to precisely assess administrative burdens following from the regulations. The method enables to compare different variants of a legal regulation planned to be established. The presented method was practically applied to the process of registration of a civil law partnership in Poland. It was proved within the conducted research that the process redesigning permits to cut significantly the costs and duration of process both for entrepreneurs and public administration. Due to application of the proposed method the precise data was received, which enabled to compare the costs of burdens in the different variants of the regulations implementation. This case empirically confirmed that application of our method could enhance the quality of public processes regulated by legislation.

Keywords: Law-making process · Legislation · Business process reengineering · Business process simulation · BPMN · Administrative burdens

1 Introduction

A legal system is efficient, when it does not squander away the limited resources allocated to it. Evaluation of how the limited resources are applied is the domain of economics encompassing the study of efficiency. Efficiency criteria in economics allow assessing whether a specific allocation of resources is proper. In the opinion of some representatives of the economic analysis of law, e.g. Posner [9], application of efficiency criteria

© IFIP International Federation for Information Processing 2021
Published by Springer Nature Switzerland AG 2021
N. Edelmann et al. (Eds.): ePart 2021, LNCS 12849, pp. 169–179, 2021.
https://doi.org/10.1007/978-3-030-82824-0_13

permits to shape the law to fulfil its fundamental purposes without wasting the limited resources. One of the purposes of the system of law is to remove inefficiencies of the market mechanism through deployment of regulations governing business activity. Regulations of the economic law generate additional costs for businesses that have to observe those regulations. This paper focuses on one of the costs of such regulations, namely, administrative burdens. Administrative burdens constitute a serious barrier in the development of enterprises in the EU. According to the data published by the European Commission [5], annual administrative burdens in the EU account for 3.5% of the EU's GDP. Of that, 60% include administrative burdens resulting from domestic legislation and 40% from the EU legislation. This paper presents a method of accurate evaluation of administrative burdens at the law-making stage. Due to the application of process modelling and simulation, it is possible to compare different variants of a legal regulation planned to be established. The presented method permits the legislators to make a decision based on measurable cost of administrative burdens to be incurred by enterprises.

The paper is organized as follows. Sect. 2 discusses the efficiency criteria and shows how they can be applied to evaluate the costs of administrative burdens. Section 3 presents the method used to assess the costs of administrative burdens based on business process modelling and simulation. Section 4 shows how the presented method has been applied in practice to analyze the process of registration of a civil law partnership. Section 5 concludes the paper and shows the areas for future research.

2   Efficiency Criteria in the Economic Analysis of Law and Their Application to Evaluation of the Costs of Administrative Burdens

The goal of the economic analysis of law is improvement of law efficiency. Economically efficient law increases social well-being. A legal system will support social well-being if it identifies and eliminates the defects of the market mechanism and removes any signs of inefficiency in the area of non-market behavior. Legal solutions that take into consideration the achievements of the rational choice theory should create adequate stimuli to influence economic calculus of legal entities, thus discouraging them from behaviors that affect efficiency, and to promote behaviors supporting effective allocation of resources [4]. The changes introduced in the legislative process should take into account the economic calculus, i.e., a balance of benefits and costs following from a specific legal solution. Vilfredo Pareto, an Italian economist, proposed the basic efficiency criterion. In Pareto's understanding, efficiency occurs when, as a result of changes in allocation of resources, the situation of any person may not be improved without deterioration of the situation of another one. In the case of law, Pareto's efficiency criterion may be applied to evaluate whether or not a specific legal regulation (e.g. introduction of licenses or permits) will have a favorable impact on efficiency. The Pareto's criterion serves to evaluate the condition (allocation) occurring as a result of introducing certain regulations. It cannot be used to determine whether the projected change of law causes efficiency to grow or decrease.

In response to the limitation of the Pareto's criterion, Nicholas Kaldor and John Hicks formulated new efficiency criterion. According to N. Kaldor, this criterion takes the following form: allocation X is preferred to Y if, as a result of transition to X, the individuals who benefited from the change are able to compensate the decreased utility of those who incurred losses due to the change and despite of that fact they still enjoy higher utility than before the change [8]. A legal regulation is efficient in Kaldor-Hicks sense if the benefits from the introduction thereof exceed the related costs. The application of this criterion in the economic analysis of law is related to the concept of wealth maximization. Efficiency in Kaldor-Hicks sense is in line with wealth maximization as the changes of law that meet this criterion, lead to an increase in aggregated wealth as a difference between benefits and costs. It results from the fact that the wealth of the parties to the exchange increases so much that they can compensate the drop in wealth of others, who incurred losses in consequences of the exchange [2].

Based on the Kaldor-Hicks criterion, R.A. Posner formed a criterion that became the most popular efficiency criterion under the economic analysis of law. Instead of the notion of utility used in the Kaldor-Hicks criterion, R.A. Posner uses the notion of social wealth. According to R.A. Posner, wealth is the value of everything that exists in a society, expressed in money [12]. The Posner's criterion is formulated as follows: the transition from the initial state X to state Y maximizes social wealth if a surplus, measured in money, of benefits over costs is achieved in Y.

The Posner's criterion is the most frequently used. The application of this criterion helps assess efficiency of various legal regulations. This assessment consists in answering the question whether the projected legal regulation will provide a surplus of benefits over costs in comparison to the existing regulation or absence thereof.

The introduction of legal regulations generates various types of costs for entities covered by them. Administrative burdens are costs incurred due to performance of administrative obligations as specified in legal regulations. What is characteristic of these costs is that they would not be incurred in absence of such regulations. Two types of administrative obligations are distinguished. The first kind include obligations imposed by the state to regulate the market, for example the registration of business activity or a permit to run a business in a specific economic sector. The second kind includes information obligations, i.e., reports, tax returns, etc.

This paper focuses on administrative burdens for at least three reasons. First, importance of administrative burdens as barriers to develop business in Europe particularly for SMEs. The second reason is that the initiatives taken so far to reduce administrative burdens are not considered sufficiently effective. The last but not least reason is that administrative burdens are not very often analyzed in terms of transaction costs, within the meaning of the economic analysis of law [4].

The importance of transaction costs for the operation of enterprises was noticed by Ronald Coase in his breakthrough paper [3]. He stressed that the costs of organizing a transaction inside an enterprise are the primary factors that explain the existence and development of businesses, while the size and scope of a business are determined by the relative entry costs. In Coase's opinion, the legal system must assure the lowest possible transaction costs. The concept of transaction costs was developed by Oliver E. Williamson [11] under the new institutional economics, who drew attention to the need to optimize transaction costs.

In this paper, we propose a method, called CAB (The Costs of Administrative Burdens), that helps to optimize administrative burdens included in the transaction costs due to the application of business process modelling and simulation. The aim of method CAB is to help legislators to make correct decisions regarding administrative burdens at the law-making stage.

3 Application of Process Modelling and Simulation to Evaluate Administrative Burdens at the Law-Making Stage

The fulfilment of administrative obligations imposed by legal regulations requires a series of activities set out in legal regulations. The sequence of activities performed is a process, therefore, to evaluate the level of administrative burdens, one may use a number of techniques developed under Business Process Management (BPM). BPM includes a set of concepts, methods and techniques that support business process modelling, analysis and management [6]. BPM is inter-disciplinary in nature, as it combines knowledge of information technology and management science [10]. In this paper, we present the application of four BPM techniques: business process modelling, analysis, reengineering, and simulation. The research presented herein is based on application of the Business Process Model and Notation (BPMN), version 2.0, as set out in standards ISO/IEC 19510[1].

We are proposing a method, called CAB, based on said techniques, which permits to assess administrative burdens depending on different variants of legal regulations. Figure 1 presents individual steps of this method.

The CAB method is applied at the law-making stage. It begins with the identification of the process that is followed from the draft of legislation and will be an administrative burden for enterprises. The result of process identification is a general description of the course of the process from the perspective of both public institutions and enterprises.

Based on this description, during the second step, a model AS-IS of the process is prepared. The process modelling is done with the use of BPMN. The prepared AS-IS model should reflect the course of the process according to the draft of legislation in as much detail as possible.

The third step is the thorough analysis of the legal, organizational and technical aspects of the process. To this end, the analysis covers all legal regulations that impact the process, both national and local. At this step also broad consultations are handled

---

[1] ISO/IEC 19510 Information technology – Object Management Group Business Process Model and Notation.

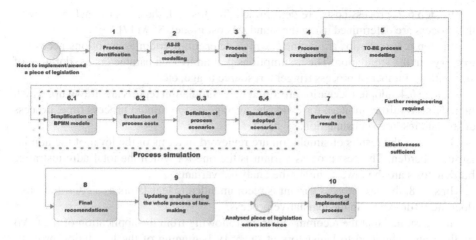

Fig. 1. The steps of the CAB method

with process stakeholders, who include not only process participants, but also other entities influencing the process. The consultations are based on interviews, questionnaires, or workshops. The analysis is made up of two stages. In the first stage, the process correctness is analyzed in order to identify process errors such as: inconsistency, incompleteness, or loops. In the second stage, process efficiency is analyzed. The purpose of the analysis is to find such fragments of the process that may be improved, e.g. bottlenecks or redundant activities.

The fourth step is process reengineering that is defined as the fundamental redesign of the process to improve its efficiency, measured by cost, quality and time [1].

Then, based on the results of the reengineering, the different process variants in the form of BPMN TO-BE models are prepared.

During the sixth step, simulation analysis is performed for the AS-IS process instance and for various TO-BE process variants. The purpose of the simulation is to evaluate efficiency of alternative process variants based on the adopted simulation scenarios. The most important value of the simulation is the possibility to assess alternative process variants as early as at the law-making activities. It is very important, because any change of the established law is time-consuming and difficult to implement. The simulation runs in four stages.

In step 6.1, in the case of complicated processes, the prepared BPMN models are simplified and adjusted to the needs of simulation. Only those process elements that affect process efficiency are taken into account. The critical path method can be used to identify those process elements that should be simulated. Moreover, process models are parametrized, which means that the durations of process activities are determined. Historical data regarding process implementation, gathered during interviews, are used for the purpose of parametrization. In the case of processes that have not yet been put into practice, the use of data from similar processes is assumed. Parameter data must be statistically significant.

In step 6.2, process costs are determined. To this end, the costs of each activity of the process are determined using the standard cost model, SCM [7].

In step 6.3, scenarios are defined, which determine certain assumptions necessary to carry out the simulation. The assumptions pertain to such parameters as: duration of simulation, number of process triggers, resource usage, etc.

In step 6.4, adopted scenarios are simulated. Simulation reports are drawn up, which include such information as, for example: average and minimum process time, process costs, and resource consumption.

In step 7, the results of simulation are reviewed in terms of the level of the administrative burden. The best process variant is the one for which the total administrative burden costs are the lowest among the analyzed variants.

In step 8, the best process variant is recommended to legislators as a contribution to documents drawn up in the legislative process.

It is assumed that the recommendations following from the application of the CAB method are submitted to legislators at the very beginning of the legislation process. Hence, it may happen that the legal regulation draft will be subject to multiple changes during the further stages of law-making activities. According to the CAB method, simulation analysis need to be applied at each stage of legislation process, whenever the draft of legislation is amended. This would help to identify how the proposed changes influence the processes and costs of administrative burdens.

Entry into life of the analyzed act of law does not conclude the CAB methodology. At this stage, processes following from the new law are ex-post evaluated to assess their real influence on administrative burdens. Carrying the analysis out basing on actual data pertaining to process implementation will help to further improve processes and in consequence reduce administrative burdens.

Since the application of the CAB method requires knowledge of the BPM techniques, it is assumed that the analysis will be carried out by external experts supporting legislators.

4   Case Study – Registration of a Civil Law Partnership

The CAB method has been used in practice to analyze the process of registration of a civil law partnership in Poland. In this case, the CAB method was modified, as the works were not related to law-making process. The main objective of the CAB method application was to verify whether the process of registration of a civil law partnership in Poland could be more effective.

Civil law partnership is a quite popular legal form of business activity in Poland. It is often used for business activity of such professionals as doctors, architects, or accountants.

In step 1, the civil law partnership registration process was identified. It was not an easy task, because in Polish legal regulations this process is set out in a number of acts of law and relevant implementing regulations. Moreover, on the part of public administration, three independent entities participate in the process: municipality offices, tax offices and branches of the Central Statistical Office. The regulations regarding the registration of a civil law partnership are supervised by various ministries, such as the Ministry of Economic Development, Ministry of Finance and others.

As the process of civil law partnership registration is already set out in regulations, in the next stage the AS-IS process model in BPNM has been prepared (see Fig. 2). iGrafx Process Central 2011 has been used as a tool for process modelling and simulation.

To prepare the model, the practical execution of the process in three entities has been analyzed: Poznań City Hall, Central Statistical Office Branch in Poznań, The First Tax Office in Poznań. These entities represent all types of public administration involved in the process. During the analysis, the duration of individual activities was measured. In addition, in interviews with individuals involved in process implementation, information on the process has been gathered.

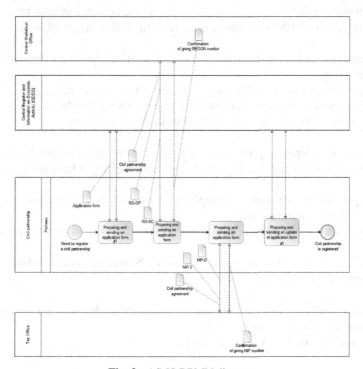

Fig. 2. AS-IS BPMN diagram

Originally, the civil law partnership registration process is comprised of four steps:

1. Each partner in a civil law partnership registers as sole proprietor. There are two registration methods available: electronically via the CEIDG[2] system or in municipality office.

---

[2] The Central Registration and Information on Economic Activity (abbreviated to CEIDG) is a register of enterprises operated by natural persons in the territory of Poland.

2. On behalf of the entire partnership, one of the partners requests that the Central Statistical Office branch assign the REGON[3] (Statistical Identification Number) to the partnership. This activity requires a visit in the office.
3. On behalf of the entire partnership, one of the partners requests the Tax Office to assign the NIP[4] (Tax Identification Number) to the partnership. This activity requires a visit in the office.
4. The partners in the civil law partnership update their respective entries in the CEIDG system by entering the REGON and NIP numbers in the civil law partnership he or she is a partner in. There are two CEIDG system entry update methods available: electronically or in the municipality office.

In the third step of the CAB method, a detailed analysis of the civil law partnership registration process and documents exchange during the process has been made. Process model in the form of BPMN permitted to identify the following problems:

- the process is not effective from the point of view of entrepreneurs registering a civil law partnership,
- during process execution, public authorities do not exchange information,
- the analysis of documents exchanged in the process shows that the entrepreneurs must submit the same data to the public administration several times.

To remove the identified problems, the process has been restructured and its model TO-BE has been developed (see Fig. 3). The following changes have been made:

- an entrepreneur submits only one application with all the information necessary to establish civil law partnership,
- the application is submitted electronically via the CEIDG system or in the municipality office,
- public administration exchanges the information between its units, without involving the entrepreneurs.

Then, to check which model offers lower administrative burdens for entrepreneurs, process simulation has been carried out.

The following simulation scenario has been adopted:

- average number of applications to register a civil law partnership in one municipality office: 968,
- each application is submitted by 1 applicant,
- simulation duration, 1 year = 264 working days,
- working time: 8 working hours.

The results of simulation shows that the registration of a civil law partnership would take on average one day after implementation of the proposed changes, instead of 18 days. (see Fig. 4).

---

[3] The REGON number is required for statistical purposes.
[4] The NIP number is required for fiscal purposes.

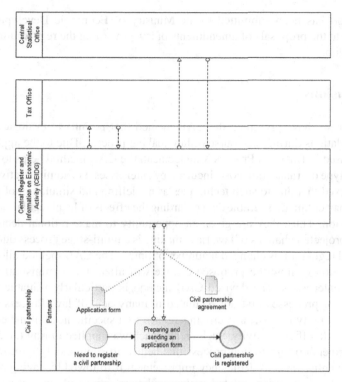

Fig. 3. TO-BE BPMN diagram

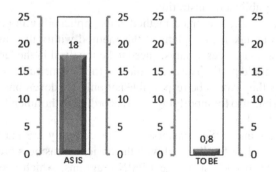

Fig. 4. Average duration of civil law partnership registration

The proposed process changes would also reduce costs incurred by entrepreneurs in relation to the registration of civil law partnership. In the TO-BE version, the registration costs incurred by entrepreneurs are by 70% lower than in the current process variant.

The simulations performed confirmed that the proposed process changes considerably improve the efficiency of the civil law partnership registration process. The improvement of efficiency pertains not only to the ratios related to the process carried out by enterprises, but will also cause the drop of costs incurred by the public administration.

The report has been submitted to the Ministry of Economic Development, as a contribution to the proposals of amendments of law governing the registration of a civil law partnership.

5 Conclusions

In this paper, we have presented the CAB method that permits to evaluate efficiency of legal regulations during the course of law-making process. Due to the application of techniques used in Business Process Management, the CAB method helps to assess the level of one type of transaction costs incurred by enterprises, i.e. administrative burdens. We have proved that due to such techniques as modelling and simulation of processes, legislators may obtain measurable data regarding the effects of legal regulations planned for introduction. Thus, they are given an opportunity to make rational decisions with regards the projected changes of law. Law-making is a multi-stage process during which the proposed regulation is changed a number of times. The CAB method allows immediate verification of how the proposed change will affect the administrative burdens incurred by enterprises. The devised CAB method is particularly valuable in case of optimization of processes that are regulated in many acts of law. Process modelling gives an opportunity to show all activities related to a specific need of the enterprises, not only a single official activity. Such an approach was applied during the analysis of civil law partnership registration process that helped to significantly improve the efficiency of the entire process. Efficiency improvement if followed by saving of time and costs incurred by enterprises related to the regulatory actions of state. What is important, the proposed improvement of processes boost efficiency of operation of not only enterprises but also public administration.

One of the value of the presented method is its applicability in practice. However some steps need to be taken to implement this method within the law-making activities. Firstly, the business process analysts need to be involved in the legislative process. BPMN specialists should participate at any stage of the law-making process. During the legislative activities they would be responsible not only for developing the BPMN diagrams from scratch but also for modifying them according to the amendments introduced to the proposals of legal acts.

Secondly lawyers and policy makers, who are currently the main actors of law-making process, should be familiarised with the basics of business process modelling. They should be able to understand the BPMN diagrams, which should not be very challenging, as the BPMN was developed to be understandable by all business users.

The CAB method should be practiced at each stage of legislative processes. Any changes of law, proposed during a legislative process, need to be analysed in terms of their influence on processes. Legislators should be aware of the consequences of their decisions.

We are aware that the application of the CAB method may prolong law-making process, but the application of this method could result in a reduction of failures in legislation. This would significantly limit the need for law amendments in the future. This would be especially important at the present time, when the number of legal acts adopted all over the world is constantly growing.

The CAB method presented in this paper demonstrates that the economic analysis of law may be enriched with methods from other fields, including the management science. The application of Business Process Management methods gives an opportunity to carry out further research activities on the improvement of the law-making process. These works may pertain to other types of regulation costs such as direct financial costs or substantive compliance costs.

References

1. Anand, A., Fosso Wamba, S., Gnanzou, D.: A Literature review on business process management, business process reengineering, and business process innovation. In: Barjis, J., Gupta, A., Meshkat, A. (eds.) EOMAS 2013. LNBIP, vol. 153, pp. 1–23. Springer, Heidelberg (2013). https://doi.org/10.1007/978-3-642-41638-5_1
2. Bełdowski, J., Metelska-Szaniawska, K.: Law & Economics-geneza i charakterystyka ekonomicznej analizy prawa (Law & Economics - genesis and description of the economic analysis of law). Bank I Kredyt **10**, 51–69 (2007)
3. Coase, R.H.: The nature of the firm. Economica **4**(16), 386–405 (1937)
4. Cooter, R., Ulen, T.: Law and Economics. 6th edn. Berkeley Law Books (2016)
5. European Commission, Commission Working Document: Measuring administrative costs and reducing administrative burdens in the European Union ({COM(2006) 691 final}).
6. Hammer, M., Champy, J.: Re engineering the Corporation A Manifesto for Business Revoluation. Harper Business, New York (1993)
7. International SCM Network, International Standard Cost Model Manual; Measuring and reducing administrative burdens for businesses. http://www.oecd.org/gov/regulatory-policy/34227698.pdf. Accessed 05 Mar 2021
8. Kaldor, N.: Welfare propositions of economics and interpersonal comparisons of utility. Econ. J. **49**(195), 549 (1939). https://doi.org/10.2307/2224835
9. Posner, R.A.: Economic Analysis of Law. Little, Brown and Co, New York (1973)
10. van der Aalst, W.M.P.: Business process management: a comprehensive survey. ISRN Softw. Eng. **2013**, 1–37 (2013). https://doi.org/10.1155/2013/507984
11. Williamson, O.E.: The Economic Institutions of Capitalism – Firms, Markets Relational Contracting. The Free Press, New York (1985)
12. Zhou, Q.: The evolution of efficiency principle: from utilitarianism to wealth maximization (2005)

Evaluating Second Generation Cross-Country Open Legal Data Infrastructures Using Value Models

Charalampos Alexopoulos[1]([⊠]) [ID], Euripidis Loukis[1], and Shefali Virkar[2] [ID]

[1] University of the Aegean, Samos, Greece
{alexop,eloukis}@aegean.gr
[2] Department for E-Governance and Administration,
Danube University Krems, Krems an der Donau, Austria
shefali.virkar@donau-uni.ac.at

Abstract. Access to legal information is of critical importance to socio-economic and political activity. Hence, the provision of capabilities to search for, locate and retrieve legal information in an efficient and structured manner to governments, businesses, lawyers and citizens is highly valuable. In order to satisfy the requirement for legal information, a 'first generation' of open legal data infrastructures that focus on providing access to national legislation and offer some basic functionalities for the providers and the users of these data, is already available in many countries. However, rapid globalization, the emergence of supra-national unions of nations, the advent of advanced data processing capabilities, and the ever-increasing complexity of legislation as it comes to mirror modern life have all contributed to the development of more advanced 'second generation' open legal data infrastructures that facilitate access to legal information from multiple national legal frameworks in multiple languages. In the face of the advent of these new technologies, it becomes vital to understand how their performance could be evaluated. This paper presents and validates a methodology for evaluating the emerging second generation of Big Open Linked Legal Data (BOLLD) e-infrastructures based on the concept of 'value model' estimations from users' evaluation ratings. The proposed approach advances beyond the traditional Information Systems (IS) evaluation approaches, as it includes assessments not only of the magnitudes of a wide range of types of value generated by such an infrastructure, but also of the relations among them. The proposed model, therefore, enables a deeper understanding of the whole value generation mechanism, and also can provide a rational definition of priorities for system improvement based on the capabilities offered to users. A first application of the developed approach is made for the evaluation of an advanced second generation BOLLD e-infrastructure developed as part of the European project ManyLaws, leading to both interesting insights as well as improvement priorities.

Keywords: Open data · Legal data · Legal informatics · e-infrastructures · Evaluation · Value model

© IFIP International Federation for Information Processing 2021
Published by Springer Nature Switzerland AG 2021
N. Edelmann et al. (Eds.): ePart 2021, LNCS 12849, pp. 180–197, 2021.
https://doi.org/10.1007/978-3-030-82824-0_14

1 Introduction

Access to legislation is of critical importance for all economic and political activity. Therefore, the provision of capabilities to search for, find and retrieve required legal information in an efficient and structured way to governments, businesses, lawyers and citizens is highly valuable. In order to satisfy differing needs for legal information many countries have developed a 'first generation' of open legal data infrastructures that focus on facilitating access to national legal legislation, and which offer a number of basic functionalities for the providers and the users of these data. However, the internationalization of economic activity, along with the emergence of supra-national unions of countries has created a demand for access to legislation not only of the home country, but also of many other nation states, and to international legislation. Simultaneously, advanced processing and analysis of this massive information – big data – have been developed in order to make it practically manageable and highly useful, and to enable such novel services as comparative analyses among countries in order to identify similarities and differences among them. Furthermore, legislation, both national and international, has become more complex, extensive, and dynamic, responding to the increasing complexity and dynamism of economic and social life as well as its problems and challenges (e.g., economic, social, political and environmental crises, digital transformations in both the private and the public sector of the economy and resulting disruptions, etc.). These factors have necessitated the development of a 'second generation' of more advanced open legal data infrastructures which enable access to legal information from many different countries, are oriented towards the elimination of the language barrier, and also offer more advanced processing capabilities and permit the analysis of this massive and dynamic legal information.

One of the most important supra-national unions of countries is definitely the European Union (EU). The main vision of the EU is to establish a well-functioning Digital Single Market, wherein European citizens can move freely and trade with their counterparts in other EU member states [1]. Digital transformation, and in particular the development, deployment and uptake of disruptive technologies, lies at the heart of the European approach to empower citizens and facilitate seamless business transactions [1]; it has a strong potential to foster economic development, but at the same time poses serious challenges and made necessary the need for effective regulations based on sound legal frameworks. The centrality of the role played by legal information in decision-making within different political, social, and economic settings entails unhindered access to the legal framework of the EU, as well as its member countries, which is vital for attaining this vision of unfettered cross-border mobility and trade. In other words, a significant prerequisite of a well-functioning Digital Single Market, within which Europeans can live, work and exploit new business opportunities, is a comprehensive knowledge of the legal and policy framework that circumscribes their actions, both in their countries and in other member states as well [2].

The European legal system is multi-layered and complex, as well as extensive, with large quantities of legal documentation having been produced since its formation. However, although European society is overwhelmed by an overload of legal information, only legal experts possess the capacity and wherewithal to follow and comprehend the latest legislation and policy evolutions and outcomes produced by ministries, parliaments, and courts at different levels of government (local, national and supra-national) – and even they oftentimes find it difficult to locate meaningful, relevant legal data [2]. A large amount of information about laws that apply in the EU member countries currently remains fragmented across multiple national databases, hidden within inaccessible systems, and scattered across public data silos. Mass customization tools, such as advanced legal information retrieval systems, offer some degree of solution to these problems, as they can help to sort, filter and present legal information in a logical and user-friendly manner. These tools and associated service have the potential to make legal information more easily accessible and comprehensible to businesses and lay users, reducing the need for recourse to expensive legal expertise [3].

In this direction the advances in the area of legal information retrieval, part of the burgeoning field of legal informatics, which can be defined as the science of information retrieval applied to legal texts - including legislation, case law, expert commentary, and scholarly works, are quite useful [4]. Accurate legal information retrieval is important in order to facilitate access to current legal documents by different groups of actors in the economy and the society. At a practical level, the retrieval of appropriate legal information, and its adequate comprehension, is at once a must and a challenge for European citizens, businesses, local administrations, national governments and institutions. In order to respond to these challenges, and to meet relevant user needs, the European ManyLaws project [3, 4] has developed a suite of user-centric services that will ensure the real-time provision and visualization of cross-country and multi-lingual legal information to citizens, lawyers, businesses and administrations, as well as advanced analyses of it (including comparisons between countries, time-wise evolutions, identification of connections as well as conflicts among laws, transpositions of EU Directives, etc.). The proposed solution is based on a platform supported by the proper environment for semantically annotated Big Open Linked Legal Data (BOLLD). The ultimate objective of the project has been to provide the technical foundation and the tools for the development of a second-generation legal data e-infrastructure, making cross-country and multilingual legal information available to everybody, in a customizable, structured and easy-to-handle way, as well as all the required processing and analysis of it in order to become practically manageable and highly useful. Achieving this objective is particularly important in the European legal context, wherein multilingualism facilitates near-universal accessibility to different Member States' legal frameworks and thereby promoting greater European integration.

This research paper presents and validates a methodology for evaluating such 'second generation' legal open data retrieval infrastructures based on the concept of 'value model' estimations from users' evaluation ratings [5–8]. This approach moves beyond the traditional Information Systems (IS) evaluation approaches, as it not only includes assessments of the magnitudes of a wide range of types of value generated by such an infrastructure, but also considers the relations among them as well (see Sect. 3 for more details). This enables a deeper understanding of the whole value generation mechanism and offers a rational definition of priorities for improvements in the capabilities offered to users. In particular, a multi-layer value flow model of such a 'second generation' legal open data retrieval infrastructure has been developed, having as its theoretical foundation the IS Success Model proposed by DeLone and McLean [9–12], supported by a methodology for estimating it using evaluation data collected from users. The proposed methodology has been used for the evaluation of the second-generation legal open data e-infrastructure developed in the abovementioned European project Many-Laws. The research presented in this paper can be considered as very useful, since second-generation open legal data e-infrastructures are quite new - still in their infancy - and are characterized by important novelties and innovations. An extensive and detailed evaluation of them is, therefore, required in order to assess the value they really generate, to identify their strengths as well as weaknesses, and to define required improvements using advanced IS evaluation approaches in order that they may evolve towards higher levels of maturity.

The research paper is structured as follows. In Sect. 2, the background of the proposed methodology is delineated. The above-mentioned evaluation methodology is then described in Sect. 3. Next, in Sect. 4, the second-generation legal open data e-infrastructure developed in the European project ManyLaws is outlined. The application of the proposed evaluation methodology to this e-infrastructure is presented in Sect. 5. Finally, in Sect. 6, the conclusions are summarized, and future research directions are proposed.

2 Background

Extensive research has been conducted on information systems evaluation [13–19], a significant proportion of which has concluded that IS evaluation is a difficult and complex task. This is because there exist many different types of IS, each having different objectives, and aiming at different types of benefits, both financial and non-financial, and also tangible and intangible. Thus, the assessment of each particular type of IS requires a different evaluation methodology, which takes into account its particular objectives as well as capabilities. In [13] two basic directions of IS evaluation are identified: (a) the 'efficiency-oriented' direction, which evaluates IS performance with respect to some predefined technical and functional specifications, focusing on answering the question of whether the IS 'is doing things right'; and (b) the 'effectiveness-oriented' direction, that evaluates the extent to which the IS supports the execution of business-level tasks or the achievement of business-level objectives, and focuses on answering the question of whether the IS 'is doing the right things'. [19] conducts a review of previous literature on the evaluation of IS. The authors conclude that IS evaluation methodologies focus mainly on the 'goal', 'environment' and 'activity' aspects of the evaluated IS: they evaluate mainly to what extent the IS contributes to the attainment of business goals, is useful to employees (who constitute that most important part of its environment, corresponding to IS 'effectiveness'), and also meets high levels of performance and accuracy (which correspond to IS 'efficiency') respectively.

Furthermore, extensive research in this area has been conducted on IS success [9–12], which has identified several dimensions/measures of it. The most widely used IS success model has been developed by DeLone and McLean [9–11]. The initial model identifies six IS success dimensions/measures, structured in three layers: (i) 'information quality' and 'system quality' (first layer); (ii) which affect 'user satisfaction' and also the 'actual use' of the IS (second layer); (iii) these two variables determine the 'individual impact' and the 'organizational impact' of the IS (third layer) [9, 11]. Subsequently, an updated version of the model was developed [10, 11], based on the experience gained from its extensive use; one which defines the following six dimensions of the success of an IS: (i) 'system quality', (ii)'information quality' and (iii)'service quality' (at the first layer), which affect (iv)'user satisfaction' and the actual (v)'use' or 'intention to use' (at the second level), and these affect (vi) the 'net benefits' that the IS generates (at the third layer). In [12] a re-specification and extension of this model is proposed, which includes perceived usefulness instead of actual use.

Based on a synthesis of the main conclusions of the IS evaluation research stream (briefly reviewed in the first paragraph of this section) on the one hand, and on the other hand the IS success research stream (briefly reviewed in the second paragraph of this section), the 'value model'-oriented IS evaluation approach has been developed [5–8]. It consists of two stages:

i) Specification of a two layered 'value model' of the specific IS under evaluation. The first layer includes 'efficiency-oriented' value measures, which are concern with the main capabilities provided the IS, as well as its technical quality (e.g., availability, response time, etc.) and usability (i.e., properties of the IS in which we can directly intervene). The second layer includes 'effectiveness-oriented' value measures, which consider the extent of support provided by the IS for the accomplishment of users' business-level objectives (i.e., the specific objectives concerning their tasks that the users want to achieve using the IS. For example. for an internal IS of a government agency, the main business objective of the public servants using it is to increase their working efficiency, while for a legal information e-infrastructure the main business objective of the lawyers using it is to improve their productivity and the quality of their performance of legal tasks), as well as the extent of use of it and overall satisfaction from it (i.e. properties of the IS in which we cannot directly intervene, but result from the first layer properties). The value model specification also includes interconnections/relations between first layer value measures and second layer ones (i.e. quantifying impacts of the former on the latter).

ii) Estimation of the above value model using evaluation data collected from users of this IS (e.g., through a questionnaire). This dimension includes a) calculation of the average ratings of the value measures of the first and the second layer; b) estimation of the above interconnections/relations between first layer value measures and second layer ones; this can be done either through the estimation of regression models, having as dependent variables the second layer value measures, and independent ones the first layer value measures, or in case of high correlations among the latter (multi-collinearity problems [20]), which is usually the case, we can calculate the correlations of the first layer value measures with the second layer ones. Based on the above results it is possible to identify strengths and weaknesses of the IS (= value measures that have received high and low user ratings respectively); and also, identify improvement priorities (= first layer value measures that have received low user ratings, and at the same time have high impact on the second layer value measures, that is, the extent to which business-level objectives have been accomplished, the overall user satisfaction, etc.

3 Evaluation Methodology

A methodology for evaluating 'second generation' big open linked legal data (BOLLD) e-infrastructures has been developed, based on the abovementioned 'value model'-oriented IS evaluation approach. Initially a value model of such an e-infrastructure has been specified, having the two-layered structure described above, elaborated using the IS Success Model of DeLone and McLean [9–12] as theoretical foundation, and also the novel capabilities offered by these 'second generation' BOLLD e-infrastructures. This is shown below, in Fig. 1. It can be seen that the model includes five first layer groups of value measures, which can be viewed as 'value dimensions': three of them map to the 'system quality' dimension of the DeLone and McLean IS success model (capabilities, or functionalities provided by the e-infrastructure, including both the 'traditional' and the novel-innovative ones, ease of use-usability, technical quality), one concerning the 'information quality' and another one concerning 'service quality'.

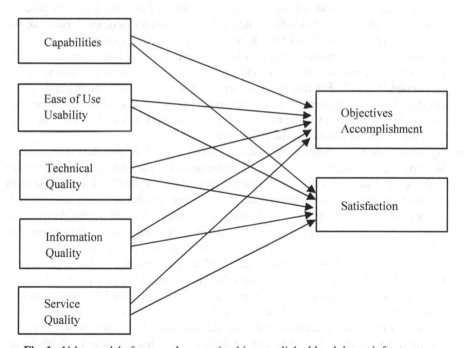

Fig. 1. Value model of a second-generation big open linked legal data e-infrastructures

The model also includes two second layer groups of value measures that are concerned with the extent of the support provided for the accomplishment of users' business-level objectives (e.g. performing various legal tasks), which is an adaptation of the 'net benefits' dimension of the DeLone and McLean IS success model, as well as the user's overall satisfaction (which is a combination of the 'user satisfaction' and the 'intention to use' dimensions, as the former).

For each of the above seven value dimensions individual value measures are defined taking into account, on one hand, the items developed for measuring the main IS success dimensions defined by relevant models (see [11] for a comprehensive review), and, on the other, the capabilities (both the traditional and the novel ones) offered by the specific BOLLD e-infrastructure. Based on these value measures, a questionnaire has been developed for collecting users' evaluation data for them. Applying these data, the value model of the e-infrastructure has been estimated based on the following algorithm that consists of the following six steps:

a) For each value dimension an aggregate variable is calculated as the average of its individual value measures' variables.
b) Average ratings are calculated for all value measures and dimensions (using for the latter the aggregate variables calculated in the previous step). This allows us to identify 'strengths' and 'weaknesses' of the BOLLD e-infrastructure.
c) For each aggregate variable of the second layer assessing one of the 'dependent' value dimensions, we estimate a regression having it as dependent variable, and having as independent variables all the aggregate variables of the first layers in order to estimate to what extent this value dimension is affected by value dimensions of the first layer. This is quantified by the R^2 coefficient of the regression [20].
d) For each value dimension of the first level we calculate its impact on the higher-level value dimensions (of the second layer), using again the aggregate variables calculated in step b. For this purpose, we can use the corresponding standardized coefficients of the regressions of the above step c, or (in case of multi-collinearity problems, which is usually the case) the correlations between the first layer of value dimension variables with second layer ones.
e) By combining the average ratings calculated in step b with the correlations calculated in step d we can construct a 'high level' value model of the BOLLD e-infrastructure at the level of value dimensions, and also a more detailed 'low level' one at the level of value measures. These value models enable a deeper understanding of the whole value generation mechanism of the BOLLD e-infrastructure, and we can also provide a colored intuitive visualization of these value models using 'hot colors' (e.g., red) for strong connections of first layer value dimensions/measures with second layer ones (e.g., having correlation higher than 0.6), and 'cold colors) for weaker connections.
f) Finally, the value dimensions and the value measures of the first layer, which are the only 'independent variables' within the control of the BOLLD e-infrastructure developer are classified, based on their average ratings by users and their average impacts on the value dimensions of the second layer ones, into four groups: low rating – high impact, low rating – low impact, high rating – high impact and high rating – low impact. High priority for improvement should be assigned to the improvement of first group of value dimensions and measures as they receive low evaluations by the users, and at the same time have strong impact on the generation of higher-level value concerning the accomplishment of users' legislation-related objectives and overall satisfaction.

4 A Cross-Border Big, Open and Linked Legal Data e-Infrastructure

In this section the main novel capabilities offered by the cross-border BOLLD e-infrastructure developed in the European ManyLaws project are briefly outlined (more detailed information on it are provided in [3, 4]):

- Parallel search in multiple EU member-state legal frameworks (including European legislation or EU directives); this process will be effectuated through the parallel translation of queried search terms, using a suitable legal vocabulary.
- Interrelation of laws and news or social media posts, using a sentiment analysis; this service will permit users to stay informed about ongoing policy trends, as well as public opinion related to the creation of new laws or the review of existing ones.
- Comparative analysis of related/connected laws from the same national legal framework; this is presented as a text visualization and will give the user the ability to identify correlations, dependencies and conflicts between different laws.
- Timeline analysis for all legal elements; this functionality provides a visualization of the progress and current status of a specific piece of national legislation (after amendment/extensions) over time, including preparatory acts and agreements.
- Visualization of the connection between an EU directive and a national legal framework. This visualization will be presented through the system as a graph, wherein the connection would be clearly identified. This functionality will allow the user to assess the degree of transposition of an EU Directive into national law.

5 Application

The proposed evaluation methodology, which has been described in Sect. 3, has been applied for the evaluation of the first version of this second-generation BOLLD e-infrastructure under development in the abovementioned project ManyLaws.

5.1 Value Model Specification

Initially a value model has been specified for the ManyLaws BOLLD e-infrastructure, based on the general specification shown in Fig. 1. This model includes all the value dimensions that the latter proposes, with the only exception of the service quality value dimension, This aspect was not included, since the e-infrastructure was not in production mode, and there were consequently no support services available to its users. Our value model is shown later in Fig. 2. It is worth noting that it includes two technical quality value dimensions pertaining to the performance and the availability of the e-infrastructure. The value measures of each of the seven value dimensions are outlined below, in Table 1. The 'Capabilities' and 'Objectives Accomplishment' value dimensions were based on the specific capabilities and objectives of the ManyLaws BOLLD e-infrastructure, while the remaining value dimensions were based on previous empirical research using the DeLone and McLean IS Success model [9–11].

188 C. Alexopoulos et al.

5.2 Data Collection

A series of workshops were held as part of the ManyLaws project, during and after the testing period in order to demonstrate the functionalities of the BOLLD e-infrastructure developed, to raise public awareness of its existence, and to allow for widespread testing of the prototype. Out of a pool of 100 potential volunteers (from the three main target groups of this e-infrastructure: legal professionals, legal researchers and public servants), 42 individuals responded and committed to pilot testing the system and implementing some predefined scenario with it. For the purposes of monitoring and evaluation within the purview of the ManyLaws project, a self-administered questionnaire was used to collect primary data from those individuals who had participated in the evaluation tests and associated workshops. The questionnaire included a series of questions that corresponded to the value measures of the abovementioned seven-value dimensions (see Table 1). These questions took the form of statements concerning some aspect of the BOLLD e-infrastructure (e.g., 'The interface of the system was pleasant and easy to look at'), and the users were asked to indicate the extent of their agreement or disagreement with each of them, using a five-point Likert scale (1 = Strongly Disagree, 2 = Disagree, 3 = Neutral, 4 = Agree, 5 = Strongly Agree). In order to maximize coverage within the shortest period of time, it was decided to make use of an online questionnaire to collect information. The questionnaire was developed and hosted on Google Forms.

These evaluation data collected from the above respondents, after being processed using the methodology described in Sect. 3, resulted finally in the construction of the value model of this novel second generation BOLLD e-infrastructure. These data will provide a first understanding of users' perceptions and assessments concerning its main characteristics and functional capabilities (first layer value), as well as the extent of support it provides for performing important legal tasks and the overall satisfaction from it (second layer value). This will allow for the identification of both strengths and weaknesses from various perspectives. Further, it will enable an initial understanding of the different importance of these first layer characteristics and functional capabilities for generating higher layer value (support for performing important legal tasks, of both national and international scope, as well as overall satisfaction), and also of priorities for improvements of these characteristics and functional capabilities.

With respect to the demographics of the 42 pilot users and respondents of the questionnaire, they could be characterized as being legal experts: most of them were public servants (46.7%), followed by legal professionals (22.2%) and then legal researchers (17.8%). A small number of participants self-identified as being businesspersons. In terms of age, 46.7% of the respondents were in the group of 45–54 years old, while 31.1% was above 75 years old. The rest vary from 18 to 74 years old. Roughly two-thirds (64.4%) of all respondents described themselves as advanced ICT users, while 26.7% self-identified as being intermediate users. Eighty percent of the pilot users stated that they used legal data primarily for professional purposes, which they find mostly online (40%) or both online and offline (60%). Finally, a large proportion of respondents reported that they spent roughly 30 min per day searching for legal information (42.2%); while others reported spending either 1–2 h (28.9%), or more than 3 h (28.9%), on the same task.

5.3   Data Analysis - Value Flow Estimation

In Table 1, below, the average rating for all value measures and dimensions (results for value dimensions in bold) are shown in the second column. With respect to the first layer value dimensions, it may be seen that the two technical quality related ones, availability and performance, are assessed as high (average ratings 4.14 and 4.05 respectively), while the remaining three - capabilities, usability and information quality – are perceived as moderate to high (average ratings 3.74, 3.73 and 3.52). Availability has received the highest average rating (4.14), so it can be considered as a strength of the e-infrastructure, while the information quality has received the lowest average rating (3.52), so it constitutes a weakness. With respect to the second layer value dimensions, we can see that both are assessed as moderate to high (average ratings 3.75 and 3.48). Proceeding to a higher level of detail, for the first layer individual value measures, we can see that most of them are assessed between moderate to high (average rating 3.5) and high (average rating 4.0). The accessibility of the platform using any browser, the availability anytime and from anywhere, and the capabilities of retrieving laws and legal documents in general have received the highest average ratings (exceeding 4.00) (strengths). In juxtaposition, the lowest average ratings have been given to the provision of only relevant results, the assessment of conflicts, comparisons or dependencies between different laws inaccuracies and the manual annotation of text (below 3.50) (weaknesses). For the second layer value measures, it may be seen that the ones concerning accomplishment of legal tasks related objectives are assessed between moderate to high (average rating 3.5) and high (average rating 4.0). For the value measures concerned with overall satisfaction with the e-infrastructure, we can see that the one associated with future use of it has received the highest average rating (between high and very high: 4.26), the one associated with paying a fee has received the lowest (less than moderate: 2.79), while the other two received average ratings between moderate and high.

As a next step we examined the extent to which the two value dimensions of the second layer are affected by the ones of the first layer (step 4). For this purpose, we estimated two regression models having as dependent variables the two value dimensions of the second layer Objectives Accomplishment (OBJAC) and Satisfaction (SAT), and as independent variables the five value dimensions of the first layer. The R^2 coefficients of these two regression models are 0.742 and 0.725 respectively, indicating that both second layer value dimensions are affected to a large extent by the ones of the first layer.

Finally, we calculated the correlations of the first layer value dimensions, as well as their value measures, with the two value dimensions of the second layer OBJAC and SAT. The results are shown in the third, fourth and fifth column of Table 1. In the fifth column, the average of these two correlations is demonstrated. We remark that the capabilities and usability, followed by the information quality, have high correlations with the two second layer value dimensions, and hence they have strong impacts on higher level value generation. The availability dimension has a moderate correlation with the two second layer value dimensions, thus its impact on higher level value generation is moderate, while the correlations of the performance dimension is not statistically significant.

Using the average ratings and correlations shown in Table 1 we can construct the value model of the BOLLD e-infrastructure; both the 'high level' one at the level of value dimensions, and the more detailed 'low level' one at the level of value measures.

Table 1. Average ratings and correlations of value dimensions and measures

Measure/ Dimension	Description	Average ratings	Correlation OBJAC	Correlation SAT	Average correlation
CAP		**3.74**	**0.824****	**0.775****	**0.800**
CAP1	Search for legal information on a particular topic in different EU Member States' legislations	3.86	0.773**	0.700**	0.736
CAP2	Retrieve a particular law or legal document	4.02	0.488**	0.425**	0.456
CAP3	Access accurate translations of a law or legal document in my language	3.90	0.718**	0.571**	0.644
CAP4	Compare laws on the same subject within the same country	3.81	0.732**	0.783**	0.757
CAP5	Compare laws on the same subject between different countries	3.71	0.676**	0.677**	0.676
CAP6	Assess the degree of transposition of EU directives into national legislation	3.79	0.718**	0.624**	0.671
CAP7	Assess the conflicts, comparisons or dependencies between different laws	3.45	0.583**	0.613**	0.598
CAP8	Trace the evolution of a piece of legislation over time	3.86	0.641**	0.592**	0.616
CAP9	Access highly informative visualizations depicting the above comparisons and contrasts	3.93	0.736**	0.572**	0.654
CAP10	Access different types of parliamentary data	3.74	0.635**	0.684**	0.659

(*continued*)

Table 1. (*continued*)

Measure/ Dimension	Description	Average ratings	Correlation OBJAC	Correlation SAT	Average correlation
CAP11	Report inaccuracies and manually annotate text	3.36	0.628**	0.642**	0.635
CAP12	Access relevant public opinion data	3.48	0.685**	0.658**	0.671
USAB		**3.73**	**0.776****	**0.829****	**0.802**
USAB1	It was easy to find the information I needed	3.64	0.545**	0.620**	0.582
USAB2	The interface of the system was pleasant and easy to look at	3.88	0.681**	0.645**	0.663
USAB3	The output/results it provides are understandable	3.81	0.749**	0.701**	0.725
USAB4	The capabilities provided by the system are compliant with the work-practices and the mentality of legal professionals	3.59	0.527**	0.696**	0.611
PERF		**4.05**	**0.122**	**0.230**	**0.176**
PERF1	The system returned rapid results to my queries	3.86	0.016	0.150	0.083
PERF2	The speed at which the system returned results remained consistent for each login session	3.74	0.065	0.140	0.102
PERF3	The pages work in my favourite browser(s)	4.55	0.291*	0.315*	0.303
AVAIL		**4.14**	**0.333***	**0.253***	**0.293**

(*continued*)

Table 1. (*continued*)

Measure/ Dimension	Description	Average ratings	Correlation OBJAC	Correlation SAT	Average correlation
AVAIL1	I was able to access and browse the platform at my convenience - at any time of the day, from anywhere	4.12	0.325*	0.274*	0.299
AVAIL2	I was able to access and navigate through the different services at my convenience - at any time of the day, from anywhere	4.07	0.292*	0.226*	0.259
AVAIL3	The platform was never offline at the moment that I wanted to use it	4.24	0.289*	0.186*	0.237
INFQ		**3.52**	**0.679****	**0.670****	**0.674**
INFQ1	The results returned by the system correspond closely to the corresponding queries	3.57	0.649**	0.640**	0.644
INFQ2	The proportion of non-relevant results to my queries provided by the system is low	3.26	0.353**	0.408**	0.380
INFQ3	The system is able to recognize different keywords from the same legal domain	3.50	0.613**	0.578**	0.595
INFQ4	The translations made by the system are reasonably accurate	3.74	0.598**	0.557**	0.577
OBJAC		**3.75**			

(*continued*)

Table 1. (*continued*)

Measure/ Dimension	Description	Average ratings	Correlation OBJAC	Correlation SAT	Average correlation
OBJAC1	To gain a better picture/understanding of the existing legislation on a particular topic in your country	3.83			
OBJAC2	To gain a better picture/understanding of the existing legislation on a specific topic in other EU Member States and also at European Directives level	3.76			
OBJAC3	To increase your productivity in performing various legal tasks involving legislation of your country	3.74			
OBJAC4	To increase your productivity in performing various legal tasks involving legislation of other EU Member States and also legislation at European Directives level	3.83			
OBJAC5	To improve the quality of performing various legal tasks involving legislation of your country	3.62			

(*continued*)

Table 1. (*continued*)

Measure/ Dimension	Description	Average ratings	Correlation OBJAC	Correlation SAT	Average correlation
OBJAC6	To improve the quality of performing various legal tasks involving legislation of other EU Member States and also legislation at European Directives level	3.74			
SAT		**3.48**			
SAT1	I am confident that the system compares favorably with other available, similar legal informatics solutions	3.52			
SAT2	I would like to use the system again	4.26			
SAT3	I would be willing to pay a subscription fee to use the system again	2.79			
SAT4	I would choose this system over other similar legal informatics products	3.33			

The former is illustrated in Fig. 2. Our model provides a compact visualization of the main dimensions/types of value generated by the e-infrastructure (quantified through the corresponding average users' ratings), the relations among them (quantified through the corresponding correlations), and the main value generation paths. This enables a better understanding of the value generation mechanism of the BOLLD e-infrastructure under consideration.

Based on these average ratings, and correlations presented in Table 1, improvement priorities were identified. At the level of first layer value dimensions, we remark that in terms of average rating two groups may be distinguished: a higher average rating one, consisting of the technical quality value dimensions PERF and AVAIL, and a lower average rating one, consisting of CAP, USAB and INFQ. Furthermore, in terms of correlations with second layer value dimensions, we can distinguish two groups of first layer value dimensions: one with higher correlations, consisting of CAP, USAB and INFQ, and one with lower correlations, consisting of PERF and AVAIL. Hence, it may

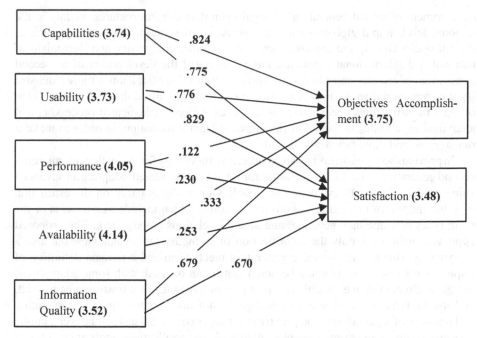

Fig. 2. Value model of the ManyLaws BOLLD e-infrastructures

be concluded that our highest priority should be given to the improvement of the CAP (capabilities), USAB (usability) and INFQ (information quality), as they have received lower ratings by the users, and at the same time have higher impact on higher level value generation concerning accomplishment of users' legislation-related objectives and overall satisfaction, especially to the information quality.

Similarly, we have identified improvement priorities at the more detailed level of value measures. In particular, we have identified 6 out of the 26 value measures of the first layer, which belong to the lower 50% (=bottom 13) in terms of average rating, and to the upper 50% (=top 13) in terms of average correlation with the two second layer value dimensions, which should be assigned improvement priority:

CAP5: Compare laws on the same subject between different countries.
CAP6: Assess the degree of transposition of EU directives into national legislation.
CAP10: Access different types of parliamentary data.
CAP11: Report inaccuracies and manually annotate text.
CAP12: Access relevant public opinion data.
INFQ1: The results returned by the system correspond closely to my queries.

6   Conclusion

Unhindered access to legislation produced at different levels of government is important for the pursuance of economic and political activities. This recognition has led to the development of a 'first-generation' of legal open data e-infrastructures, mainly at the national level. Rapid globalization, the emergence of supra-national entities such as the European Union, and the ever-increasing volume, complexity and dynamism of national and international legislation has necessitated the development of a 'second generation' of cross-country BOLLD e-infrastructures that offer a much more extensive legal information than the first-generation ones. It is recognized that this new iteration of legal infrastructures needs also to offer the user more sophisticated processing and analytical capabilities to handle of this massive legal information, in order to make it manageable and more practically useful.

In previous sections of this research paper, a methodology for evaluating the emerging second generation of BOLLD e-infrastructures has been presented, adopting an advanced value model oriented IS evaluation approach. Our model is based on the estimation of value models of these BOLLD e-infrastructures, which include assessments of the main types of value they generate, and also the relations among them. The proposed approach enables not only the identification of strengths and weaknesses, but also a deeper understanding of the value generation mechanism and a rational definition of improvement priorities. It should be noted that it can be used, with some adaptations, for the evaluation of the 'traditional' first generation BOLLD infrastructures as well, and also for future more advanced second-generation ones, contributing to the evolution and maturity of legal information provision for supporting legal tasks of lawyers, public servants, business and even individual citizens. A first application of this approach was made for the evaluation of an advanced second generation BOLLD e-infrastructure developed under the aegis of the European project ManyLaws, leading to interesting insights, as well as improvement priorities. The present study also makes a significant contribution to existing literature, and that body of knowledge concerned with the value model construction approach to IS evaluation.

More research is required relating to the further application of the proposed methodology for the evaluation of next versions of the same BOLLD e-infrastructure, and also of other advanced second generation BOLLD infrastructures, based on larger 'professional' users' groups. There also remains scope for further enquiry into the extension of this BOLLD e-infrastructures' evaluation methodology, with the potential addition of more first and second layer value dimensions and value measures.

References

1. European Union: Shaping Europe's Digital Future – Factsheet (2020). https://ec.europa.eu/commission/presscorner/detail/en/fs_20_278
2. Virkar, S., Alexopoulos, C., Stavropoulou, S., Tsekeridou, S., Novak, A., Charalabidis, Y.: User-centric decision support system design in legal informatics: a typology of users. In: Charalabidis, Y., Cunha, M.A., Sarantis, D. (eds.) Proceedings – ICEGOV 2020 13th International Conference on Theory and Practice of Electronic Governance, 23–25 September 2020, Athens, Greece, pp. 711–722. ACM Press (2020)
3. Charalabidis, Y., Loutsaris, M.A., Virkar, S., Alexopoulos, C., Novak, A.-S., Lachana, Z.: Use case scenarios on legal machine learning. In: Ben Dhaou, S., Carter, L., Gregory, M. (eds.) Proceedings - ICEGOV 2019 12th International Conference on Theory and Practice of Electronic Governance, 3–5 April 2019, Melbourne, VIC, Australia, pp. 364–373. ACM Press (2019)

4. Virkar, S., Tsekeridou, S., Romas, I., Alexopoulos, C.: Towards comprehensive legal information search and retrieval: learning and building from evaluated projects. In: Proceedings - Internationales Rechtsinformatik Symposion, IRIS 2020, 27–29 February 2020, Salzburg, Austria (2020)
5. Pazalos, K., Loukis, E., Nikolopoulos, V.: A structured methodology for assessing and improving e-services in digital cities. Telematics Inform. (SCOPUS) **29**, 123–136 (2012)
6. Loukis, E., Pazalos, K., Salagara, A.: Transforming e-services evaluation data into business analytics using value models. Electron. Commer. Res. Appl. **11**(2), 129–141 (2012)
7. Charalabidis, Y., Loukis, E., Alexopoulos, C.: Evaluating second generation open government data infrastructures using value models. In: 47th Hawaii International Conference on System Sciences (HICSS), pp. 2114–2126 (2014)
8. Loukis, E., Leou, T.: Evaluating complex government SAAS through value flow model estimation. In: Proceedings of 13th Mediterranean Conference on Information Systems (MCIS 2019), Naples, Italy (2019)
9. DeLone, D.H., McLean, E.R.: Information systems success: the quest for the dependent variable. Inf. Syst. Res. **3**(1), 60–95 (1992)
10. DeLone, D.H., McLean, E.R.: The DeLone and McLean model of information systems success: a ten-year update. J. Manag. Inf. Syst. **19**(4), 9–30 (2003)
11. DeLone, W., McLean, E.: Information systems success measurement. Found. Trends Inf. Syst. **2**(1), 1–116 (2016)
12. Seddon, P.B.: A respecification and extension of the DeLone and McLean model of IS success. Inf. Syst. Res. **8**(3), 240–253 (1997)
13. Smithson, S., Hirscheim, R.: Analysing information systems evaluation: another look at an old problem. Eur. J. Inf. Syst. **7**, 158–174 (1998)
14. Farbey, B., Land, F., Targett, D.: Moving IS evaluation forward: learning themes and research issues. J. Strateg. Inf. Syst. **8**(2), 189–207 (1999)
15. Willcocks, L., Graeser, V.: Delivering IT and e-Business Value. Butterworth-Heinemann, Boston (2001)
16. Irani, Z.: Information systems evaluation: navigating through the problem domain. Inf. Manag. **40**(1), 11–24 (2002)
17. Gunasekaran, A., Ngai, E.W.T., McGaughey, R.E.: Information technology and systems justification: a review for research and applications. Eur. J. Oper. Res. **173**, 957–983 (2006)
18. Irani, Z., Love, P.: Information systems evaluation - a crisis of understanding. In: Irani, Z., Love, P. (eds.) Evaluating Information Systems - Public and Private Sector. Butterworth-Heinemann (2008)
19. Prat, N., Comyn-Wattiau, I., Akoka, J.: A taxonomy of evaluation methods for information systems artifacts. J. Manag. Inf. Syst. **32**(3), 229–267 (2015)
20. Greene, W.H.: Econometric Analysis, 7th edn. Prentice Hall Inc., Upper Saddle River (2011)

Analysing the Implementation of Electronic Communication Strategies Through Legislation

Valerie Albrecht(✉) 📵 and Anna-Sophie Novak 📵

Centre for E-Governance, Danube University Krems, Dr.-Karl-Dorrek-Straße 30,
3500 Krems, Austria
{valerie.albrecht,anna-sophie.novak}@donau-uni.ac.at

Abstract. E-government strategies have come a long way and often undergone several revisions until now. The scientific community has identified building blocks, singular cases and especially success factors for their implementation. However, as of now there is little evidence regarding the legal implementation of these strategies. To contribute to this gap in the scientific literature, in this paper we examine three central European countries regarding the implementation of legal measures that have been suggested or implied by their current e-government strategies. To achieve a focused observation of the legal frameworks, we decided to concentrate on the element electronic communication, which has recently gained relevance in European e-government. To achieve this, we carry out a document analysis as well as a legal analysis of current strategic and legal documents for the three cases. Our results show differences in strategy formulation that are defined by overarching European trends as well as an existing legal basis for electronic communication between public authorities and citizens that will need to be adapted for new ways of electronic communication in the future.

Keywords: E-government strategies · Electronic communication · Digital transformation · Government services · Strategy implementation · Legislation

1 Introduction

E-government strategies have played an important role in the digitalisation of the public sector for some time now. However, in many countries new digital strategies or revisions of these are currently still in development. As one of the early adopters and best practice examples of e-government, Austria is currently working on the development of a new digital strategy, namely the "Digital Action Plan Austria" [1]. Administrative aspects and digital public services are a decisive part of digital strategies and new policies will benefit from building on earlier experiences. Consequently, a prerequisite of being able to formulate these learnings is the analysis of existing strategies and their implementation. While legislation is often seen as a barrier for the implementation of digital strategies [2] it can be an important driver that provides the framework for a secure and trustworthy digital service infrastructure in the public sector.

© IFIP International Federation for Information Processing 2021
Published by Springer Nature Switzerland AG 2021
N. Edelmann et al. (Eds.): ePart 2021, LNCS 12849, pp. 198–209, 2021.
https://doi.org/10.1007/978-3-030-82824-0_15

Such endeavours not only mirror national strategic and legislative initiatives but are also the basis for an interoperable cross-border digital public service. Only recently, trustworthy, secure interactions that allow for a digital communication between the public sector and citizens, accompanied by regulatory frameworks, have been specified in the Berlin Declaration on Digital Society [3]. The principles codified in this and similar documents become part of national digital strategies and should consequently be translated into comprehensive legal frameworks. This article analyses the implementation of these strategic measures into legislative practice.

2 Background

With a rising number of e-government strategies in countries worldwide, the success of their implementation becomes increasingly visible. Consequently, methods and frameworks to analyse these strategies [4] and evaluate their implementation [5] are being developed. These new frameworks allow for a more critical reflection of strategic documents [4] while addressing changing developments of digital public services and creating a basis for the citizen-oriented provision and development of new services [6]. Additionally, frameworks of important elements of these strategies are being identified [7]. In this range, a wide array of possible focus points for e-government strategies exists [8], which are, however, often closely related to policy domains [9]. Consequently, e-government strategies not only provide a long-term outlook and a holistic perspective for the development of e-government services, but also address previously identified barriers [10]. They are based on an extended analysis and the framework of demand and envisaged outcome [11] and often need to consider a wide array of external factors, such as infrastructure, the impact of technologies, and others [12]. Building on Meijer's definition of an e-government strategy describing a "strategy for e-governance innovation means setting long-term goals and implementing actions for realizing e-governance" [10] the implementation of these strategies plays a central role to achieve the goal of their drafting and promulgation.

One aspect of this implementation is the translation of these strategies into rule of law. Legislative frameworks have already been identified as important aspects of e-government strategies [7]. However, the scientific literature so far mainly focuses on legislation as processes that are part of public service delivery [13] or as a barrier to successfully implementing e-government projects [2, 14, 15]. Scientific articles reviewing current legislation show a need for further connecting digitalisation efforts and legal realities [16]. Legislation becomes especially important when these strategies, e.g. through the application of new channels or technologies, facilitate structural change, as in electronic communication [17].

When contextualising electronic communication, it is important to distinguish a technological definition with a focus on e.g. broadband transmission [18] and electronic communication in the service provision context of e-government, which is our focus. This second type of electronic communication is charactised by a larger amount of automatisation, real-time data validation and consequently an increased responsiveness [19]. With special respect to the European framework, an essential part of electronic communication is interoperability [20]. Closely related to electronic communication frameworks is the question of qualified and trusted electronic identification [21].

When examining these strategies, many existing studies focus on either historic developments [9], regional success factors and characteristics [7, 8] or future-technology oriented strategies [22] in specific countries. While the literature shows an extensive discussion of the formulation of these strategies as well as their implementation or the implementation of specific digital public services, respectively, little research has been done on the legal implications of e-government strategies as well as international comparative analysis. To address this gap, we will examine e-government strategies of the DACH area (Germany, Austria, and Switzerland) for their practical effects on legislation by conducting a document and a legal analysis. By doing this, we strive to answer the following research question: **To what extent are electronic communication aspects of e-government strategies implemented into legal measures in German-speaking countries (DACH)?**

3   Method

To answer this question we examined three different cases on a national level with regard to current relevant strategic e-government documents as well as their legal counterparts. To enable a focused review we chose one specific aspect, electronic communication, for a more in-depth and deductive approach. This section explains our methodology by presenting the process of case selection and the means with which the respective cases have been analysed.

3.1   Case Selection

The Federal Republic of Germany, the Republic of Austria, and the Swiss Confederation, although countries with varying levels of e-government and administrative differences, show apparent similarities in administrative federalist structures, platform-oriented e-government models as well as the usage of strategic documents to manifest and communicate these efforts. The four case studies examined were close in terms of a federal administrative tradition, a common official language and geographic proximity. This has led to a variety of studies observing administrative and digitalisation trends in these countries [23, 24]. However, they have yet to be examined regarding their e-government strategies and the respective legal implementation of these strategies.

3.2   Document Analysis

Document Analysis as a qualitative research method can support the process of gaining insights into the formulation of as well as trends that can be found in policy documents [25]. As a valuable tool for qualitative enquiry, the method requires critical evaluation and can involve a broader contextualization of the documents [26]. Wach and Ward [25] describe the definition of "key areas of analysis" (p. 2), which we applied by focusing on one specific element of e-government to be analysed. Since we observe only a single factor of e-government strategies, i.e. electronic communication, a holistic analytical framework cannot be applied to the strategies at hand. Instead, we will adapt Hofmann's analytical framework [4] and focus on.

1. The contextualization of electronic communication in the strategy,
2. The goals and actions of electronic communication within the strategy,
3. Relevant stakeholders of electronic communication, if mentioned in the strategy,
4. The national context of electronic communication as well as
5. Conditions and consequences of implementing electronic communication.

The documents that have been identified as strategic e-government documents in the observed countries according to Sect. 3.1 "Specific political communications on digital public administration" of the EU Digital Public Administration factsheets [1, 27, 28] and consequently have been included in the analysis. Only strategies on the national level with the explicit aim of communicating a digital or e-government strategy have been included, and to ensure coherence between the strategic and legal documents, only the German versions of each document have been included. Finally, the following documents have been selected:

- Austria: Federal E-Government Strategy (The ABC guide of eGovernment in Austria) [29]
- Germany: National eGovernment Strategy (NEGS) [30], and "Shaping Digitalisation" (Digitalisierung gestalten – Umsetzungsstrategie der Bundesregierung) [31]
- Switzerland: eGovernment Strategy (2020–2023) [32]

3.3 Legal Analysis

We identified seven documents as relevant legal documents in the observed countries:

- Austria: E-Government Act [33], and Explanatory Notes [34]
- Germany: E-Government Act [35], De-Mail Act [36], and Explanatory Notes [37]
- Switzerland: E-Government Act [38] and Explanatory Notes [39]

4   Results

For the selected cases, we analysed four strategic and seven legal documents. This section presents the results of each analysis according to country.

4.1 Results of Document Analysis

We analysed all documents in their German version to ensure coherence between the strategic and legal documents. With the German counterparts of keywords related to "communication", "electronic traffic" (translation, would be part of communication in English), "digital post", "electronic channel" and "electronic delivery" statements on the issue of electronic communication have been identified. During the coding process we additionally found the closely related issue of "identification". We applied these codes to identify strategic measures concerning electronic communication in the four strategic documents. In a second step the so identified parts have been observed according to the aforementioned adaptation of Hofmann's [4] framework.

4.1.1 Austria

The Austrian e-government strategy especially focuses on the aspects of current (i.e., the time of the strategy publication) electronic communication as well as delivery and its legal aspects. On third place, codes concerning electronic traffic and framework conditions are tied. In the strategy document, electronic communication is being contextualised as an essential factor of e-government, in coherence with understandings from the scientific literature [19]. Electronic communication in Austria is presented as a mature and holistic complex that is based on an elaborate and trustworthy back-end architecture, and allows easy as well as secure access to public services. An important part of this framework is electronic delivery, a tool that, according to the strategy document, is used increasingly and integrated in existing portals. The medium-term goal here is the replacement of paper-based processes through electronic communication between citizens and services, while e-government in Austria generally strives to allow electronic communication everywhere without media discontinuity. Currently, half of Austrian citizens use digital communication with public authorities, one additional third plans to do so [40]. The legal aspect accompanying this strategic project is the implementation of a right for electronic communication with public authorities for citizens. An additional plan is the integration of electronic delivery into a central portal by providing a digital postbox. This postbox shall function as a one-stop-shop for electronic delivery of official documents to Austrian citizens. Together with businesses, who are also mentioned as receiving parties of electronic public sector communication, citizens are the main stakeholders of the planned innovation initiatives. With a central digital postbox like this, electronic communication between the public sector and citizens has the potential to be centralised in the front-end, no matter the federal jurisdiction for a particular service delivery. Many technological framework conditions for these user-centered plans are already met, e.g. with the ELAK (electronical authority file) and with the delivery act first legal prerequisites are fulfilled. However, technological advances and international standards raise new issues, such as the need for a legal framework for a secure and trustworthy electronic identification and more general structural and organisational changes in the public sector.

4.1.2 Germany

For Germany, two documents have been available, an e-government strategy as well as a general strategy for digitalisation. As for the other countries, only the excerpts concerning electronic communication between the public sector and its stakeholders have been evaluated. The e-government strategy itself mainly provided a little information on plans for electronic communication and digital citizen accounts. The digitalisation strategy presented specific measures regarding electronic communication in specific areas of public life. To provide a holistic overview of German e-government endeavours, the results of both documents will now be examined together. In both documents, a broad view on electronic communication has been prevalent, that includes access to and interactions with the public sector. This holistic approach is also mirrored in the goals, which center on the development of a secure and easy access point to, as far as possible, digitised public services via electronic citizen accounts with a secure authentification possibility, and comprehensive service integration, e.g. with a new digital postbox and e-payment options. These access points should be available for citizens as well as private businesses. This complex is supported by the implementation of German laws that require the pilotation of online services as well as European regulations and standards. In this context, uniform contacts as well as cross-border identification solutions are required. On a national level, plans for a central provision of infrastructure and basic services are stated, which requires extensive coordination for digital services on all federal levels. While legal requirements for the online access law and the e-government law have been included in the considerations of these strategies, new challenges emerge regarding the implementation of single digital gateway requirements and secure cross-border identification.

4.1.3 Switzerland

The Swiss e-government strategy is far more general than the other observed documents. With its easy to understand language, short overviews and wealth of visual illustrations, its target audience seems to be a broad public as the addressee of political communication. Still, general statements on electronic communication could be identified. Especially prevalent is- the formulation of electronic channel and identification technologies. The Swiss strategy emphasis the existing possibilities of electronic interaction with public authorities as well as the goal of an attractive public sector that makes electronic communication with public authorities the first choice for citizens and private businesses. While this user-centricity seems to be the central element of digital public service design, the strategy itself states that the public sector is an actor and not a facilitator of digitalisation. At the same time, and even though Switzerland is not a member state of the European Union, the strategy emphasis the adherence to European Principles, such as digital-by-default. Additionally, basic requirements for electronic communication, such as a secure and official electronic identity, have been implemented and are to be expanded, especially with regard to the usage of public sector databases. Consequently, even though little to no legislation has been mentioned in the strategy, legal frameworks for secure data exchange, digital identity and digital-by-default communications will be needed for the implementation of this user-centric vision.

4.2 Results of Legal Analysis

This section presents the results of the legal analysis.

4.2.1 Austria

In Austria, electronic communication with public authorities is regulated principally in the E-Government Act (E-GovG) [33]. Electronic communication includes communication with authorities and electronic delivery (although the electronic delivery specifically is regulated in a separate law). On January 1, 2020, the right to communicate electronically with public authorities entered into force (1a E-GovG). Furthermore § 1b EGovG regulates the obligation for companies to accept electronic deliveries from authorities:

"Companies [...] shall participate in electronic service". This avoids the need to phys-ically visit the authorities. As is common practice under the current procedural law, the authority concerned must announce on the Internet any technical requirements or organizational restrictions on electronic communications.

It is debatable whether the right to communicate electronically with public authori-ties is a right for citizens or an obligation of the authorities [41]. The title of the section of the law "Right to Electronic Communications" suggests that it is a right for citizens and businesses. Conversely, those subject to the law are not obliged to make use of electronic communication. This is also made clear in the explanatory notes: "The introduction of this new right does not, however, change the admissibility of other intended forms of contact with courts and administrative authorities, such as by means of physical submis-sions" [34]. § 25 of the E-GovG clarifies that a right to electronic communication con-versely implies the obligation for the administration to create the technical prerequisites for electronic receipt or transmission. The regulation provides a three-year transitional period for the establishment of the technical arrangements. This allowed the authorities concerned sufficient time to plan and expand their electronic communication services.

Excluded from the right to communicate electronically are procedures that cannot be handled electronically. The explanatory notes [34] to the law mention, for example, documents that are issued exclusively in physical form (passport) or enclosures such as samples in the patent system. By way of example, the explanations list procedures in which biometric data must be taken after the application has been submitted. Moreover, the right to electronic communication cannot be granted without restriction in cases of judicially ordered deprivation of liberty, since "the legal and factual framework con-ditions in prisons thus differ significantly from those in freedom" [34]. § 1b EGovG regulates the obligation for companies to accept electronic service: "Companies [...] shall participate in electronic service". According to the wording of § 1b EGovG, com-panies must participate in electronic delivery. Unlike citizens, companies therefore have no freedom of choice regarding electronic delivery but are obliged to participate passively in it. This results in the obligation to participate passively in electronic service, but not the obligation to participate actively. However, no sanctions are ordered in the event that the obligation to participate in electronic delivery is not fulfilled [42]. Moreover, delivery to non-registered recipients is not possible. Therefore, companies that do not register do not miss a service. In the absence of legal or factual consequences, this is a "toothless" regulation. In conclusion, the right to electronic communication exists in Austria inso-far as the technical possibilities are made available by the authorities. Citizens are not obliged to use any electronic communication that may be made available.

4.2.2 Germany

As in Austria, the German e-government act requires authorities to provide electronic access for citizens (§ 2 EGovG) [35]. It is not obligatory for public authorities to com-municate electronically with citizens, nor is it obligatory for citizens to communicate electronically with public authorities [43]. The regulation merely imposes on public authorities the obligation to create electronic access that can be used voluntarily. The law deliberately leaves open how this access is to be designed in a technology-neutral manner. All public authorities are obliged to provide electronic access, for example by e-mail. The law goes further in obligating federal authorities. They must also open electronic access via De-Mail and ID cards. De-Mails main objective is to send and receive messages and documents via the Internet confidentially, securely and verifiably [44]. De-Mails are similar to conventional e-mails - however, they have important features that e-mails often lack: The identities of sender and addressee can be clearly verified and cannot be falsified and the messages are transmitted exclusively via encrypted channels and stored in encrypted form. They are therefore not accessible to unauthorized persons at any time and can neither be read nor changed [37].

4.2.3 Switzerland

Switzerland has a variety of e-government related legislation that often includes technical aspects as well as differing frameworks in the regions. A comprehensive e-Government Act (EMBaG) was planned, but failed due to resistance from the cantons [45]. The cantons have decided not to go ahead and instead want to pursue the organization 'Digital Administration Switzerland' [46]. The planned EMBaG [38] contained in its Art 4 regulations on electronic communication and provided that electronic means should be used for the interaction of federal authorities with each other and of the cantons and municipalities with each other and the interaction between authorities and companies and the interaction between authorities and natural persons. Article 4 (1) EMBaG should have explicitly required the federal authorities subject to this law to communicate electronically - the law does not specify which means the federal government should use to achieve this goal [39]. After the planned EMBaG failed due to the resistance of the cantons, there is no legal basis in Switzerland for electronic communication between authorities and citizens at the federal level.

5 Analysis and Discussion

This section discusses the results gained from the analysis of the scientific literature and the digital strategies in order to answer the research question: **To what extent are electronic communication aspects of e-government strategies implemented into legal measures in German-speaking countries (DACH)?**

The following aspects regarding electronic communication can be found in e-gov measures of the DACH countries: While the three countries show a similar administrational service structure and, over the past years, have shown efforts to increasingly improve and further develop their e-government strategies, significant differences can be observed in their formulation of e-government strategies. While the Austrian e-government strategy shows an extensive technical background and more immediate and concrete goals with the establishment of a digital public service communication as standard, Germany pursues a holistic approach with its inclusion of existing laws, digital citizen, respectively business, accounts as well as service digitalisation. Switzerland at the same time focuses on the communication aspect and puts attractiveness for the users at the center of its endeavours. These differences might be founded in the differences between the stakeholders these documents are aimed at as well as their structure. While Switzerland focuses on accessible communication, Austria provides a focus on an overview of its technical and strategic endeavours, and Germany under-lines a holistic approach with sector-specific measures. Despite these differences, all three countries show the relevance of electronic communication in technology, practice as well as legislation and hint on (cross-border) identification standards as emerging challenges.

From a legal perspective the right for electronic communication is generally already implemented, usually for services on the national level. This is a particular challenge for federal states such as Germany, Austria and Switzerland. Even if legal regulations are introduced at the national level, it is the federal states that conduct the majority of cases involving contact with citizens, and it is therefore the federal states and municipalities where mandatory electronic communication would make the greatest difference. In gen-eral, a trend can be observed at the federal level from a legal point of view: Firstly, the authorities are obliged to communicate electronically with each other; secondly, busi-nesses are/could be obliged to participate passively and actively in electronic delivery. The next step, which has not been taken in any of the three selected countries, but very much so in countries such as Norway, would be the obligation of citizens to participate actively and passively in electronic communications with the authorities. In summary, Austria and Germany have taken important legal steps by anchoring electronic com-munication at the federal level. It remains to be seen how the situation will develop in Switzerland. The involvement of the federal provinces and the municipalities in the obligation to use electronic communications must be further pursued.

A summary of the analysis shows that technological aspects of the analysed e-government strategies are already implemented, and the goal of a digital first elec-tronic communication between citizens and the public sector shows itself in the right for digital communication in several nations. This right for electronic communication mainly affects public authorities, while other steps have more immediate consequences for service users. Our research also seems to indicate a relation between strategic focal points and legislation maturity for electronic communication. Austria, with its empha-sis on a strong technical foundation has already implemented laws to ensure electronic communication between the public sector and citizens. Germany has an extensive legal foundation for preparing digital communication, but currently develops new strategic measures that surpass former tools, such as De-Mail. Switzerland, however, is still in the process of preparing the legal basis for its user-centric e-government vision.

6   Conclusion and Outlook

We examined the implementation of a specific aspect of DACH digital strategies into law, and consequently provided an overview of the legal frameworks for electronic com-munication between citizens, respectively businesses, and the public sector. Our results show the application of strategic projects in several maturity levels of legislation and we conclude that future strategic and legislative action in this field has to focus on a framework for digital communication, secure and interoperable identification as well as public services on the state level. However, our results are limited to official strategic sources that do not necessarily contain legally binding policy projects. Additionally, we could not include current strategies and legislation that might address the gaps we identified, but is currently still undergoing political evaluation. Another issue that we aimed to address during the coding is the difference in definitions of core e-government and electronic communication concepts in the three countries. While coding and analysis showed common aspects, core principles of differing administrational cultures will influence the implementation of legislation. Future research should add another level of analysis to the observation and connect strategic and/or legal documents with the practical implementation of these factors. A comparison with best practices for electronic legislation, such as Norway or Denmark, might also be possible. On a European level, the focus on the interaction of interoperable frameworks for electronic communication and identification will become increasingly important for the implementation of the Berlin declaration principles.

References

1. European Commission: Digital Public Administration factsheet 2020 Austria (2020)
2. Glyptis, L., Christofi, M., Vrontis, D., Giudice, M.D., Dimitriou, S., Michael, P.: E-government implementation challenges in small countries: the project manager's perspective. Technol. Forecast. Soc. Chang. **152**, 119880 (2020)
3. Ministerial Meeting During the German Presidency of the Council of the European Union: Berlin Declaration on Digital Society and Value-Based Digital Government, Berlin (2020)
4. Hofmann, S., Madsen, C.Ø., Distel, B.: Developing an analytical framework for analyzing and comparing national e-government strategies. In: Viale Pereira, G., et al. (eds.) EGOV 2020. LNCS, vol. 12219, pp. 15–28. Springer, Cham (2020). https://doi.org/10.1007/978-3-030-57599-1_2
5. Elsheikh, Y., Alqasrawi, Y., Azzeh, M.: On obtaining a stable vote ranking methodology for implementing e-government strategies. J. King Saud Univ. Comput. Inf. Sci. (2020). https://doi.org/10.1016/j.jksuci.2020.11.035
6. Lindgren, I., Madsen, C.Ø., Hofmann, S., Melin, U.: Close encounters of the digital kind: a research agenda for the digitalization of public services. Gov. Inf. Q. **36**, 427–436 (2019)
7. Walser, K., Hosang, R., Meyer, M.: Kompetenzen und Technologien für die Verwaltung: Entwicklung eines thematisch-strukturellen Elementenrasters für E-Government-Strategien-Fallstudie Schweizer Kantone (2016)
8. Ruano de la Fuente, J.M.: E-government strategies in Spanish local governments. Local Gov. Stud. 40, 600–620 (2014)
9. Jæger, B., Löfgren, K.: The history of the future: changes in Danish e-government strategies 1994–2010. Inf. Polity: Int. J. Gov. Democr. Inf. Age **15**, 253–269 (2010)
10. Meijer, A.: E-governance innovation: barriers and strategies. Gov. Inf. Q. **32**, 198–206 (2015)
11. Wirtz, B.W., Daiser, P.: E-Government: strategy process instruments. In: Wirtz, B.W. (ed.) Deutsche Universität für Verwaltungswissenschaften Speyer, Lehrstuhl für Informations-und Kommunikationsmanagement (2015)
12. Brown, D.: Electronic government and public administration. Elektroninė valdžia ir viešasis administravimas, pp. 61–68 (2006)
13. Angelopoulos, S., Kitsios, F., Kofakis, P., Papadopoulos, T.: Emerging barriers in e-government implementation. In: Wimmer, M.A., Chappelet, J.L., Janssen, M., Scholl, H.J. (eds.) Electronic Government. LNCS, vol. 6228, pp. 216–225. Springer, Heidelberg (2010). https://doi.org/10.1007/978-3-642-14799-9_19
14. Adu, K.K., Patrick, N., Park, E.G., Adjei, E.: Evaluation of the implementation of electronic government in Ghana. Inf. Polity: Int. J. Gov. Democracy Inf. Age **23**, 81–94 (2018)

15. Ahmad, M., Othman, R.: Implementation of electronic government in Malaysia: the status and potential for better service to the public. Public Sect. ICT Manag. Rev. **1**, 2–10 (2007)
16. Cerrillo-i-Martínez, A.: The regulation of diffusion of public sector information via electronic means: lessons from the Spanish regulation. Gov. Inf. Q. **28**, 188–199 (2011)
17. Strejcek, G., Theil, M.: Technology push, legislation pull? E-government in the European Union. Decis. Support Syst. **34**, 305–313 (2003)
18. Briglauer, W., Cambini, C., Fetzer, T., Hüschelrath, K.: The European Electronic Communications Code: a critical appraisal with a focus on incentivizing investment in next generation broadband networks. Telecommun. Policy **41**, 948–961 (2017)
19. Anand, A., Vaidya, S.D., Sharahiley, S.M.: Role of integration in scaling of an e-Government project. Trans. Gov. People Process Policy **14**, 65–80 (2020)
20. Heim, M., Nikolic, I.: A FRAND regime for dominant digital platforms. J. Intell. Prop. Info. Tech. Elec. Com. L. **10**, 38 (2019)
21. Pelikánová, R.M., Cvik, E.D., MacGregor, R.: Qualified electronic signature – eIDAS striking Czech public sector bodies. Acta Univ. Agric. Silviculturae Mendel. Brun. **67**, 1551–1560 (2019)
22. Kim, S.-T.: Next generation e-government strategies and asks for the smart society - based on Korea's case. J. e-Governance **36**, 12 (2013)
23. Akkaya, C., Krcmar, H.: Towards the implementation of the EU-Wide "Once-Only Principle": perceptions of citizens in the DACH-region. In: Parycek, P., et al. (eds.) Electronic Government. LNCS, vol. 11020, pp. 155–166. Springer, Cham (2018). https://doi.org/10.1007/978-3-319-98690-6_14
24. Kristo, R.C., Cruz Medina, E.: Innovation among SMEs in the DACH region; assessment of the status quo and the development of an innovation framework. Wien (2017)
25. Wach, E., Ward, R.: Learning about qualitative document analysis (2013)
26. Bowen, G.A.: Document analysis as a qualitative research method. Qual. Res. J. **9**, 27–40 (2009)
27. European Commission: Digital Public Administration factsheet 2020 Germany (2020)
28. European Commission: Digital Public Administration factsheet 2020 Switzerland (2020)
29. Barotanyi, B., et al.: Behörden im Netz - Das österreichische E-Government ABC. Bundesministerium für Digitalisierung und Wirtschaftsstandort, Wien (2017)
30. IT-Planungsrat: Nationale E-Government-Strategie Fortschreibung 2015 (2015)
31. Bundesregierung: Digitalisierung gestalten - Umsetzungsstrategie der Bundesregierung. Presse- und Informationsamt der Bundesregierung (2020)
32. Schweiz, E.-G.: E-Government-Strategie Schweiz 2020–2023. Bern (2019)
33. Austrian Parliament: Bundesgesetz über Regelungen zur Erleichterung des elektronischen Verkehrs mit öffentlichen Stellen (E-Government-Gesetz-E-GovG), Bgbl. Nr. 10/2004, as amended on 24 th July 2013 (2004)
34. ErläutRV 1457 BlgNR 25. GP 5
35. Bundestag, D.: Gesetz zur Förderung der elektronischen Verwaltung sowie zur Änderung weiterer Vorschriften, p. 25. Bundesgesetzblatt (2013)
36. Bundestag, D.: De-Mail-Gesetz vom 28. April 2011 (BGBl. I S. 666), das zuletzt durch Artikel 14 des Gesetzes vom 20. November 2019 (BGBl. I S. 1626) geändert worden ist. Bundesgesetzblatt (2011)
37. Bundesamt für Sicherheit in der Informationstechnik - BSI: De-Mail, Sicherer elektronischer Nachrichtenverkehr – einfach, nachweisbar und vertraulich. Bonn (2016)
38. Schweizerische Eidgenossenschaft: Vorentwurf Bundesgesetz über den Einsatz elektronischer Mittel zur Erfüllung von Be-hördenaufgaben (EMBaG) (2021)
39. Schweizerische Eidgenossenschaft: Erläuternder Bericht, Vorentwurf Bundesgesetz über den Einsatz elektronischer Mittel zur Erfüllung von Behördenaufgaben (EMBaG), p. 27 (2021)

40. Scheiber, P.M., et al.: eGovernment MONITOR 2020. Kantar für Initiative D21 und TUM (2020)
41. Horn, B.: E-Government 2020: Das Recht der BürgerInnen auf elektronischen Verkehr mit Behörden – Verpflichtung zur Schaffung der Voraussetzungen für elektronische Anbringen und Zustellungen. jusIT 2019/6, 219 (2019)
42. Liebenwein, S.R.: Victoria: eZustellungNEU. Österreichisches Anwaltsblatt 01 2020 (2020)
43. Warnecke, T.: Das Bürgerportalgesetz. Vertrauliche Kommunikation im e-Government und e-Commerce? Multimedia und Recht **13**, 227 (2010)
44. Bundestag, D.: Entwurf eines Gesetzes zur Regelung von De-Mail-Diensten und zur Änderung weiterer Vorschriften (2010)
45. Konferenz der Kantonsregierungen: Stellungnahme, Bundesgesetz über den Einsatz elektronischer Mittel zur Erfüllung von Behördenaufgaben (EMBaG), vol. Plenarversammlung vom 26. März 2021 (2021)
46. Eidgenössisches Finanzdepartement EFD: Digitale Verwaltung Schweiz: Für die digitale Transformation im Bundesstaat (2021)

The Accountability of Intelligence and Law Enforcement Agencies in Information Search Activities

Pál Vadász(✉) 🆔 and Zsolt Ződi 🆔

Information Society Research Institute, National University of Public Service,
Budapest, Hungary
pal.vadasz@uni-nke.hu

Abstract. The development of technology has challenged legislation in several areas during the last decade. The increase in the amount of data and computer performance, and new software solutions such as artificial intelligence and computer linguistics based intelligent search require a reassessment of the legal barriers to their operations. On the one hand, law enforcement agencies and security services demand increasing access to these technologies to come up to the social expectations in the field of security. On the other hand, civil rights organizations require an ever-stronger oversight of law enforcement agencies and security services to avoid their possible abuse of the most advanced technologies. The paper argues that the only way to resolve this dilemma is to improve the accountability of law enforcement agencies and national security services, thereby increasing public trust. Procedural and technical methods to perform this task are examined. The corresponding EU legal framework is analyzed.

Keywords: Accountability · Law enforcement agencies · Security services · Whistleblowers · Targeted search · Bulk search · Log analysis

1 Introduction: The Freedom Versus Security Dilemma

Citizens' confidence in law enforcement agencies and the security services or intelligence community (henceforth LEA and IC organizations or just organizations if it is contextually evident) is a relative concept that varies in time and space. In the deep layers of the consciousness of Central- and Central-Eastern-European nations the state has, for centuries, been more a repressive organization serving an elite than a group of civil servants working for citizens and providing security as a service from the taxes they pay. People do not feel the same way everywhere. In Switzerland, a referendum [1] recently decided that LEA and IC organizations should be able to legally listen to telephone conversations, and carry out online searches, because Swiss citizens are less afraid of the state than of terrorists or organized crime and expect that state organizations use all available means to protect their personal security.

© IFIP International Federation for Information Processing 2021
Published by Springer Nature Switzerland AG 2021
N. Edelmann et al. (Eds.): ePart 2021, LNCS 12849, pp. 210–220, 2021.
https://doi.org/10.1007/978-3-030-82824-0_16

Networks involved in organized crime, terrorism, child pornography, illegal arms and drug trades, and human trafficking take advantage of the most modern information and communication technology (henceforth ICT) arsenal available without being too worried about legal hurdles. The complexity of data generated by these activities presents LEA and IC organizations a virtually impossible task unless they keep up with the most modern technologies.

On the one hand, LEA and IC organizations are therefore seeking to make full use of the arsenal available to them. On the other hand, civil rights organizations have a legitimate expectation that these activities are carried out within strict legal boundaries to avoid unnecessary intrusion into the privacy of citizens and violations of human rights.

Various publications strongly argue either for or against the increased legal limitations, without showing a way out of this dilemma. This paper accepts the arguments of both sides, however, as a new approach, endeavors to cut the Gordian knot by highlighting the importance of the substantially improved accountability both organizationally and, as a new dimension due to the enhanced artificial intelligence (henceforth AI) and natural language processing (henceforth NLP) technologies, technically.

The purpose of this paper is threefold, as follows. To identify the key information search technologies whose use limitation artificially weakens the effectiveness of such organizations. To examine the means and methods by which the conflict between freedom and security could be resolved or at least reduced. To examine the legal environment in terms of how and to what extent it restricts LEA and IC organizations from using state-of-the-art information search technologies.

2 Background and Challenges

A full review and analysis of the literature on the accountability of LEA and IC organizations would go far beyond the space available here. Most publications do not, of course, focus on information search only, but rather take a holistic view of LEA and IC organizations' activities [2–4].

Two trends have been observed since the 2001 terrorist attacks. Terrorist organizations and organized criminal groups are using increasingly sophisticated and modern information and communication technologies. The legal frameworks of all known countries are accepting – if very slowly – this changing environment and are gradually reducing the restrictions on the use of key technologies.

There is an abundant literature on the overwhelming secrecy of LEA and IC organizations, on the lack of transparency, insufficient oversight, and poor accountability. Such is the Carnivore case [5], the hot dispute involving the British Investigatory Powers Bill (the so-called snoopers' charter) [6], the BND[1] practice in 2016 [7] that was again curtailed in Germany in 2020 [8], or GCHQ[2], held responsible for breaching privacy rights [9]. The quintessence of these studies is that they directly or implicitly demand a strict legal framework to limit the technical capabilities of these organizations.

Much less is publicized by the LEA and IC organizations about their demands and the need for loosening control. Seminal work was published by David Anderson Q.C. [10]

---

[1] Bundesnachrichtendienst, the foreign intelligence agency of Germany.

[2] Government Communications Headquarters, the signals intelligence service of the UK.

that examined both sides of the coin by interviewing all UK LEA and IC organizations as well as civil rights groups with particular focus on the targeted versus bulk search dilemma. This report is one of the very few that elaborates on the specific need and practices of the organizations in their everyday activities. Anderson found that bulk search is not only extremely useful but inevitable in certain cases. He states that stored data provide essential input for AI applications without which they just cannot function. Also, his team cautiously indicates that superficial bulk search followed by focus only on strong suspects is less intrusive, than a deep drill-down into the private life of someone who, at the end of the day, turns out to be innocent.

3 Major Technological Breakthroughs

In information search, the basic requirements are novelty, timeliness, degree of processing, authenticity, and availability [11]. The most widely used information search within LEA and IC organizations is either open-source intelligence (OSINT) or enterprise content search run on internally stored data. It is a natural requirement of LEA and IC organizations to obtain data, which is as complete as possible, and to do so as quickly as possible, preferably in real-time, with as few restrictions as possible and bringing to the surface as many hidden data connections as possible.

Over the last decade, new technologies have emerged, the use of which has become paramount for LEA and IC organizations. ICT infrastructure has developed enormously. The development of text mining technologies on an exponentially growing amount of data is evident. The reliability of video and image recognition has reached 98% or above. The proliferation of non-relational database technologies has become widespread. Breakthroughs in the application of multi-layer neural networks in semantic language technologies have reached new levels since 2017, in terms of automatic translation, natural language-based so-called question and answering (Q&A) and predictive analytic capabilities.

Although ICT technology covers a wide area, including communication interception, encryption etc., the crucial areas are the four principles of data protection laws: purpose limitation and mass data collection, data retention, the interconnectivity of data bases and profiling. Most legal boundaries can be grouped into these four categories.

The confinement of search by purpose limitation (targeted search) or, in other words the prohibition of mass data collection (bulk, dragnet or strategic search) is one of the most controversial issues. To illustrate the problem, one should imagine the unnatural situation in which drug finder dogs are only allowed to sniff those bags that have been authorized by a judge beforehand, and not all of them at the airport arrival hall [10].

The data retention confinement prohibits the storage of collected data over a certain date, i.e., these must be permanently deleted. The technical consequence is that the training data for enrichment evaporates, thus paralyzing the AI search applications [10].

The limitation of interconnecting databases means that relevant information in one database cannot be freely matched with that in another. For example, the fact that a local report that a student pilot is only interested in taking off but not in landing techniques is not compared to the FBI database of terrorists, can lead to 11/9/2001. The problem is topical in the EU [12].

And finally, the limitation of profiling, particularly by AI-based face-recognition is again one of the controversial topics of the day. This means that the recognition and following of terrorists is made substantially more difficult.

There is no room in this paper to discuss the consequences of AI biases.

4 Examples of Abuses of LEA and IC Organizations

Several cases of abuse by secret services are well known. Reference can be made to the Echelon system [13] or the Snowden files [14]. There are countless publications on the Orwellian dystopias arising from the abuse of human rights by the NSA[3] or GCHQ and the like. But there are also strong arguments to support the use of modern technologies by LEA and IC organizations. This debate has resulted in a process of rethinking the legal framework in several advanced democracies, including the USA, the UK and, within the EU, Germany, France, the Netherlands, and Sweden [15].

The fundamental danger, irrespective of the country, is political interference in the operation of LEA and IC organizations, which jeopardizes their professional independence and democratic objectives. Such political meddling can, inter alia, be illustrated by a few examples, as follows:

- influencing opposition political parties or movements, such as in the Öcalan case [16];
- observation of members of their own or allied parties, such as in the Watergate case [17];
- action against civil persons or organizations, such as in the Politovskaya case [18];
- monitoring of journalists, for example, the monitoring of French journalists for their sources [19];
- action against inside informants (whistleblowers), such as in the case of Mordechai Vanunu [20];
- disclosure of classified information, such as in the Valerie Plame case [21].

Having considered the legal and organizational mechanisms which ensure the checks and balances cited above, it is obvious that no control mechanism can be effective if the people carrying out the oversight are influenced through an invisible structure such as a party hierarchy, a religious order, a freemason's lodge, or the like. Examples are easy to find. These include Stalin's Soviet system, the National Socialist's capture of the state after 1933, or the ODESSA[4], which infiltrated West-German society after World War II.

NGOs illustrate the possibility of circumventing the laws which guarantee individual rights. These methods are by their nature less verifiable, but they most certainly cannot be ignored. The essence of the *"one hand washes the other"* model is that what is forbidden in one country is not forbidden in another. This can help to circumvent national laws. The cooperation between the NSA and GCHQ is a striking example. Both are rather limited in monitoring their own nationals, but it is not forbidden to look at nationals of

---

[3] National Security Agency, the signals intelligence service of the USA.

[4] *Organization der ehemaligen SS Angehörigen*, organization of persons formerly belonging to the SS.

the other country, since, as foreigners they are not subject to national legal restrictions. Data exchange is permitted [22].

Outsourcing of tasks to private organizations is not unknown within LEA and IC circles [23]. It is quite difficult to officially control the activity of a foreign private subcontractor financed through unofficial channels. Such organizations can be entrusted with sensitive tasks that could be unpleasant to report on to a parliamentary committee [24].

5 Organizational Methods to Support Accountability

5.1 Accountability

The problem of accountability can be very simply formulated: how to exercise democratic control over organizations whose functioning is essential for the security of the state, while their operation is essentially secretive. The antagonism is clear: the control mechanisms want to know as much as possible, while LEA and IC organizations want to disclose as little as possible. How do you supervise institutions if you do not see what they do? And how should they function if any leak puts at risk the success of operations, the survival of structures built over a very long time, or even people's lives? This is particularly true of operations which are illegal in a hostile environment. Control is based on the creation of checks and balances. In democracies, there are basically two kinds of solutions to this problem. On the one hand, to balance rights and duties between LEA and IC organizations and the institutions that control them. On the other hand, monitoring mechanisms can be established outside the implementing organizations [25]. It should be noted that democratic control and the freedom of operation of LEA and IC organizations are not mutually exclusive concepts. On the contrary: the freedom of operation of the Dutch secret services is perhaps one of the most extensive within the EU, while the oversight is one of the strongest [15].

5.2 Remedies to Enhance Oversight

Some of the tools and institutions considered by the literature as a method of checks and balances are as follows.

- The services watch each other.
- The appointments of Directors-General are subject to parliamentary approval. Thus, the executive power is subject to personal scrutiny by, for example, the National Security Committee of the National Assembly.
- Compliance audit.
- LEA and IC organization heads report to Parliamentary committees. The depth at which a parliamentary committee can see into an organization's internal affairs differs from country to country. There are countries where this is possible only at a strategic level, while in other countries the committee can investigate specific details. It matters what classified information have member access to.
- Ad hoc parliamentary committees can be appointed by the legislature to investigate specific cases.

- The work of LEA and IC organizations is overseen by a responsible minister whose power may differ from one country to another.
- In most countries judicial decisions can also allow operations that restrict individual rights, such as data acquisition and processing.
- Any EU citizen can appeal to the European Court of Justice.
- Civil societies can organize protests.
- Think tanks monitor events and influence processes through public forums.
- The free press can reveal abuses.
- Social media can be a platform for free critical expression, even in an anonymous form.
- Committees of respected people with high integrity can investigate matters and formulate independent views.
- Whistle-blowers can call the attention of the public to a particular issue.
- Finally, the data protection authorities may monitor the processing of personal information by LEA and IC organizations.

5.3 Whistle-Blowers

Whistle-blowers have received particular attention recently. As seen above, in situations where the system of checks and balances function only superficially because the real line of command runs under the surface, the only functioning independent sources of information are whistle-blowers. The verdict on whistle-blowers is ambiguous. Civil society considers them heroes, or even martyrs, while their employers regard them as traitors. Edward Snowden, one of the best-known whistle-blower, was honored with statues in New York, Berlin, and Glasgow, while he has a good chance of being sentenced to life imprisonment or even being injected with poison in the United States. Mark Felt, Deep Throat, did not have the courage to reveal until hours before his death that he had informed Bob Woodward and Carl Bernstein of the background to the Watergate affair, which ultimately led to the fall of President Nixon. Perhaps less well-known is the case of Katharine Gun, a translator at GCHQ, who, in 2003, released classified documents related to the UN Security Council's decision-making procedure regarding the existence of Iraq's weapons of mass destruction. The charge was dropped due to a brilliant move by the defense, and she was unexpectedly released.

6 Technical Tools for Accountability

Before dealing with the subject of data protection, one must highlight that, apart from legal and organizational-procedural guarantees, there is an alternative to improving accountability, which is less addressed in the literature, and which would require greater attention. This is a method involving technical controls. It is worth mentioning that the FRA study strongly criticizes the poor technical background of the oversight bodies in the EU [15].

The distillates from any system (such as in the two cases outlined below) must be stored in places that are not accessible to internal personnel, and the resulting data must be indelible and unalterable. Obviously, all analytical tools only look at those event logs or records that each individual application environment provides, i.e., *"they are hooked up"*. Permanently or provisionally disconnected proceedings are not recorded, and therefore not analyzed.

6.1 Log Analysis

Log analysis consists of analyzing the collection of electronic tracks, log files (audit trails, event logs) of transactions and events generated by the operation of an IT system (network, operating system, applications) with the help of an application designed for this specific purpose. Examples of such events include the opening of a file or a directory, printing, entering, exiting, or copying files without permission. The log file is usually a structured database (the records are structured in the same way, e.g., after normalization a list of telephone calls or credit card numbers), but its size is vast and therefore cannot be processed by human effort. The log analyst analyzes the logfile using statistical methods and AI to highlight non-routine events, called anomalies (e.g., illegal copying). Log analysis has been used for a long time to detect events which deviate from the norm. Its use is not unknown in public administration and in the private sector for checking compliance or fraud detection, for example. However, not much on the subject can be found in the publications related to LEA and IC accountability.

6.2 Database Extraction

Another technology available is the permanent filtering of databases within an organization under appropriate conditions for an engineering and human analysis unit which ensures accountability. The filtering mechanism should ensure that all data relevant to accountability is passed on for verification (even encrypted) and that confidential operational data is not removed from the system unnecessarily.

Appropriate conditions (both human and technical) must be provided in the classified environment. Anyone who receives insight into these system mappings should have the highest security clearance and periodic vetting.

7 Legal Instruments of Accountability

7.1 EU Legal Framework – Data Protection

The EU's data protection regulation is aware of and articulates the dilemma of freedom versus security. The current EU legislation on the processing of personal data is based on the GDPR [26] while the rules concerning the law enforcement agencies are in Directive 2016/680 (Law Enforcement Directive—LED) [27]. The LED regulates data protection only in the field of law enforcement agencies and does not concern the activities of national security services; the regulation of the secret service and its data protection aspects are currently within the competence of the member states.

The LED was adopted with the GDPR. The logic of regulation is that the GDPR should be used as a background norm, with the exceptions defined in the GDPR itself.

Recital 19 of the GDPR defines the exception for law enforcement agencies: "*The protection of natural persons regarding the processing of personal data by competent authorities for the purposes of the prevention, investigation, detection or prosecution of criminal offences or the execution of criminal penalties, including the safeguarding against and the prevention of threats to public security and the free movement of such data, is the subject of a specific Union legal act. This Regulation should therefore not apply to processing activities carried out for those purposes.*"

The main difference between the GDPR and the LED is, of course, the legal basis for data processing: whereas the most common legal basis for data processing in the GDPR is the data subject's consent, in LED it is either "*public interest*", or "*performance of official authority*". The principles for data processing are very similar in the two norms. According to LED, personal data should be processed "*lawfully and fairly*", collected only "*for specified, explicit and legitimate purposes*", and "*kept in a form which permits identification of data subjects for no longer than is necessary for the purposes for which they are processed*" [27]. It can therefore be concluded that the principles of purpose limitation, data minimization and storage limitation should also apply to law enforcement organizations.

In 2017, the Article 29 Working Party [28] published an opinion on the subject [29]. The opinion deals with a wide range of issues, including processing special categories of personal data, automated decision-making, profiling, data subjects' rights, and the powers of the data protection authority in the context of LED. In relation to purpose limitation, the document states that the core problem lies in prevention issues. "*The question whether certain data have served their purpose and are no longer necessary, arises particularly when data storage is allowed for preventive purposes*" [30]. The document sees the solution in the combination of an overall maximum time limit and periodic reviews. It recommends that the storage of data should be based on a risk assessment. It refers to the solutions contained in the judgments of the European Court of Human Rights and the European Court of Justice as regards specific period-limitations, and other solutions [27].

Regarding the special data, (such as health, political opinion, race, etc.) the LED requires that they can only be processed if "*strictly necessary*" ([29], Article 11). The WP 29 recommendation also proposes further risk analysis, the introduction of additional procedural guarantees and technical measures in this area. According to the WP 29, profiling also poses significant risks to the rights and freedoms of individuals and therefore requires adequate protection measures [27]. Another important requirement is that the data subject should always retain the right to obtain human intervention in these cases. A new, additional principle that is becoming increasingly significant is that profiling cannot lead to discrimination [31].

The data subject also has the right regarding data processing under the LED to get information on the data processing in a "*concise, intelligible and easily accessible form, using clear and plain language*" ([27], Article 12 (1)) but there are obviously serious restrictions laid down in Article 15. (e.g., it should not obstruct official or legal inquiries, investigations, or procedures, or prejudice the prevention, detection, investigation, or prosecution of criminal offences.) The scope of the exceptions is so broad that the WP 29 reminds the "*national legislators that any exemptions from the fundamental rights and legitimate interests of the natural person should be applied as the exception rather than the rule and that omitting information may be allowed within an investigation only for as long as such a restriction constitutes a necessary and proportionate measure"* ([29], Article 22).

In summary: the logic of EU regulation is that it has created specific regulations for law enforcement organizations, which are based on very similar principles to the GDPR: it includes purpose limitation, prohibition of unlimited storage, right of access for the data subject, etc. The data protection regulations of national security services are a matter of national competence, and currently there is no EU standard.

7.2 European Court of Human Rights (ECtHR) Case Law

The ECtHR has issued several judgments protecting privacy (*"Right to respect for private and family life"* – Art. 8.) under the European Convention on Human Rights. The second paragraph of Art. 8. states that public authorities are entitled to intervention *"such as is in accordance with the law and is necessary in a democratic society in the interests of national security, public safety or the economic well-being of the country, for the prevention of disorder or crime, for the protection of health or morals, or for the protection of the rights and freedoms of others"*.

The ECtHR, which is the guardian of the Convention, has contributed to the development of the Convention through specific interpretations of necessity and proportionality. For example, in the MM vs. United Kingdom (24029/07 - 13 November 2012) and Huvig vs. France (1105/84 - 24 April 1990) cases, it stated that any intervention must have its domestic legal basis, namely laid down in a law to which the parties concerned have access and may adapt their action. Several judgments dealt with what the term *"necessary in a democratic society"* meant (e.g., Handyside vs. United Kingdom (5493/72 of 7 December 1976) and The Sunday Times vs. United Kingdom. (6538/74 of 6 November 1980). In those rulings, the Court stated that *"necessary"* means that an intervention is a pressing social need, rather a way of better achieving certain objectives, or making it easier to achieve them. There have also been numerous judgments on proportionality, like S & Marper vs. United Kingdom (30562/04 and 30566/04 (4 December 2008), in which unlimited storage of DNA samples was prohibited by the court. The ECtHR case law regarding the dilemma of mass surveillance (or, as it is called by the Court, *"strategic monitoring"*) versus targeted surveillance is interesting. In the Weber vs. Germany case [32], the ECtHR considered the issue closely and concluded that *"strategic monitoring"* should have adequate guarantees (i.e., only a higher body can order it with a sufficiently powerful reason, data should be destroyed when it is no longer needed, and should not be transmitted to other authorities). But overall, strategic monitoring is not in itself a disproportionate interference with private life.

8 Conclusion

The present paper covers the relationship between LEA and IC organizations and the legal framework of data protection in view of recent disruptive technologies. The dilemma between freedom and security still exists today and has even been sharpened by new ICT developments. The paper highlights the key legal boundaries that confine the application of modern technologies by LEA and IC organizations. Instead of arguing either for or against more technological freedom, the paper takes sides for both, but strongly argues for enhanced accountability. Organizational, procedural and - as a barely covered new area - technical methods are presented to improve the accountability of LEA and IC organizations to ensure greater confidence among citizens.

References

1. Gerny, D.: Das Nachrichtendienstgesetz auf einen Blick. https://www.nzz.ch/schweiz/abstim mung-vom-25-september-das-nachrichtendienstgesetz-auf-einen-blick-ld.111204. Accessed 21 March 2021
2. FRA: Surveillance by intelligence services: fundamental rights safeguards and remedies in the EU, vol. 1, p. 8. European Union Agency for Fundamental Rights, Vienna (2017)
3. Weber, R.H., Staiger, D.N.: Privacy versus security. In: Kulesza, J., Balleste, R. (eds.): Cyber-security and Human Rights in the Age of Cybervelliance. Rowman & Littlefield, Lanham (2016)
4. Born, H., Wills, A.: Overseeing Intelligence Services, A toolkit, DCAF, Geneva (2012)
5. Ventura, H.E., Miller, J.M., Deflem, M.: Governmentality and the war on terror: FBI project carnivore and the diffusion of disciplinary power. Crit. Criminol. **13**, 55–70 (2005). https://doi.org/10.1007/s10612-004-6167-6. Accessed 26 May 2021
6. Schafer, B.: Surveillance for the masses: the political and legal landscape of the UK Investigatory Powers Bill. Datenschutz Datensich **40**, 592–597 (2016). https://doi.org/10.1007/s11 623-016-0664-0. Accessed 26 May 2021
7. Meyer, D: Spy agency back in court over snooping: you're abusing mass surveillance powers. https://www.zdnet.com/article/spy-agency-back-in-court-youre-abusing-your-mass-surveillance-powers/. Accessed 24 May 2021
8. Rojszczak, M.: Extraterritorial bulk surveillance after the German BND act judgment. Eur. Const. Law Rev. 1–25 (2021). https://doi.org/10.1017/S1574019621000055
9. Goodwin, B.: GCHQ bulk interception programme breached privacy rights, Strasbourg court rules (2021). https://www.computerweekly.com/news/252501356/GCHQ-bulk-interc eption-programme-breached-privacy-rights-Strasbourg-court-court-rules?utm_campaign= 20210526_GCHQ+bulk+interception+programme+breached+privacy+rights%2C+Strasb ourg+court+rules&utm_medium=EM&utm_source=EDA&asrc=EM_EDA_163354630
10. Anderson, D.: Report of the Bulk Powers Review. Crown copyright, London (2016)
11. Kahaner, L.: Competitive Intelligence, p. 104. Touchstone-Simon & Schuster, New York (1997)
12. Quintel, T.: Connecting Personal Data of Third Country Nationals: Interoperability of EU Databases in the Light of the CJEU's Case Law on Data Retention. University of Luxembourg Law Working Paper No. 002-2018 (2018)
13. Schmid, G.: Report on the existence of a global system for the interception of private and commercial communications (ECHELON Interception System). 07th 11th European Parliament Session Document A5–0264/20012001. http://cryptome.org/echelon-ep-fin.htm. Accessed 25 March 2021
14. Macaskill, E., Dance, G.: NSA Files: Decoded. http://www.theguardian.com/world/intera ctive/2013/nov/01/snowden-nsa-files-surveillance-revelations-decoded#section/1. Accessed 25 March 2021
15. FRA: Surveillance by intelligence services: fundamental rights safeguards and remedies in the EU, vol. 2, European Union Agency for Fundamental Rights, Vienna (2018)

16. Öcalan v. Turkey. http://hudoc.echr.coe.int/eng?i=001-69022. Accessed 25 March 2021
17. Dickinson, W.B., Mercer, C., Polsky, B.: Watergate: Chronology of a crisis, 1, p. 133, 140, 180 and 188. Congressional Quarterly Inc., Washington D.C. (1973)
18. Archangelsky, A.: Murder in Moscow: Anna's legacy. https://doi.org/10.1177/030642201667 0350. Accessed 01 June 2021
19. Lichtfield, J.: Sarkozy accused of using security service to spy on journalists. The Independent (2010). https://www.independent.co.uk/news/world/europe/sarkozy-accused-of-using-security-service-to-spy-on-journalists-2124599.htm
20. Mordechai Vanunu gets 18 years for treason - Archive 1988 (1988). https://www.theguardian.com/world/2018/mar/28/mordechai-vanunu-israel-spying-nuclear-1988
21. Iley, C.: Valerie Plame Wilson: housewife CIA spy who was a 'fair game' for Bush. http://www.telegraph.co.uk/culture/film/8318075/Valerie-Plame-Wilson-the-housewife-CIA-spy-who-was-fair-game-for-Bush.html. Accessed 25 March 2021
22. Ball, J.: US and UK struck secret deal to allow NSA to 'unmask' Britons' personal data. http://www.theguardian.com/world/2013/nov/20/us-uk-secret-deal-surveillance-personal-data. Accessed 25 March 2021
23. Voelz, G.J.: Contractors and intelligence: the private sector in the intelligence community. https://doi.org/10.1080/08850600903143106. Accessed 01 June 2021
24. Shorrock, T.: Spies for Hire. Simon and Schuster Paperbacks, New York (2008)
25. Caparini, M.: Controlling and overseeing intelligence services in democratic states. In: Born, H., Caparini, M. (eds.) Democratic Control of Intelligence Services. Routledge, New York (2016)
26. Regulation (EC) No 2016/679 of the European Parliament and of the Council of 27 April 2016 on the protection of natural persons regarding the processing of personal data and on the free movement of such data and repealing Regulation (EC) No 95/46 (General Data Protection Regulation, GDPR)
27. Directive (EU) 2016/680 of the European Parliament and of the Council of 27 April 2016 on the protection of natural persons regarding the processing of personal data by competent authorities for the purpose of the prevention, investigation, detection, prosecution, or enforcement of criminal penalties, and on the free movement of such data, and repealing Council Framework Decision 2008/977/JHA. (Privacy Policy, LED)
28. Article 29 Working Party was an advisory body made up of a representative from the data protection authority of each EU Member State, the European Data Protection Supervisor, and the European Commission. After the entering into force of the GDPR it ended its functioning
29. WP 258: Opinion on some key issues of the Law Enforcement Directive (EU 2016/680) adopted on 2017 November 29. https://iapp.org/media/pdf/resource_center/wp258_police_directive-11-2017.pdf. Accessed 25 March 2021
30. Opinion 01/2014 on the WP 211 - Application of the necessity and the proportionality concepts and data protection within the law enforcement sector (2014). https://ec.europa.eu/justice/article-29/documentation/opinion-recommendation/files/2014/wp211_en.pdf. Accessed 31 May 2021
31. FRA: Towards More Effective Policing Understanding and Preventing Discriminatory Ethnic Profiling: A Guide. European Union Agency for Fundamental Rights (2010). https://fra.europa.eu/sites/default/files/fra_uploads/1133-Guide-ethnic-profiling_EN.pdf. Accessed 30 May 2021
32. Weber and Saravia v Germany (2006). http://hudoc.echr.coe.int/eng?i=001-76586. Accessed 01 June 2021

Author Index

Printed in the United States
by Baker & Taylor Publisher Services